POWER RPG III

Advanced Concepts, Tips, and Techniques

Doug Pence
and Ron Hawkins

First Edition, November 1995

DISCLAIMER

Midrange Computing
5650 El Camino Real, Suite 225
Carlsbad, CA 92008

First Edition, Rev. 0   V3R1

TABLE OF CONTENTS

Preface

[The educated differ from the uneducated] as much as the living from the dead.

—Aristotle

The objective of the authors of this book was to put together a collection of tips, tools, and techniques that would benefit any AS/400 programmer, whether a junior programmer right out of school, or a seasoned veteran with 10 years of experience.

Any RPG/400 programmer reading this book will almost certainly learn techniques that will both increase his or her productivity as well as improve the quality of the software produced.

From designing software to attain maximum performance to learning how to use advanced problem solving tools, this book presents a wide range of topics that are important to any RPG/400 programmer. It offers in-depth coverage of basic subjects— like data structures, string handling, and subfiles—and also tackles the more intricate areas like APIs (Application Program Interfaces) and using journaling as a debug tool. The book also contains a variety of tools designed to improve programmer productivity and efficiency.

The RPG language on the AS/400 offers a veritable plethora of ways to perform almost any job. Often, knowing the best way to do the job is a result of being familiar with all of the tools at your disposal. It is for this reason that this book should find its way into every RPG/400+ reference library.

Chapter 1

Performance Starts with Program Design

Throughout this chapter we focus on reducing I/O and maximizing the use of main memory. To understand how to write programs that perform well on the AS/400, you must understand which functions most degrade system performance. The primary bottleneck on most midrange systems is related to I/O processing or memory management. Creating, deleting, opening, closing, reading, and writing to data files drain system performance, making your software appear to run slowly. Over utilization of system memory causes the system to "thrash" and spend the majority of its resources moving objects from memory to disk and vice versa. Most software on the AS/400 and its predecessors fall victim to one or the other of these problems.

I/O AND ITS EFFECT ON AS/400 PERFORMANCE

I/O processing is slow because it is still slave to a mechanical process. The data is stored on some form of magnetic media and must be retrieved or written using the moving parts of whatever the storage device happens to be.

Despite major technical achievements in this area within the last decade, I/O processing remains the culprit of most performance problems on the AS/400. Features like *journaling* and *mirroring* have been added to the operating system for stability and to allow us to make software systems more reliable, but their use can further amplify the I/O processing bottleneck problem. The good news is that there are a number of things that you can do as a programmer to help alleviate this problem. Let's begin with the basics.

Don't Need It? Don't Use It!

From a performance standpoint, opening and closing files are two of the most time-consuming events that take place on the AS/400. When an RPG program is called, the data files are usually opened automatically by the system. If the programs you are working with have a large number of files (sometimes this is unavoidable), program initiation can seem to take forever while the program is loaded and all of the files are opened.

Ways this delay can be reduced are if the file opens are *user-controlled*, if the files are already open with a *shared data path,* or *both*.

User-controlled File Opens

User-controlled file opens give you the option of only opening a file if and when you intend to use it. As you can see by the example in Figure 1.1, you can code your program to open files as you need them instead of when the program loads. You can either set a flag in the program indicating that the file has been opened already so you will not attempt to open it again, or you can use an error indicator on the open statement, as shown in Figure 1.2. Failure to perform one step or the other results in a nasty little RPG error.

Figure 1.1: User-controlled Opens Using Conditional Flags

```
FCUSTOMERIF  E         K        DISK                           UC
C           OPNCUS    IFNE *ON                      FILE NOT ALREADY
C                     OPEN CUSTOMER                  OPEN, OPEN IT
C                     MOVE *ON        OPNCUS  1
C                     ENDIF
C           CUSKEY    CHAINCUSTOMER                99
```

Figure 1.2: User-controlled Opens Using Error Indicators

```
FCUSTOMERIF  E         K        DISK                           UC
C                     OPEN CUSTOMER             99
C           CUSKEY    CHAINCUSTOMER             99
```

If you code your file opening routines at strategic points within your program, it is possible that certain files may never be opened at all. For example, if the program contains multiple screens that are processed conditionally depending upon user response, the program could be coded so that only those files that are associated with the selected screens are ever opened. There is a double bonus in this situation because files that are never opened obviously need not be closed either.

Secondly, but perhaps more importantly from an overall performance standpoint, user-controlled files offer an excellent opportunity to distribute program overhead so that it is less noticeable to the user.

The example in Figure 1.3 illustrates how you can code the program so that the opening of the files is occurring at the same time the program is waiting for a response from the user. While EXFMT was a wonderful addition to the RPG language, those of us who have been in the midrange market for a while remember when we had to code the display file as a primary or demand file. Separate steps were required to write and read each screen format.

Figure 1.3: User-controlled Opens between Writing and Reading Display File Format

```
FDISPLAY CF  E                    WORKSTN
FCUSTOMERIF  E           K        DISK                           UC
C                        WRITEFORMAT              DISPLAY FILE FORMAT
C            OPNCUS      IFNE *ON                 FILE NOT ALREADY
C                        OPEN CUSTOMER              OPEN, OPEN IT
C                        MOVE *ON        OPNCUS  1
C                        ENDIF
C            OPNSLS      IFNE *ON
C                        OPEN SALESMEN
C                        MOVE *ON        OPNSLS  1
C                        ENDIF
C                        READ FORMAT              99 WAITS FOR INPUT
```

In this example, the WRITE and READ op codes replace Execute Format (EXFMT).
Notice that several user-controlled file opens have been placed in between the WRITE
and the READ. When this program executes, the screen panel displays and then the files
open while operator attention is focused on the screen. Coding the program this way
creates a condition where the files are being opened while the program is waiting on the
user, instead of the other way around.

When using this particular technique of reading and writing the display formats, you must
compile your display file as DFRWRT(*NO) so it does not defer writing a screen until a
read operation is encountered. Failure to comply with this requirement results in a
condition where the screen does not appear until the read operation is executed.

When using user-controlled file opens, you may choose to ignore the closing of the files
and let the program handle that part of it when the last record indicator is encountered. If
the delay caused when the program ends is causing you problems, you may want to try
using the RETRN op code instead of setting on LR (this is discussed in further detail later
in this chapter, "RPG Program Calls").

The Shared Data Path

Another technique that helps to reduce program initiation overhead uses a method called
shared data paths. This method can be very useful when programs and subprograms use
the exact same data files. By opening the data or display files using shared open data
paths, subsequent high-level language programs can be opened in about half the time.

The example in Figure 1.4 is a sample initial program that is called when a user first signs
on to the system. The Open Database File (OPNDBF) command opens the data files that
are used by the application most often, and the Override Database File (OVRDBF)

command specifies that the open data path is to be shared. When the files are opened with a shared data path, the menu is displayed. Program calls to application programs within this same session use the existing open data path instead of creating a new one.

Figure 1.4: Sign-on CL Program to **Pre-open** *Files and Display Initial Menu*

```
PGM
MONMSG     CPF0000
           OVRDBF    FILE(CUSTOMER)  SHARE(*YES)
           OVRDBF    FILE(SALESMEN)  SHARE(*YES)
           OPNDBF    FILE(CUSTOMER)  OPTION(*ALL)
           OPNDBF    FILE(SALESMEN)  OPTION(*ALL)
           GO        CUSTMENU
ENDPGM
```

Another method of employing the open data path methodology is to build or change the file so that the data path is always shared on the file. Notice that the Create Physical File (CRTPF), Change Physical File (CHGPF), Create Display File (CRTDSPF), and Change Display File (CHGDSPF) commands give you the option of compiling the objects in such a manner that the data path is always shared.

You may want to share the open data path of a display file when you have several programs within a single job stream that happen to share the same display file. Employing this technique gives you the same advantages as it would if we were talking about a database file.

RPG IV, the Next Generation

Now that ILE/400 is available with Version 3, Release 1 (V3R1), you are allowed to read a record with one program and update it with another (as long as the open data path is shared). Another change with this release is that it allows you to share open data paths within a job or an activation group.

To summarize, if your application uses the same physical or display files over and over again, those files may be opened and closed many times within a single job stream. This can cause big delays in application program initiation and help to create a situation where overall system performance is degraded significantly. Using shared data paths can help alleviate these problems and help to improve overall system throughput.

Words of Caution

The term *shared* may be somewhat misleading because not all sessions have access to the open data paths. Only programs within the same session share the open data path.

There is also a warning to heed if you use the library list to manipulate which file on the system is to be used. When a file has been pre-opened with a shared open data path, an application program uses that file whether it is currently in your library list or not. The program simply uses the open data path of the shared file. If you do not have files with the same name in multiple libraries, this is not a problem for you.

Another thing to remember when using open data paths is that the file is always in use as long as the session exists. It does not matter whether or not a program is actually running. This can be a potential problem at times when a job needs dedicated access to a file (e.g., file saves). Files with shared data paths remain "in use" until the files are closed or the session is terminated.

Also, you can not assume that the file pointer will be where you want it when a program is initiated. If you are going to do any type of sequential read operation, remember to set your file pointer appropriately. You do not need to worry about this when the open data path is not shared because each program in the job stream will open and keep its own independent file pointer.

You also need to pay attention to how you open the file. In other words, you will experience problems if you open a file as *input only* and then try to update the file.

There are other security and operational issues to consider before trying this particular method. More information on this technique is offered in the IBM AS/400 *Database Guide*, the *CL Reference Manual*, and the *ILE RPG/400 Programmers Guide*.

THE PATH YOU CHOOSE MAY BE THE MOST IMPORTANT PART OF YOUR JOURNEY

The path through your data is often the most critical decision you can make with regard to how an application performs. As stated earlier in this chapter, I/O has a dramatic effect on performance.

For example, if you choose to read a file by index instead of arrival sequence, you are making a choice to greatly increase the amount of work the system has to do. The AS/400 high-level languages (HLLs) do not perform as well when reading a file by index as they do when they read data in arrival sequence. This is because, when a program reads a data file by an index key, the system must first read the key and then go out to get the physical data. So the HLL program must double the I/O processing right off the bat. Also, because the physical data is being accessed in a random fashion, the data can not be blocked (retrieving multiple records on every I/O operation) as it would be when the file is processed in arrival fashion. This increases the system resources that are used when the HLL program is run.

When running one of your RPG programs, you may have noticed a message in your job log stating that the key was to be ignored and the data was being processed in arrival sequence. This occurred because, at compile time, the system noticed that there was nothing in your RPG program that required the file to be processed randomly. In other words, there were no I/O operations, like CHAIN or SETLL, that required a key. Consequently, the system decided that, to be more efficient, the HLL program should process the data in arrival sequence and assigned a minimal blocking factor as well (more on blocking when we discuss reading files by the index).

Design Considerations with Regard to I/O Processing

When designing a new program, the choice is whether to read records in arrival sequence, to read by an index, or to use OPNQRYF or FMTDTA (sort) to sequence the data into the desired path. Unfortunately, the answer is: It depends. Answer these two, key questions before you decide which method to employ:

- Is the program interactive or will it run in batch?

- How big is the file that is being processed?

Most of the time when coding an interactive program, you do not have much of a choice. You will have a tough time trying to convince your salespeople that they are better off working with a subfile of their prospects in arrival sequence. He or she will want the subfile presented in a sequence that makes him or her more productive, with little or no regard to system performance. Who can blame them? Addressing system performance is your job, not theirs.

Batch programs should almost always be written to use FMTDTA or OPNQRYF. Even if there is already an index available for the sequence you desire, the program is likely to run faster if you get the data into the proper arrival sequence prior to processing it.

Avoid Reading Files by the Index Whenever You Can

If the program you are writing involves a data file with a handful of records (in the hundreds), it may be more efficient to read the file by keyed index. This is because there is a certain amount of overhead required to run FMTDTA or OPNQRYF. However, if the file you are reading has 250,000 records, you will notice a definite performance improvement if you put the data into the appropriate sequence first. Two options available to perform this task are either Format Data (FMTDTA) or Open Query File (OPNQRYF).

Since the addition of the ALLWCPYDTA(*OPTIMIZE) to the OPNQRYF command, there are few reasons to use the FMTDTA (sort) command. This new option allows the system to decide whether or not it is more efficient to sort the data.

Using OPNQRYF can range from the very simple to the very complex. Let's say, for example, that you have a daily sales report that has been written to read a logical file over your 250,000-record customer file by customer name. The code in Figure 1.5 could be embedded into a CL driver program to put the customer file (CUST) into customer name sequence prior to running the RPG program. The RPG program could then be changed to read the CUST file in arrival sequence.

Figure 1.5: Using OPNQRYF to Sequence Data into the Appropriate Arrival Sequence

```
OVRDBF FILE(CUST) SHARE(*YES)
OPNQRYF FILE((CUST)) ALWCPYDTA(*OPTIMIZE) KEYFLD((CUSNAM))
```

The net result of this change is a significant performance improvement. I/O is reduced because the system does not need to read the index first and then go out and get the data. The system also automatically blocks the data and multiple records are read each time the system has to go to the disk.

LOGICAL FILES ARE A VALUABLE TOOL, BUT DON'T OVER USE THEM

The logical file is one of the most treasured gems in our toolbox, but most of us have abused the privilege of using it at one time or another. Why shouldn't we? The Sales Department asked us for a new report and we do not seem to have a data path that puts the data in the exact sequence they are looking for. It would be so easy to add that new logical file over the Customer Master file, write the report, and get the request off our desk.

DON'T DO IT!

Before adding a new logical file, consider the consequences of your actions. Depending upon the DDS and compile options you use when you create the logical file, you are potentially creating additional system overhead for your AS/400 every time that file is updated. Even if you build the file so that the index maintenance is delayed, the index still has to build at some point.

The decision to create a new logical file should be based upon the run-time environment (batch or interactive) for which it is required. Logical files should not be created for programs that will run in a batch environment.

There are other disadvantages to logical files as well. Logical files require disk space for the index. There is also a certain amount of system overhead that the system incurs when keeping track of logical files and the physical files with which they are associated.

USING SETOBJACC TO REDUCE I/O AND MAXIMIZE MEMORY USAGE

Throughout this chapter, we have encouraged you to reduce the impact of the mechanical process of reading disk as it pertains to your application. One way to do this is to maximize use of your system memory.

The Set Object Access (SETOBJACC) command is used to pull objects (primarily programs, database files, and their access paths) into memory to reduce the amount of disk I/O required by the system. If a database file's index and data can be processed from memory rather than disk, the mechanical part of the task is removed from the equation and the processing is performed significantly faster. Obviously, how well this works depends upon a variety of things like the amount of main memory you have on your system, the time of day the job runs, and the size of the files or programs with which you are working.

The benefits of moving a physical file that must be processed randomly (by key) into memory will far outweigh the benefits of doing the same for a file that will be read in arrival sequence for two reasons:

- When you compile your RPG program, the compiler checks to see if you are processing a file in arrival sequence. If so, the system automatically *blocks* records when the program is run. *Blocking* is a term used to describe when the system retrieves multiple blocks of your data on each I/O request because the system determined the order in which you will be reading the records. How many blocks of data are retrieved depends upon algorithms within the operating system.

  Blocking is not effective on randomly accessed files because the system must work overtime to load records into memory that are not in the sequence the program expects. In fact, blocking can actually degrade the performance when applied to randomly accessed files.

- When you are reading a file by an index key, the system must first read the index record and then go out to seek the physical data.

The maximum advantage is attained if you can put both the physical file and its access path into main memory simultaneously. All of the I/O requests from within your program occur in memory rather than on disk.

Using the SETOBJACC command to put a file into memory is kind of like record blocking, except that you can bring the entire file into memory at once. In the case of randomly accessed files, you want to bring both the data and the access path into memory, if you can. This can have a tremendous impact on program performance because the mechanical process of the disk I/O has been eliminated.

It should be noted here that the SETOBJACC command is not useful when the file is specified as output only. This is because the output operations are already "buffered" in memory (remember that all records are added to the end of a file unless you are reusing deleted records) and do not cause high levels of I/O activity.

There are basically two flavors to the SETOBJACC command: plain vanilla and tutti-frutti. Plain vanilla is very simple and great to use when your system is dedicated to a single task (like month end or daily startup). Tutti-frutti is a little more involved, but the benefits derived can be substantial.

Make Mine Vanilla, Please

Most AS/400 shops have certain times of the day, week, or month when dedicated processing can occur. If you have this luxury, you may want to look at this flavor of the SETOBJACC command to speed up the dedicated jobs that run at such times.

For our example in Figure 1.6, we take our customer physical file (CUST) in our library (FILES) and place it into main memory. Our job is to process the file randomly by key, so we also specify the MBRDATA parameter so that both the data and the access path are pulled into main memory (we could have indicated that just the access path or data be brought in).

Figure 1.6: Using SETOBJACC to Put Objects into Main Storage

```
SETOBJACC OBJ(FILES/CUST) OBJTYPE(*FILE) POOL(*JOB) MBRDATA(*BOTH)
```

When the SETOBJACC command is run, the system takes a "snapshot" of memory just prior to pulling your object into memory. It then sends a message to your job log that lets you know how much benefit you will gain from running the command. Figure 1.7 is an example of what the message looks like.

Figure 1.7: Message Sent When Running the SETOBJACC Command Showing Object Size and Space Available in the Memory Pool

```
19K of CUST brought to pool with 996K unused.
```

The message states that, prior to bringing 19K of the CUST file into memory, 996K of memory was available. Memory may not be available because main storage is not cleared of your objects just because a job ends. The objects in memory are left there until the space is needed for something else. If the message tells you that 0K was available prior to attempting to bring your object into memory, clear the memory pool first.

For our example, let's assume the job is running interactively. In this case, the parameters for the CLRPOOL command are very simple (Figure 1.8).

Figure 1.8: Clearing the Memory Pool

```
CLRPOOL POOL(*JOB)
```

The CLRPOOL command clears all objects out of the main storage pool so there is plenty of room for the objects that we want to place there. The down side is that your job will be moved out of the main storage pool as well. We recommend signing off to end your job after running the CLRPOOL command. When you sign back on, the memory pool is cleared and you will have initiated a new job.

With a clear memory pool, you are free to run the SETOBJACC command to put the objects you will be using into main memory. You can then run the rest of your job as you would normally. The only step left is to clear your objects from memory once your job is completed. There are two ways to do this. You can use the CLRPOOL command as we did prior to placing objects into memory, or you can use the SETOBJACC command with slightly different parameters (Figure 1.9).

Figure 1.9: Clearing Objects from Main Storage After Using SETOBJACC to Put Them There

```
SETOBJACC OBJ(FILES/CUST) OBJTYPE(*FILE) POOL(*PURGE)
```

Time for Tutti-frutti

The tutti-frutti method would be used in nondedicated environments, but the same basic principles and advantages we experienced in the plain vanilla version apply. The difference is that, in the tutti-frutti version, you set up your own memory pools to store your most heavily used objects.

Memory Pools

Memory pool is simply a term used to describe the segregation of memory. When you install memory on the AS/400, it is automatically placed into the memory pool designated *BASE. If you leave your default system configuration alone, all of your subsystems will get their memory from this pool.

When processing in a nondedicated environment, it is best to create your own subsystem. When you create a subsystem and allocate memory to it, the memory the new subsystem uses is taken from the *BASE storage pool. The command to allocate 500K to pool number 2 in the SETOBJS subsystem is shown in Figure 1.10. Ensure that you have enough memory in the *BASE memory pool before executing the command. If there is not enough, decrease the size of some other subsystem that will return the memory to the *BASE pool. This can be done while working in the WRKSYSSTS command display.

Figure 1.10: Creating a Subsystem for SETOBJACC

```
CRTSBSD SBSD(QGPL/SETOBJS) POOLS((1 *BASE)(2 500K 1))
```

The 500K figure is for example only. You need to adjust it based on the size of the objects you are going to put in it. When you run the SETOBJACC command, it displays a message (like that shown in Figure 1.7) telling you the size of the object put into memory as well as the available space in the pool before the object was put in.

The example in Figure 1.7 shows that the object CUST has a size of 19K and was put into a memory pool that had 996K available prior to executing the SETOBJACC command. If there is not enough space available for the whole file, it might still be advantageous to bring in as much of the file as you can. Obviously, it's better to fit the whole object in the pool if possible. But remember, it's not the size of the object that is important, it's the number of times the file is being accessed. You can still improve response time by bringing a 20K file (or half of a 40K file) into memory if that file is accessed a jillion times a day.

The next step is to start the subsystem and initialize the memory pool. You should automate this process by making it part of your daily start up routine. The command in Figure 1.11 starts the subsystem and clears pool 2 in our SETOBJ subsystem, which is where we are going to load our files. Do not become confused by the numbering system of the pools. The AS/400 operating system divides memory into pools and numbers them. Pool 1 is the machine pool and pool 2 is the *BASE pool. All other pools are numbered consecutively from there. In addition, each pool can be segregated up to 10 times. We segregate ours twice, and put the memory in pool 2.

Figure 1.11: Clearing the User-created Private Main Storage Memory Pool

```
STRSBS SBSD(QGPL/SETOBJS)
CLRPOOL POOL(SETOBJS 2)
```

We can now bring the file into memory using the command in Figure 1.12. The SETOBJACC command executes extremely quickly, taking no more than a few seconds for most files.

Figure 1.12: Using SETOBJACC to Put Objects into a Private Main Storage Pool

```
SETOBJACC OBJ(FILES/CUST) OBJTYPE(*FILE) POOL(SETOBJS 2) MBRDATA(*BOTH)
```

Memory is Fast, Disk I/O is Slow

Bringing a file or program into memory (which is done with relatively few I/Os) can eliminate thousands of disk accesses throughout the day and prove to be a tremendous savings in transaction throughput. It requires some planning as to which objects should be in memory, but the rewards can far exceed the effort.

As you can see, the difference between plain vanilla and tutti-frutti is not all that great. Enjoy the improved performance and *bon appetit*.

TOO MUCH OF A GOOD THING CAN KILL YOU

We stress that you should concentrate on reducing I/O and maximize utilization of your system memory. But, like many good things in life, it is easy to go overboard.

If your system does not have enough memory or you are over-utilizing it in an effort to reduce I/O, your overall system performance can be degraded because your system is thrashing. In this case, there are too many objects contending for system memory and the system is trying to keep up by expending all of its resources moving pages temporarily from memory to disk and vice versa. This is similar to the drop-off in performance you notice on your PC when you do not have enough memory to run a job and "virtual memory" is used.

There are a variety of tools that can help you analyze if this is a problem on your system. We recommend that you take a class on Work Management if you think this may be an issue on your system.

REUSING DELETED RECORDS

The odds are pretty good that most of the physical files on your system can be broken down into three categories:

- Files that almost never change.

- Files that have records written to them regularly, but records never get deleted.

- Files that frequently have records written and deleted from them.

We concern ourselves with the second and third types in this section. Because the information in these types of files does not remain static, they can reach conditions that adversely affect performance if they are not maintained properly.

When you must read a file randomly by key, system performance is better when the physical data in the file is in the same order as the key by which you are reading it. This is because a single I/O operation is more likely to get a block of data that holds more than one record that must be processed. If the sequence of the data and the index do not match, the I/O operation will likely result in only a single record being processed before the system must go out and get another block (and the same block may need to be read later). The end result is that many more I/O operations may need to take place for the job to complete.

When a record is added to a file, the data normally is added to the end of the file, unless the REUSEDLT parameter was specified for the file. When REUSEDLT has been specified for a physical file, the system attempts to "reuse" records that were previously deleted whenever you add new records to the file. This parameter must be specified when the file is built (CRTPF), or you can change the file using the Change Physical File (CHGPF) command.

Using the REUSEDLT parameter can adversely affect system performance. The system has to search for deleted records every time a new record is added. This may or may not be a big deal, depending upon the size of the file as well as the percentage of deleted records. Secondly, because new records may be inserted into spots where deleted records previously existed, programs that were designed to process the file in arrival sequence may perform differently than what was intended initially.

THE REORGANIZE PHYSICAL FILE MEMBER (RGZPFM) COMMAND

Regardless of how records get added, if the index is added to randomly, the index and the data will not be in the same sequence after the add is performed. As we have repeatedly discussed, the greatest bottleneck for system performance is I/O. One way to combat this is to perform maintenance on files that experience heavy traffic. The Reorganize Physical File Member (RGZPFM) can be used to put the data and index back into the same sequence and, at the same time, remove any records that are flagged for deletion. Any programs that process the file randomly benefit from this process because the I/O is likely to be reduced (record size can affect this too because it directly relates to how many records are retrieved on a single I/O process).

The primary functions of the RGZPFM command are to remove deleted records from a physical file and to change the sequence of the records to match a selected index (usually this is the primary key to the physical file). If you have a physical file that is usually read by a specific logical file, it may be advantageous to reorganize the records in the file so they match the key of that particular logical file.

It can be surprising how much disk space gets tied up in deleted records if your data files never get reorganized. When a record gets deleted on the AS/400, it still takes up the same amount of space on disk until the record gets reused (if the file was designated to use the REUSEDLT option) or the RGZPFM command is run. The file must not be in use when the RGZPFM command is run, so it may be a problem in some shops that do not have scheduled down time to perform system maintenance tasks.

If you do not specify any additional parameters, the RGZPFM command simply removes the deleted records from the physical file. If you choose to use the KEYFILE parameter, it can be used to resequence the data to match the key of the physical file or to match the path of a selected logical file. The examples in Figures 1.13 through 1.15 show our customer file being reorganized to remove deleted records only, to remove the deleted records and resequence the file into physical file key order, and so the data will be in customer name order (that is the path of the CUSBYNAM logical file), respectively.

Figure 1.13: Using RGZPFM to Remove Deleted Records from a File

```
RGZPFM FILE(CUST)
```

Figure 1.14: Using RGZPFM to Remove Deleted Records and Resequence the Data to Match the Key to the Physical File

```
RGZPFM FILE(CUST) KEYFILE(*FILE)
```

Figure 1.15: Using RGZPFM to Remove Deleted Records and Resequence the Data to Match the Key of a Logical File

```
RGZPFM FILE(CUST) KEYFILE(CUSBYNAM)
```

THE *RGZPFFLTR* COMMAND

The Reorganize Physical File Filter (RGZPFFLTR) command (explained in more detail in Chapter 11) can be a valuable tool if your shop has the luxury of being able to schedule unattended down time to perform system maintenance. The command can be setup as an autostart job that automatically reviews all of the files on your system to determine which files need to be reorganized. How it determines whether the RGZPFM process is required or not is based upon a percentage value you use when you call the RGZPFFLTR command.

The percentage refers to the level of deleted records in a file that you deem to be acceptable. For example, if you think that all files that have at least 10 percent of the records in them deleted should be reorganized, you would set the parameter at 10 percent.

In any case, the files that meet the prescribed percentage criteria are reorganized automatically into the order of the key of the physical file. This utility could take some time to run, depending upon the number of files that meet the specified criteria and the speed of your system, but the overall impact on system performance and DASD utilization could be appreciable.

PERFORMANCE AND THE PROGRAM CALL

The ability to break down job streams into smaller subprograms is one of the wonderful things about the AS/400. RPG and CL can be used to break down larger jobs into smaller, more manageable components that can be used elsewhere. These modular components can be thought of as *reusable code*. They can be called from a variety of places to perform the same function. We think it is a good idea to code your programs with this thought in mind!

One example of this type of module is our window subfile program, used to decide to which printer a report should be sent (this sample program is in Chapter 2). You can call this program from any RPG or CL program and the operator is able to select a printer. The selection values are returned to the calling program parameters.

The program can be called from any other program that has been designed to request printed output. The fact that the same program can be called from many different places makes the code reusable. The greatest value to reusable code is that every time you enhance the reusable code, you are enhancing the utilization of all programs that call it.

As with most good things, however, there is a price to pay. Breaking down longer job streams into smaller, more manageable components can have an adverse effect on system performance. It is for this reason that IBM announced ILE in V3R1. ILE can be used to *bind* the programs in the job stream together so the system does not need to do so much work locating and loading the various components.

Even without program binding, a number of techniques can be employed to help reduce the impact on performance. Now let's discuss changes you can make to your CL and RPG programs to reduce the effect of program calls.

CL Program Calls

CL program calls have a few downsides that RPG does not have, so here are a few tips to keep in mind when your are working with CL programs:

- If your CL program is designed to contain a loop where a program is called multiple times, use a qualified program name (indicating the library and program name) on your call instead of letting the library list determine where the program resides. Unlike RPG, the CL program does not keep internal pointers telling it where the program was found originally.

- If you have a choice of calling a CL program or an RPG program that both perform the same function, choose the RPG program. A CL program requires more overhead to call than an RPG program.

- If programs within the job stream will use the same files, seriously consider sharing open data paths (as discussed earlier). Reduced I/O nets you the greatest gain in performance.

RPG Program Calls

There are also several tips you can use to reduce system overhead when performing program calls from RPG. Here are a few we have come up with:

- If an RPG program is going to be called more than once in the job stream, consider using the RETRN op code instead of setting on LR. This keeps the program resident in memory so it does not need to repeatedly incur the overhead required for program initialization and file open and close operations. In making this change, however, you need to pay attention to file pointers, field usage, and indicator settings. Because the program does not terminate, these values are going to be what they were when you last exited the program.

- As previously mentioned, if you have a choice of calling a CL program or an RPG program that both perform the same function, choose the RPG program. A CL program requires more overhead to initiate than an RPG program.

Again, focus on the reduction of I/O operations. User-controlled file opens and shared open data paths can be used to reduce the effect of file open and close operations. Appropriate use of the SETOBJACC command or sharing open data paths can be used to minimize the effect of I/O on your programs.

REDUCING THE SIZE OF YOUR PROGRAMS

One way to reduce memory utilization on your system is to reduce the size of the programs that are being run. Logic tells us that, if the programs being loaded into memory were half the size, twice as many could fit in memory at once. There is a simple way to attain this goal without reprogramming or reducing the functionality of your system— remove program observability in your programs.

When a program is compiled, the system takes your source member and translates it into a program object that the machine can read and execute. As part of the compile process, the system automatically adds in program overhead to allow the program to be debugged. This extra program overhead that the compiler automatically built in is called *observability*.

Observability is a very valuable part of your toolbox when you are writing, implementing, and beta testing a new system. Without it, we would not be able to run Debug and it would take us much longer to diagnose problems. But, once a system goes into production, you are not as likely to be running Debug all of the time. Why not use the Change Program (CHGPGM) command to remove the observability and cut the size of your programs in half? You can always restore observability by recompiling the program.

The results from removing observability vary, but we have seen some programs shrink to 40 percent of their original size. To run a test for yourself, simply display the size of a program by running the Display Program (DSPPGM) command. Then use the Change Program (CHGPGM) command to remove observability. Running the DSPPGM command again will reveal how much you were able to reduce the size of your program. In our example in Figure 1.16, we remove observability from the CUSPGM program in library TESTLIB by keying the CHGPGM command.

Figure 1.16: Remove Program Observability and Reduce Program Size with CHGPGM

```
CHGPGM   PGM(TESTLIB/CUSPGM) RMVOBS(*ALL)
```

REDUCING SCREEN I/O IN YOUR INTERACTIVE PROGRAMS

Another way to improve overall system performance is to minimize the amount of data that must be passed to and from display panels from within your interactive programs. Rather than reduce the amount of information on the screens, you can move toward this goal by reducing redundant and reiterative data.

Many interactive programs are designed to send an entire display panel full of data on every output to the screen. Sometimes the data being sent to the screen is almost identical to the information that is already displayed, with only one or two fields or display attributes changing from the previous display. This can create a situation where there is a lot more system traffic than is necessary. It is particularly noticeable if these programs are being run on terminals that are running over remote lines, where you can actually see the terminal "paint" the lines on the screen.

When a display panel is sent to the screen, display attributes must be sent as well as the data. These attributes control which fields are high-intensity, reverse-image, underline, nondisplay, input-capable, and much more. There is a lot of data beyond what you see that must be sent for every screen operation.

There is a way you can code your interactive programs so only the data and attributes that have changed since the previous screen I/O operation are sent to the screen. This method consists of utilizing the Put with Explicit Override (PUTOVR), Override Data (OVRDTA), and Override Attribute (OVRATR) DDS keywords.

PUTOVR is a DDS record-level keyword that essentially allows the system to "look" before presenting a display panel to see what needs to be sent to the screen. If the system determines that the display panel being sent is not already on the screen, the entire panel is displayed. On the other hand, if the display panel is already displayed, only fields that have the OVRDTA or OVRATR keywords in effect are sent to the screen. Using this technique can have a significant impact on how much data needs to be sent to the screen.

Using our example in Figure 1.17, we have used the PUTOVR keyword on the FORMAT1 display panel. Note that our customer number and customer name fields both have been coded to utilize the OVRDTA keywords. The CUSNBR field also has been coded with the OVRATR keyword.

Figure 1.17: Using the PUTOVR, OVRDTA, and OVRATR DDS Keywords

```
A             R FORMAT1
A                                       PUTOVR
A                                     1 35'Customer Lookup'
A             PGMNAM     35    B  4 25DSPATR(RI)
A                                     4  5'Customer Number:'
A             CUSNBR      5    B  4 22OVRDTA
A                                       OVRATR
A  40                                   DSPATR(HI)
A             CUSNAM     35       +2OVRDTA
```

When FORMAT1 is initially written to the screen, the entire display panel is sent because the system detects that FORMAT1 is not already on the screen. On subsequent output operations to the screen, only the CUSNBR and CUSNAM fields are sent because they have been coded with the OVRDTA fields. Note that the PGMNAM field has not been coded with the OVRDTA keyword because it will not change after the initial output to the screen.

Also in our example, only the CUSNBR field has been assigned the OVRATR keyword. This means that the only field on the screen whose display attributes may change after the initial display is the CUSNBR field. If the indicator controlling the High Intensity attribute (indicator 40) is turned on, the field is updated on the following output to the screen. If the OVRATR keyword was not coded with the CUSNBR field, the display attributes do not change and the attributes in effect on the initial output operation remain in effect as long as the screen is displayed.

Both the OVRDTA and OVRATR keywords may be conditioned by indicators. You may want to go a step further than this example and condition these keywords so they are only active when the data or attributes are going to change.

Do Not Overlook the Obvious

If your system is experiencing performance problems (and whose isn't?), there are a number of things you should look for prior to changing programs. Some of the same things that make the AS/400 such a wonderful computer to work on can also lead to degraded performance. Just a few of the things that can cause degraded performance are:

- DASD (disk storage) that is over 80-percent utilized. Check your utilization with the Work with System Status (WRKSYSSTS) command. The AS/400 operating system needs room to work. If it does not have enough room, the system has to work overtime trying to find the space.

- Running jobs interactively that are better suited for batch environments. This is especially true if the job in question requires heavy I/O processing. Any job that runs for more than 30 seconds and does not require operator intervention or action is a candidate for batch processing.

- Moving batch jobs to subsystems that were set up to run interactive jobs. These jobs run with the incorrect run-time attributes and adversely affect interactive performance.

- Inadequate memory. You are far better off to have too much than too little. You may be able to remember when 640K (640,000 bytes) was considered to be enough for a personal computer. Just try to run some of today's programs on 640K! These days, all computers require more memory in order to run. We have already shown you how to get more performance out of your system if you have enough main memory.

- Query and SQL. While these are wonderful tools, you need to ensure that they are not regularly run in an interactive environment. You pay a huge performance price if users on your system abuse this privilege.

- Message Logging Levels. How much information is being written to your job logs? This can have an effect on system performance if more information is being recorded than is required. (We teach you all about the message logging levels in Chapter 10.)

- Journaling. If you use journaling, you pay a price for the overhead required. You are doubling the amount of the I/O operations required for the files undergoing journaling.

THE BLAME GAME

Numerous articles and publications that focus on the performance of RPG operation codes give the impression that using one operation code over another will have a serious impact on system performance. While we certainly do not deny that the AS/400 performs some operations better than others, we think the dramatic increase in processing power we have seen in the last few years greatly offsets the minimal impact of changing RPG operation codes.

Admittedly, by competitive performance standards, the AS/400 does not perform multiplication and division functions very well. It tends to lag when performing lookups on large arrays or when comparing very large fields to one another. Using file translation or the Translate (XLATE) operation code can cause delays.

But the odds are that you would not be using the function if you did not need it. Your time searching for improved performance would be far better served looking for I/O bottlenecks and memory over-utilization.

PERFORMANCE, PERFORMANCE, PERFORMANCE

Users simply will not be able to get fast enough performance. It is one of the rules in today's computing environment. The faster computers get, the more performance users expect. Who can blame them?

The simple truth is that the AS/400 is competing with lightning-fast, single-user systems that were not designed to run in a multiuser environment. They do not require all of the excess overhead that is considered to be mandatory in the "midrange" market. Of course they can be loaded with comparable layers of software to perform networking, database management, security, print spooling and spool management, and the multitude of other standard operating system functions we have come to expect from our beloved AS/400.

Unfortunately, most comparisons are not and will not be apples to apples. The AS/400 will continue to be considered a dog by some in the computing world, and it probably will never get the industry-wide reputation it so richly deserves.

It is up to the people at our level to get everything out of the system that we possibly can. You should consider your quest for better performance to be your own personal search for the holy grail. It is not whether you arrive at your destination that is important; rather, it is how much you learn along the way.

Chapter 2

Subfiles Belong in Every Programmer's Toolbox

The subfile originally appeared on the IBM System/38 as a simple method of storing data (usually a subset of a collection of database records) in memory for the purposes of presenting them as part of a display file. Like most of the System/38 operating system, the subfile was later migrated to the AS/400 where it has been greatly enhanced since that time.

A subfile is defined similarly to the way you define a database file. In fact, the subfile can be read, chained to, written to, or updated much like a database file. There are some characteristics that differentiate the subfile from the database file, however. You can store data in *hidden* fields—fields that are not displayed, but can be used when you process the file later. You can control which record the cursor is positioned at without having to keep track of a zillion indicators. You can present or process a group of records on the display at the same time with a single command. This list could go on and on, but the primary advantages are speed, performance, ease of coding/maintenance, and the ability to select several records to be processed within a single operation to the workstation.

In this chapter we cover subfile fundamentals as well as some advanced topics, and code four very different kinds of subfiles. If you are a novice programmer, you should feel comfortable working with subfiles when you complete this chapter. If you are an intermediate- or advanced-level programmer, you may find a few gems within these pages.

THE BASICS

The two principle components of any subfile are the control record and the subfile record. Being true to its name, the control record is used to control the presentation of the subfile through a series of keywords, which generally are controlled with indicators. These keywords are used to indicate how many records are in the subfile, which function keys are allowed, how many records are displayed at one time, etc. The control record can also include input/output fields just as any other record format, and is often used to display the headings of each field in the subfile.

In Figure 2.1, we see a subfile presented in a DDS window. This subfile is used to help an operator select a printer when requesting a printed report or list. The control record (represented by the shaded area) presents the operator with five different options:

- Enter part or all of the printer description and press Enter to advance automatically to the description closest to the characters keyed.

- Enter a 1 in front of the desired printer record and press Enter to indicate the selected choice.

- Press the page keys to scroll forward or back through the printer description records.

- Press F12 to cancel and return to the previous screen.

- Press F3 to exit the application.

Figure 2.1: Subfile Control Record (shaded area)

```
:.............................................................:
:                                                            :
: Options: 1=Select                                          :
:                                                            :
: OR Key partial description: _____               :
:                                                            :
: Opt  Code          Description                             :
:  _   LASER6    ACCOUNTING - CHECKS                         :
:  _   LASER7    ACCOUNTING - INVOICES                       :
:  _   LASER3    ACCOUNTING - LASER PRINTER                  :
:  _   PRT03     COMPUTER ROOM - INVOICE PRINTER             :
:  _   LASER1    COMPUTER ROOM - LASER PRINTER               :
:  _   PRT02     COMPUTER ROOM - LETTER QUALITY              :
:  _   LASER2    FRONT DESK - LASER PRINTER                  :
:                                            More... :
:  F3=Exit  F12=Previous                                     :
:                                                            :
:.............................................................:
```

The subfile record is where we define each data field in the subfile. The fields can be specified as input, output, or hidden fields (not displayed). The example in Figure 2.2 shows that the subfile record (represented by the shaded area) has three visible fields:

- An input-capable option field (Opt) to allow the operator to indicate the desired selection.

- The printer ID (Code) that is coded as output only.

- Extended description of the printer (Description), also coded as output only.

Figure 2.2: Subfile Record (shaded area)

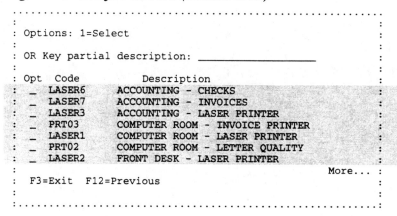

```
:.............................................................:
:                                                            :
: Options: 1=Select                                          :
:                                                            :
: OR Key partial description: _____               :
:                                                            :
: Opt  Code          Description                             :
:  _   LASER6    ACCOUNTING - CHECKS                         :
:  _   LASER7    ACCOUNTING - INVOICES                       :
:  _   LASER3    ACCOUNTING - LASER PRINTER                  :
:  _   PRT03     COMPUTER ROOM - INVOICE PRINTER             :
:  _   LASER1    COMPUTER ROOM - LASER PRINTER               :
:  _   PRT02     COMPUTER ROOM - LETTER QUALITY              :
:  _   LASER2    FRONT DESK - LASER PRINTER                  :
:                                            More... :
:  F3=Exit  F12=Previous                                     :
:                                                            :
:.............................................................:
```

In the example in Figure 2.2, we easily could have coded the printer ID field (Code) as a hidden field and only displayed the description on the screen. The printer ID field would still be available when we went to process the subfile.

Another thing to notice in the preceding example is that the literal More... is displayed near the bottom of the screen. This indicates that pressing the Page Down key results in the presentation of a new page of subfile records. This feature is discussed in more detail under the heading "The Subfile End (SFLEND) Keyword."

THE SUBFILE RECORD FORMAT (SFL) DDS

When coding a subfile, you must always define the subfile first, and then the control record. The DDS for the subfile record is similar to DDS for a database file, except that you are coding a file that will be presented to the screen and reside only in memory.

A subfile record format must have at least one display field (the exception to this rule is a message subfile, which we talk about later in this chapter). The field locations on the detail records represent the line and position of the fields as they will appear on the first subfile record displayed. The system figures out where the subsequent records belong on the screen based upon the value of the Subfile Page Size (SFLPAG), which is defined in the control record format.

Figure 2.3 shows the definition of a sample subfile record format. Note that the SFACCT field is defined as a hidden field with a data type of H and there are no line or position entries. This field stores data that we can use later when processing the file, but the data in SFACCT is not displayed on the screen. The SFLSEL and SFCUST fields are displayed beginning on the seventh line in positions 2 and 5, respectively.

Figure 2.3: DDS for a Subfile Record Format

```
A             R SFLRCD                    SFL
A               SFACCT        10H
A               SFSEL          1A  B  7  2
A               SFCUST        30A  O  7  5
```

THE SUBFILE CONTROL RECORD FORMAT (SFLCTL) DDS

The subfile control record gives you the ability to indicate how the subfile should be presented and should react when various conditions present themselves. There are four record-level keywords that are mandatory for every subfile control record format (see Table 2.1).

Table 2.1: Mandatory DDS Keywords for a
Subfile Control Record Format

Keyword	Description
SFLCTL	Indicates that the record format will control a subfile. It must be coded directly after the subfile record format that it is to control.
SFLDSP	Indicates to the system that the subfile should be displayed when an output operation is performed on the subfile control record. An option indicator is usually coded with this keyword. If you perform an output operation to the subfile control record while this keyword is active and there are no subfile records to display, your program receives an error message. By indicating an option indicator on the SFLDSP keyword and only turning it on if there happen to be subfile records to display, you avoid the error message.
SFLPAG	Describes the size of the subfile "page." Generally speaking, this keyword describes how many subfile records appear on the screen at one time. If each subfile record format takes up only one line of the screen, this number matches the number of lines on the screen taken up by the subfile (SFLPAG is 7 for the example in Figure 2.2). On the other hand, if each subfile record format uses two lines, SFLPAG is half of the number of lines required by the display file. Note that not every subfile record must take up the same number of lines (a variable number of lines is allowed if you are using the field selection technique that is discussed later in this chapter).
SFLSIZ	Defines the number of records in the subfile. How this keyword affects the operation of the subfile depends upon whether or not the Subfile Page (SFLPAG) and the Subfile Size (SFLSIZ) are equal (more on this subject later in the chapter). The system may change the value in this field, depending upon conditions that we discuss later in this chapter.

The SFLDSPCTL keyword (described in the next section) is also required if you are performing any input operation with the subfile control record.

The rest of the keywords that may be used on a subfile control record cover a wide variety of functions. The length of the list may seem a little intimidating, but you will find that many of the keywords are rarely used. In this chapter, we cover the keywords that we feel are most pertinent. The optional subfile control keywords (as of V3R1) are listed in Table 2.2.

Table 2.2: Optional DDS Keywords for a Subfile Control Record Format

Keyword	Description
SFLCLR	When you perform an output operation to the subfile control record with this keyword active (conditional indicators are advised), the subfile is cleared of all data. SFLCLR is similar to the Subfile Initialize (SFLINZ) keyword, except that no subfile records exist after execution of this keyword. You need to remember to turn off the conditioning indicator for the Subfile Display (SFLDSP) keyword after performing the SFLCLR operation. Failure to do so causes an error message if you try to perform a subsequent output operation to the subfile control record and you have not written any subfile records first.
SFLCSRRRN	This optional keyword is used to return the relative record number of the subfile record where the cursor is, back to the program. The parameter for the keyword is the name of the signed numeric hidden field that you must define in the control record that is used to hold the subfile relative record number.
SFLDLT	This conditional keyword is used to delete a subfile. This operation normally is not required with most subfiles because closing the display file accomplishes the same goal. The exception to this rule is if you already have the maximum number of subfiles (12) on the screen, and you need to get rid of one to make room for another.
SFLDROP	This conditional keyword is used when the subfile record format requires more than one line on the display. When a subfile record takes more than one line on the display, it is *folded*. When an output operation is performed on the subfile control record with the SFLDROP keyword

Keyword	Description
	active, the subfile records are truncated so that they fit on a single display line (the additional information does not appear) and more records will fit on a single page. Execution of the SFLDROP keyword on records that have already been truncated results in the display of the records in a folded state.
SFLDSPCTL	This conditional keyword indicates whether or not the subfile control record format should be displayed when you send an output operation to it. You must use this keyword if you plan to perform any input operations on the subfile control record format (even if no fields are displayed).
SFLEND	Tells the system what action to take when the end of the subfile is encountered. Options on this keyword allow for a plus sign (+), More..., and Bottom, or a graphical scroll bar (on graphical displays only). We discuss SFLEND later in this chapter (see "The SFLEND Keyword").
SFLENTER	This optional keyword is used to indicate that the Enter key (or other function key) act as a Page Up key.
SFLFOLD	This optional keyword is similar to the SFLDROP keyword, except the multiple-line subfile records initially are brought up in a folded state (instead of truncated). Performing an output operation to the subfile control record format with this keyword active switches the subfile records from a truncated to a folded state and vice versa.
SFLINZ	Used to initialize a subfile to blanks, nulls, and zeros (depending upon the field type). The optional keyword is similar to the SFLCLR keyword, except that the subfile is initialized (records will exist) instead of cleared.
SFLLIN	Used to describe multiple-column subfiles. This optional keyword can be used when you want to show more than one subfile record on a single display line. The additional parameter is used to specify how many spaces to place between the displayed records. When used, the records are written from top to bottom and then left to right. In other words, the first set of records appears top to bottom in the first column, the next set

Keyword	Description
	appears top to bottom in the next column, and so on.
SFLMODE	This optional keyword may be used in conjunction with the SFLDROP or SFLFOLD keywords. The required parameter is used to define a hidden field that returns whether or not the subfile is displayed presently in a folded or a truncated mode. You must define the parameter as a hidden, 1-byte alphanumeric field in the subfile control record format.
SFLMSG	This conditional keyword displays a message when an output operation is performed on the subfile control record format. More on this subject later when we discuss error handling with a message subfile.
SFLMSGID	Can be used to conditionally display messages from the specified message file when an output operation is performed on the subfile control record. We cover this in more depth when we discuss error handling with a message subfile.
SFLPGMQ	This optional keyword can be used in conjunction with the SFLINZ keyword to build a message subfile. The entire message subfile can be built with a single output operation on the subfile control record format. This keyword is unique in that it may appear on the subfile record format or the subfile control record format.
SFLRCDNBR	Allows you to indicate which page of the subfile should be displayed when an output operation is performed on the subfile control record format. If you do not specify this keyword, the system automatically presents the first page of the subfile to the screen. The field associated with this keyword must contain the relative record number of the subfile record you wish to see on the first page. The CURSOR parameter of this keyword can be used to indicate that the cursor is to be positioned automatically at the relative record number in question. The *TOP parameter can be used to indicate that the relative record number specified should represent the record that you wish to position at the top of the screen. If you omit this parameter, the SFLRCDNBR keyword ensures that the record specified appears somewhere on the screen.
SFLRNA	Used in conjunction with the Subfile Initialize (SFLINZ) keyword to

Keyword	Description
	indicate that, when the subfile is initialized, it is left with no active records.
SFLROLVAL	Used to describe an input field on the subfile control record. The operator uses the input field to indicate how many to page up or down. When this keyword is omitted, the system automatically pages the entire value specified in Subfile Page (SFLPAG).
SFLSCROLL	This field is used to return the relative record number of the subfile record at the top of the screen back to your program when scroll bars are being used. Scroll bars are an optional feature that can be specified on the Subfile End (SFLEND) keyword if you happen to be using graphical displays.

A sample subfile control record has been coded in Figure 2.4. Note that the SFLCTL, SFLDSP, SFLPAG, and SFLSIZ required keywords are all present. We have added Subfile Display Control (SFLDSPCTL) so that our subfile control record is displayed when we write an output operation to the control record. Subfile End (SFLEND) was added so the literals More... or Bottom is displayed on our subfile depending upon how indicator 41 is conditioned when we perform the output operation.

Figure 2.4: DDS for a Subfile Control Record Format

```
     A          R SFLCTL              SFLCTL(SFLRCD)
     A                                SFLSIZ(0010)
     A                                SFLPAG(0010)
     A                                SFLDSP
     A                                SFLDSPCTL
     A   41                           SFLEND(*MORE)
```

You are going to find that writing subfile programs is not that difficult. However, there are more issues that we need to discuss before we begin coding.

LOADING THE SUBFILE

Two methodologies may be employed when loading subfiles. One method is to write enough records to fill a single page of the subfile and then execute the subfile control format. This type of subfile is generally referred to as a *page-at-a-time* subfile. The second method of loading a subfile is to write all database records to the subfile before executing the control format. We refer to this second type as a *fill-'er-up* subfile.

The fill-'er-up subfile type should *only* be used when there is a fixed, small number of records that ever will be displayed. Remember that these records are being written into main storage memory, and your program is not the only resource contending for that valuable space. If too many programs contend for main memory, the system spends all of its time moving objects in and out of main storage and performance suffers. Second, why perform all of the extra I/O required to fill the subfile? Remember that someone is sitting and waiting at the keyboard while this task is performed. Use the advice that your parents gave you and just take what you need.

If there is a large (or an unknown) number of records to be written to the subfile, you should *always* use the page-at-a-time style of subfiles.

THE RELATIONSHIP BETWEEN SUBFILE SIZE (SFLSIZ) AND SUBFILE PAGE (SFLPAG)

Regardless of whether you are employing page-at-a-time or fill-'er-up subfiles, there are two primary categories of subfiles. These types are distinguishable based upon the relationship between the number of records allowed in the subfile (SFLSIZ) and the number of records to be displayed in a single subfile page (SFLPAG).

When SFLSIZ and SFLPAG are the Same

When SFLSIZ and SFLPAG are the same, the maximum number of records allowed in the subfile can never exceed the number of records to be displayed on a single page. The SFLDROP, SFLFOLD, and SFLROLVAL keywords are invalid for this type of subfile because they refer to functions that require more than one page of records to exist in the subfile. Likewise, when an operator presses the Page Up or Page Down keys, control is always returned to the RPG program.

Field selection can be employed on this type of subfile where you use indicators to determine which fields appear in the subfile. Introduction of this type of inconsistency in the data makes the SFLINZ, SFLLIN, SFLRCDNBR, and SFLRNA keywords invalid as well.

When SFLSIZ and SFLPAG are Not Equal

When the values specified for SFLSIZ and SFLPAG are not the same, the system processes the Page Up and Page Down keys without returning control to the RPG program as long as there are records in the subfile to scroll through. When the beginning or end of the subfile is encountered within the scrolling process, control is returned to the RPG program where the decision to write more records or perform some other function can be made.

Typically with this type of subfile, you initially load enough records into the subfile to present a single page and then perform the output operation on the subfile control record format. If the operator presses Page Down, control is returned to the RPG program (there are no more records in the subfile to display) where your program writes an additional page of data to the subfile without clearing the original records and then repeats the process. Using this method, if the operator presses Page Up (after pressing Page Down at least once), the paging is handled entirely by OS/400 without ever having to return control to the RPG program until the beginning of the subfile is encountered.

Another characteristic of this type of subfile is that the subfile automatically extends itself to contain additional records if you write a subfile record with a relative record number greater than the value specified in the SFLSIZ keyword. It continues to extend itself up to 9,999 records, which is the maximum that may be specified for a subfile.

Deciding the initial size of the subfile can be important. If SFLSIZ is too big, memory is wasted, which could hurt overall response time. If the SFLSIZ is too small, the system may be working overtime to extend the size of the subfile continuously. In general, we like to code the SFLSIZ as two or three times the SFLPAG.

THE PAGE KEYS AND THEIR RELATIONSHIP TO THE SUBFILE

As we discussed earlier, the system handles rolling when the page keys are pressed, as long as there are records to display. If you have coded the fill-'er-up style of subfile, you do not need to code anything to handle the page keys at all (including the Roll and Page keywords in the subfile control record) because OS/400 performs the task for you.

On the other hand, if you have coded the preferred page-at-a-time subfile, you have a little more work to do. When the subfile hits the end or start of the file (depending upon which page key is pressed), control is passed back to the RPG program so more records can be written.

The Page Down Key for Page-at-a-time Subfiles

When the Page Down key is pressed and the last page of records that have been written to the subfile is displayed, control is returned to the RPG program. A new page of subfile records is added then (without clearing the previous records) and the subfile is displayed. This process continues as long as there is data left to be written to the subfile. Once the condition is reached where no more data exists with which to populate the subfile, the indicator that corresponds with the Subfile End (SFLEND) keyword is set on and the subfile is displayed once again. In Figure 2.4, indicator 41 represents the SFLEND indicator.

The Page Up Key for Page-at-a-time Subfiles

If the user presses the Page Up key and the first page of the subfile is currently displayed, control is returned to the program as well. The database file must first be repositioned so the database file pointer corresponds to the first record in the subfile. To complete the setting of the database file pointer, the program must then read backwards until it has read enough records to fill a subfile page.

Because the program is rolling backwards through the data, the subfile must be cleared before writing a new set of subfile records so that pages won't get out of sequence. This is done by performing an output operation to the subfile control record with the indicators set so that either the Subfile Clear (SFLCLR) or Subfile Initialize (SFLINZ) keyword are active at the time. You must remember to reset your indicators after clearing the subfile or you will experience problems with subsequent output requests.

After the database file pointer has been reset and the subfile has been cleared, we can loop back up as if the user had pressed the Page Down key.

CONTROLLING WHICH PAGE OF THE SUBFILE YOU SEE FIRST

When the last page of the subfile is not currently displayed and the Page Down key is pressed, the system rolls the screen to the next page in the subfile without ever returning control to the RPG program. On the other hand, if the user presses the Page Down key and the last page of the subfile is displayed, control is returned to the program and we simply continue reading the database records (as long as there are records to read) and writing to the subfile records.

Once we have loaded another page, we redisplay the subfile. The problem with this is that, when a subfile is displayed, the default setting is to display the subfile from the beginning of the subfile. In other words, the first page is always displayed initially. Consequently, if we write additional pages to the subfile and perform an output operation on the subfile control record, the first page of the subfile is displayed again and it looks as if nothing happened. The user must press the Page Down key a second time (where control would not be returned to the RPG program because subfile records already exist) to see the additional pages that were written. Fortunately, there is a solution to this problem. We can control which page of the subfile is displayed by using the Subfile Record Number (SFLRCDNBR) keyword.

To use the SFLRCDNBR keyword, define a four-character, zoned numeric field (with zero decimal positions) within the subfile control record that is used to store a subfile relative record number as we have in Figure 2.5. Generally, we code this field as a hidden field. The program must load this field with the relative record number of a record that is in the page we want displayed. The system then displays that page, but the record corresponding to the relative record number we loaded into the SFLRCDNBR field is not necessarily at the top of the screen.

Figure 2.5: Using the SFLRCDNBR Keyword

```
    A          R SFLCTL                    SFLCTL(SFLRCD)
    A                                      SFLSIZ(0020)
    A                                      SFLPAG(0010)
    A                                      SFLDSP
    A            SFLRRN       4  0H         SFLRCDNBR
```

Using the example in Figure 2.5, we can use the SFLRCDNBR keyword to control which page of the subfile is to be displayed. To use this option, we load the appropriate subfile relative record number into the SFLRRN field prior to performing an output operation to the subfile control record format. If there are 30 records in the subfile and we want the third page to be displayed, we put any number between 21 and 30 into the SFLRRN field to attain our desired results.

If you want a specific record to appear at the top of the subfile screen, load the appropriate relative record number into the SFLRCDNBR field and use the *TOP parameter in the DDS. This gives you control over which specific record appears at the top of each screen.

You can also use the SFLRCDNBR field to control where the cursor is positioned within the subfile by using the CURSOR parameter. This offers a good alternative to using the position cursor (PC) display attribute within your subfile. The problem with using the display attribute to position the cursor is that the position cursor attribute remains in effect until you update the subfile record with the conditioning indicator off. Subsequent output requests to the subfile control record may have the cursor positioned where you no longer want it.

THE SUBFILE END (SFLEND) KEYWORD

The SFLEND keyword is used indicate to the program operator whether or not there are more records that may be displayed in the subfile. This keyword is only activated when there are no more records to be written to the subfile.

When we are coding the fill-'er-up subfile, we can go ahead and set the conditioning indicator for the SFLEND keyword on from the outset because we know that all the records that ever will be written to the subfile are being written from the start.

But when we are coding page-at-a-time subfiles, we are only going to write records to the subfile as needed, so we do not turn the conditioning indicator on until there are no more records to write. In most cases, this means that we have reached an end-of-file condition on the database file that we happen to be loading into the subfile.

There are three different output options that may be employed when using the SFLEND keyword. The parameter used with the SFLEND keyword indicates to the system which output option you want to use. These optional parameters are *MORE, *PLUS, and *SCRBAR.

Using the SFLEND Keyword with the *MORE Parameter

The *MORE parameter of the SFLEND keyword is probably the most familiar because it is used to display the More... and Bottom literals on the screen much as you see on many output displays throughout the AS/400 operating system. The *MORE keyword tells the system to display More... at the end of every page of the subfile unless the conditioning indicator is on *and* the last page of the subfile currently is displayed, in which case the literal Bottom is displayed. The drawback to using the *MORE parameter on the SFLEND keyword is that you must leave an entire unused line where the More... or Bottom literals appear. This unused line is automatically the line that directly follows the last record of the subfile (output line of the first subfile record + SFLPAG + 1 line). If you fail to leave the line blank when using the *MORE parameter, your Display File will not compile.

Using the SFLEND Keyword with the *PLUS Parameter

The default option on the SFLEND keyword is *PLUS where a plus sign (+) is displayed in lieu of the More... literal. When the last page of the subfile is displayed and the SFLEND conditioning indicator has been turned on, no plus sign (+) is displayed. This method can be an advantage in that it does not require the extra blank display line that *MORE requires, but its intent is not as clear to some program operators. When present, the plus sign (+) automatically overlays the last three positions of the last subfile record on a page, which may cause a problem if you are not careful when laying out your subfile record on the screen.

Using the SFLEND Keyword with the *SCRBAR Parameter

The final output option parameter for the SFLEND keyword is *SCRBAR, where a graphical scroll bar can be utilized. This option was made available as part of V3R1 and obviously, only applies to graphical workstations with device descriptions that support a pointer device (generally a mouse). When using the *SCRBAR parameter, you can also specify the *MORE or *PLUS parameter, so the system knows which option to exercise when the application is run from a nongraphical workstation.

The scroll bar works much as it would with other graphical interfaces in that it has a cursor to indicate how big the subfile is and where you are within it. The cursor can be moved with the pointing device and the subfile is repositioned accordingly.

You must leave the three right-most characters in your subfile record blank to leave room for the scroll bar to appear on the screen. This restriction is similar to the extra blank line that must be left when using the *MORE parameter.

By the very nature of the page-at-a-time and fill-'er-up subfiles we have discussed, the scroll bar option is a lot more attractive with the latter than it is with the former. If you use the page-at-a-time subfile, the cursor within the scroll bar could be somewhat misleading because it represents the number of records that currently are in the subfile and not those that ultimately could end up there. When used in a fill-'er-up subfile, the cursor is obviously a much more fair representation of where the operator is within the file.

Figure 2.6 shows what a subfile scroll bar looks like. We code the program that presents this display later in this chapter.

Figure 2.6: Example of a Subfile Scroll Bar

```
 Options:  1=Select or press ENTER to cancel

 Option    State       Description
    █         AK          ALASKA            ▲
    _         AL          ALABAMA           ▣
    _         AR          ARKANSAS
    _         AZ          ARIZONA
    _         CA          CALIFORNIA
    _         CO          COLORADO
    _         DE          DELAWARE          ▼
```

CODING THE "CUSTOMER SUBFILE" DISPLAY FILE

Having said all that, writing the code necessary to create and display a subfile is actually fairly simple. The first subfile program we will code is a page-at-a-time subfile used to display a customer file in customer number sequence. This program is not all that functional, but a good example of a variety of the concepts we have been discussing.

As you can see from Figure 2.7, the program operator has the option of pressing the page keys to scroll through the customer file, or pressing Enter to end the program. Every time the Page Down key is pressed, we add a new page of subfile records and perform an output/input operation (EXFMT) to the subfile control record. When the operator presses the Page Up key, our program clears the subfile (so subfile records are not written out of order), resets the database pointers, rebuilds the subfile, and performs the I/O operation.

Figure 2.7: Sample "Customer Subfile" Display

```
                         Customer Subfile


     Press PAGE keys, or Enter to Cancel

     Customer Name            Customer Number
   JEFF'S COMPUTER CABLES        1
   SORRENTO ELECTRICAL SUPPLY    10
   ENCINITAS PAINT               11
   JOLLYTIME LANDSCAPE           12
   WESTONHILL PROPERTY MANAGEMENT 13
   SOUTH BAY PLUMBING            14
   CHULA VISTA SPRINKLER SUPPLY  15
   SANTEE ELECTRICAL             16
   BAYSIDE REALTY                17
   ESCONDIDO NURSERY             18
   HOME DEPOT                    2
   WESTERN LUMBER                3

                                              More...
```

Let's examine the subfile record and subfile control record as they have been defined in the DDS specifications shown in Figure 2.8. As required, the Subfile Record (SFLRCD) is defined before and directly prior to the Subfile Control Record (SFLCTL). The SFLCTL keyword indicates which subfile record (SFLRCD in this case) is being controlled by the subfile control record format.

Figure 2.8: DDS for "Customer Subfile"

```
     A           R SFLRCD.              SFL
     A             SFNAME      30A  O  7  2
     A             SFACCT      10A  O  7 36
     A           R SFLCTL             SFLCTL(SFLRCD)
     A                                SFLSIZ(0024)
     A                                SFLPAG(0012)
     A    21                          SFLDSP
     A    22                          SFLDSPCTL
     A    23                          SFLCLR
     A    24                          SFLEND(*MORE)
     A                                ROLLDOWN(27)
     A                                ROLLUP(28)
     A             RRN          4  0H  SFLRCDNBR
     A                             1 29'Customer Subfile'
     A                                DSPATR(HI UL)
     A                             4  5'Press PAGE keys, or Enter to-
     A                                 Cancel'
     A                             6  2'    Customer Name          -
     A                                    Customer Number'
     A                                DSPATR(HI UL)
```

The subfile control record contains the four mandatory keywords required for every control record format: Subfile Control (SFLCTL), Subfile Display (SFLDSP), Subfile Size (SFLSIZ), and Subfile Page (SFLPAG).

Note that, in our example, Subfile Size (SFLSIZ) and Subfile Page (SFLPAG) have different values. SFLPAG has a value of 12 (meaning that up to 12 records appear on the screen at one time) and that SFLSIZ is 24 records (indicating that the subfile will usually consist of about two pages of data). If more than 24 records are written to the subfile, the system automatically extends the size of the subfile to the number of records needed, but users may notice a slight pause in response time while the system performs this task.

We also have conditioned the Subfile Display (SFLDSP) keyword (telling the system when to display the subfile records) on an indicator. If we fail to condition this keyword and an attempt is made to display subfile records when no records have been written to the subfile, the system responds with an error message. We only turn on the conditioning indicator (21) for the SFLDSP keyword if a record is written to the subfile.

The Subfile Display Control (SFLDSPCTL) keyword tells the system when to display the control record. This keyword is required on this subfile because we are performing input requests on the subfile control record format and we have information on the subfile control record format that we wish to display. We have conditioned the SFLDSPCTL on an indicator (22) because we do not want the subfile control record to be displayed when we perform an output operation on the subfile control record to clear the subfile.

An indicator (23) is used to condition the Subfile Clear (SFLCLR) keyword that is only turned on when we want the subfile cleared. For our purposes in this program, this condition is met when the operator presses Page Up. Failure to properly condition this keyword could result in the subfile being cleared on each output operation to the control file record.

The status of the Subfile End (SFLEND) keyword is based upon an indicator (24), which we turn on once we find the end of our customer database file. Turning on this indicator causes the Bottom literal to appear when the last page of the subfile is displayed. When all other pages are displayed, the Page Down key is enabled and the More... literal appears just below the last subfile record.

The ROLLDOWN and ROLLUP keywords are coded to set on indicators 27 and 28 (depending on which key is pressed). Note that the PAGEUP and PAGEDOWN keywords have been added as DDS keywords to be used in lieu of the ROLLUP and

ROLLDOWN keywords. They work the exact same way as their counterparts, except that PAGEUP is the equivalent of ROLLDOWN and PAGEDOWN is the equivalent of ROLLUP.

We use the RRN field to control which page of the subfile is displayed. The subfile relative record number we load into the Subfile Record Number (SFLRCDNBR) field (RRN) determines which page of the subfile is displayed. In this example, we have not specified any parameters for this keyword to indicate where the cursor should be (we have no input fields), and we do not care if the record we specify in the RRN field is at the top of the screen or not.

CODING THE "CUSTOMER SUBFILE" RPG PROGRAM

The RPG program in Figure 2.9 typifies what is involved in writing a page-at-a-time subfile. We read enough database records to fill a page of the subfile and then perform an Execute Format (EXFMT) on the subfile control record so the operator can decide what the next course of action should be. Taking this approach ensures that we have done the minimal number of disk I/O operations on the database file, and that initially there is very little memory required to store our subfile. Because we can not be absolutely certain how many records our customer database file may contain, this is the most logical method to use when designing this subfile.

Figure 2.9: RPG Program for "Customer Subfile"

```
      FTESTDSP CF   E                    WORKSTN
      F                                           RRN    KSFILE SFLRCD
      FCUSTOMERIF  E         K          DISK
      C                     READ CUSTOMER                41 READ FIRST RECORD...
      C                     MOVEA'0100'    *IN,21           SETUP SFL CONTROL
      *    27 = page up -- 28 = page down
  B1  C          *IN27      DOUEQ*OFF                       STAY IN THE LOOP
      C          *IN28      ANDEQ*OFF                       AS LONG AS PAGE KEYS
  B2  C                     DO   12        X       30       ARE PRESSED
  B3  C          *IN41      IFEQ *OFF
      C                     MOVELNAME      SFNAME           POPULATE SUBFILE
      C                     MOVE CUST#     SFACCT
      C                     ADD  1         RRN     40 21    ACTIVATE SFLDSP
      C                     WRITESFLRCD                     IF RECORD IS WRITTEN
      C                     READ CUSTOMER                41
  X3  C                     ELSE
      C                     MOVE *ON       *IN24            ACTIVATE SFLEND
  E3  C                     ENDIF
  E2  C                     ENDDO
      C                     EXFMTSFLCTL                     DISPLAY/READ SUBFILE
  B2  C          *IN27      CASEQ*ON       RLBACK           PAGE UP PRESSED
  E2  C                     ENDCS
  E1  C                     ENDDO
      *
      C                     MOVE *ON       *INLR
```

```
       *
    C          RLBACK     BEGSR
    C          1          CHAINSFLRCD                   41      RESET DATABASE
    C          SFACCT     SETLLCUSTOMER                         POINTER
    C                     MOVEA'0010'   *IN,21
    C                     WRITESFLCTL                           CLEAR SUBFILE
    C                     MOVEA'0100'   *IN,21
    C                     MOVE *ZEROS   RRN
B1  C                     DO   12                               READ ENOUGH RECORDS
    C                     READPCUSTOMER                 41 TO FILL A PAGE
B2  C          *IN41      IFEQ *ON
    C          *LOVAL     SETLLCUSTOMER                         IF BEGINNING OF THE
    C                     READ CUSTOMER                 41 FILE IS REACHED,
    C                     LEAVE                              START OVER
E2  C                     ENDIF
E1  C                     ENDDO
    C                     ENDSR
```

The first steps performed in our example are to read the first database record and to set the initial conditioning indicators for our subfile control record format. We set on the conditioning indicator (22) to display the subfile control record format so that it appears on our first output operation.

We then enter a loop that populates the subfile with the first 12 records (that is the size of our subfile page). The loop has been coded so that the subfile remains active as long as the page keys are pressed. When the Enter key is pressed, the program exits the loop and the program terminates (indicator LR is set on).

By adding 1 to the RRN (SFLRCDNBR) field, we ensure that the most recent page of the subfile is always displayed. New pages of the subfile continue to be added to the subfile every time the Page Down key is pressed, until the end of the customer database file is reached. At that point the Subfile End (SFLEND) indicator (24) is turned on. This causes the literal Bottom to be displayed.

If the Page Up key is pressed, we execute the RLBACK subroutine, which clears out the subfile and repositions the database file pointer. If the subfile is not cleared, we are adding records to the subfile that are out of sequence.

To reposition the database file pointer, the RLBACK subroutine first chains to the very first record in the subfile that was written to get the record key that will be used to reposition the file. This is more efficient than reading backwards through either the database file or the subfile because we may have accumulated many pages of data in the subfile before rollback was ever pressed. Remember that OS/400 handles the roll back process through the subfile records (without ever returning control to the RPG program) as long as there are subfile records to read.

That was not so difficult, was it? You have taken one of the most widely misunderstood and feared subjects among beginner and intermediate AS/400 programmers and made it look easy. Your confidence with subfiles should be soaring now.

Let's have some fun and move on to that window subfile with the scroll bar we saw back in Figure 2.6. But before we write our next subfile program, we need to cover a few more basic concepts. Because this is a window subfile, we will be dealing with a few DDS window keywords. We are also going to be introduced to a subfile where the operator can perform input.

Writing Subfiles within a DDS Window

Finally! The ability to put subfiles within DDS windows was announced when V2R3 was released. Subfiles have become such a major component of our day-to-day programming that the ability to put them within a window was a very natural progression.

Even though we do not cover the DDS window keywords until the next chapter, do not let that deter you. As you see in Figure 2.10, the code required for the purposes of this example involve only two new DDS keywords, and they are very simple. There are, however, some new issues that we need to cover, before getting into this next example.

Figure 2.10: DDS for State Lookup Window Subfile

```
A              R WINDOW
A                                    WINDOW(3 4 13 53)
A                                    RMVWDW
A              R SFLRCD              SFL
A   42                               SFLNXTCHG
A                SFLRRN     4S 0H
A                SFLSEL     1A  B  5  4DSPATR(HI)
A                SFDESC    30A  O  5 19
A                SFLCOD     2A  O  5 12
A              R SFLCTL              SFLCTL(SFLRCD)
A                                    OVERLAY
A                                    SFLDSP
A                                    SFLDSPCTL
A   24                               SFLEND(*SCRBAR *MORE)
A                                    SFLSIZ(0050)
A                                    SFLPAG(0007)
A   42                               SFLMSG('Invalid Selection Entry')
A                                    WINDOW(WINDOW)
A                SETPOS     4S 0H    SFLRCDNBR(CURSOR)
A                CURPOS     5S 0H    SFLSCROLL
A                                  2  2'Options:'
A                                  2 11'1=Select'
A                                    DSPATR(HI)
A                                  2 20'or press ENTER to cancel'
A                                  4  2'Option    State         Description  -
A                                    '
A                                    DSPATR(HI UL)
A              R DUMMY
A                                    KEEP
A                                    ASSUME
A                                  1  2' '
```

Reading Subfile Records That Have Been Changed

The fact that OS/400 can handle much of the rolling within the subfile without returning control to the RPG program poses a rather unique problem. If our subfile has more than one page of data in it, we do not know which page was displayed at the time input was performed. Nor do we know if input was performed on more than one subfile record.

We could address these potential problems by setting up a loop within our RPG program that chains through the subfile using the subfile relative record number to see if any input was keyed into our input fields. This is not very efficient, however, and does not help us if a record has been updated.

The Read Changed Record (READC) RPG operation code is the answer to this particular problem. When used in conjunction with the Subfile Next Change (SFLNXTCHG) subfile record-level keyword, your program can be coded so that only subfile records that have been modified are read. So, instead of coding a loop to go through all subfile records, you code it so only the records that have been changed are read.

The rub with this particular method of processing is that, if your program detects an error in the entered data and the subfile is redisplayed, you will not read the record in error again unless the operator changes data on the record in error. If you condition this keyword on an indicator, you can beat this problem by setting on the option indicator and performing an UPDAT operation to the subfile record prior to the next EXFMT on the control file record format. This updates the modified data tag and the record is read on the next READC loop whether the operator changes any data in the subfile record or not.

Don't Blank Out That Screen, Dummy!

When using the DDS window keywords, you may have already experienced the frustration of screens inexplicably being blanked out when you try to present your DDS window.

If you call an external RPG program that displays a window over a previously displayed screen format, the screen displayed by the preceding program is blanked out before the window is displayed. This seems to defeat the purpose of using a window.

One solution to this problem is to add a dummy format containing the KEEP and ASSUME keywords to the display file that contains the window. Note that there is a DUMMY format in Figure 2.10 that is never called. Removing it, however, results in the problem described above.

Subfile Error Messages

This next example in Figure 2.10 also uses one of the two simplest forms of subfile messages. We use the Subfile Message (SFLMSG) keyword to display error messages on the screen. When the conditioning indicator is turned on and an output operation is performed on the subfile control record format, the message text that is specified along with the SFLMSG keyword is displayed in the message area at the bottom of the screen.

The SFLMSGID is the other simple subfile message method. This keyword is used like the SFLMSG keyword, except that you specify the message ID and the qualified name and location of the message file.

These methods include conditioning by indicators, so they do not give you a lot of flexibility. When you have programs with a large number of potential errors or you want to pass variable data into the messages, you are better off using message subfiles. We discuss these situations later in this chapter.

I'd Like Scroll Bars with That Subfile, If You Please...

As we discussed earlier when we were describing the Subfile End (SFLEND) keyword, you can now use scroll bars for graphical workstations that have a pointing device. Because our State Lookup subfile is coded as a fill-'er-up type of subfile, it was a practical option for this example.

Notice in Figure 2.10 that we are using the *SCRBAR parameter on the SFLEND keyword. We also used the *MORE parameter, so workstations that are incapable of showing the scroll bar use the More... and Bottom literals instead of the less user-friendly plus sign (+).

Because we are using the scroll bar, we were able to demonstrate the field level SFLSCROLL keyword as well. This keyword returns the relative record number of the subfile record that happens to be at the top of the screen back to your RPG program. The field to hold the returned relative record number must be coded as a five-digit, signed numeric hidden field.

CODING THE STATE LOOKUP WINDOW SUBFILE DISPLAY FILE

Let's examine the DDS in Figure 2.10 that we are using for our State Lookup window subfile program. You are already familiar with most of the keywords we will use.

This program is different from those that we have looked at so far in that our program presents three different record formats (WINDOW, SFLCTL, and SFLRCD) to the screen at the same time.

The DDS for the WINDOW record format is simple. It only tells the system that we are using a DDS window that begins on line 3, in position 4, is 13 lines deep, and is 53 characters across. The RMVWDW keyword has been added so the system will remove existing DDS windows from the screen prior to presenting this one. The WINDOW keyword tells the AS/400 that this format is a DDS window and the system handles the rest of the work for you.

The Subfile Record (SFLRCD) in our example uses the Subfile Next Change (SFLNXTCHG) keyword just discussed. It also has a hidden field (SFLRRN) in which we store the subfile relative record number. It comes in handy when we want to control the positioning of our subfile. We then have an input-capable field called SFLSEL, which a program operator can use to key a selection option. The other two fields are used to store the state code and description.

Our subfile control record has the standard required keywords (SFLSIZ, SFLPAG, SFLDSP, and SFLCTL). This particular subfile is coded as a fill-'er-up subfile because we know that we have a small, fixed number of records that can possibly be loaded into the subfile. The fact that there are only 50 states leaves us in a position to know the exact number of records contained in the subfile. By putting all of the records in the subfile up front, we are in a position to let the system handle all of the rolling for us when the page keys are pressed. Note that the Subfile Size (SFLSIZ) is 50, and the Subfile Page (SFLPAG) is 7.

We have also coded the SFLDSPCTL keyword into our control record. This is required because we will be requesting input from our subfile and also because we have information in the control record that we would like displayed on the screen.

We use the SFLRCDNBR field to control which page of the subfile is displayed and where within the subfile the cursor is positioned, by loading the appropriate values into the SETPOS field.

The WINDOW keyword tells the system that this subfile is presented within a window and identifies the name of the window.

CODING THE STATE LOOKUP WINDOW SUBFILE RPG PROGRAM

As you see from the code in Figure 2.11, it does not take very much code to get our window subfile program up and running. This window subfile routine may be called from any program where you want to allow an operator to look up the valid state codes. The selected state code is returned to the calling program in the RTNCOD parameter.

Figure 2.11: RPG for State Lookup Window Subfile Program

```
    FSLIDEDSPCF   E                   WORKSTN
    F                                         SFLRRNKSFILE SFLRCD
    FSTATES   IF  E          K        DISK
    I             SDS
    I                                    *PARMS    PARMS
    C             *ENTRY    PLIST
    C                       PARM               RTNCOD 2
    C                       MOVE *BLANKS   SFLSEL
    C                       Z-ADD1         SETPOS
    C                       WRITEWINDOW
B1  C                       DO   50
    C                       READ STATES                        24
B2  C             *IN24     IFEQ *OFF
    C                       MOVE STATE     SFLCOD
    C                       MOVE STDESC    SFDESC
    C                       ADD  1         SFLRRN
    C                       WRITESFLRCD
E2  C                       ENDIF
E1  C                       ENDDO
    *
B1  C             GETOUT    DOUEQ*ON
    C                       EXFMTSFLCTL                     DISPLAY/READ SUBFILE
    C                       MOVE *OFF      *IN42
    C                       MOVE CURPOS    SETPOS           SET CURSOR
B2  C             *IN41     DOUEQ*ON                        READ CHANGES LOOKING
    C                       READCSFLRCD               41 FOR SELECT REQUEST
B3  C             *IN41     IFEQ *ON
    C                       MOVE *ON       GETOUT           GET OUT IF ENTER
X3  C                       ELSE                            PRESSED W/O SELECT
B4  C                       SELEC
    C             SFLSEL    WHEQ '1'                         GET OUT IF RECORD
    C                       MOVE SFLCOD    RTNCOD           SELECTED
    C                       MOVE *ON       GETOUT 1
    C             SFLSEL    WHNE *BLANKS
    C                       MOVE *ON       *IN42            FALL THRU TO ERROR
    C                       MOVE SFLRRN    SETPOS
    C                       UPDATSFLRCD
    C                       OTHER
    C                       ITER            .
E4  C                       ENDSL
    C                       LEAVE
E3  C                       ENDIF
E2  C                       ENDDO
E1  C                       ENDDO
    *
    C                       MOVE *ON       *INLR
```

The program initially writes the window record format to the screen and then reads through the STATES database file and loads the subfile with each record read from the file. This is typical for a fill-'er-up style of subfile.

Once the subfile has been loaded, the program is ready to process and edit input from the operator. An I/O request is made of the subfile control record and the current cursor position is fed back into the SETPOS field that represents our SFLRCDNBR field. This is done because we can not know where the actual cursor position is at the time we read the control record. Remember, the system is controlling our rolling when page keys are pressed, so our current cursor position could be anywhere in the subfile.

Rather than reading all of our subfile records to see if the operator made a selection, we use READC so we may read only the records that have changed. If we find that no records have changed, we can assume that the operator wanted to terminate the program and simply pressed Enter without making a change.

If records have changed, there are only three possibilities:

- The operator made a valid selection by keying a 1 in front of the desired selection.

- An invalid selection was made (a value other than 1 was keyed).

- The selection field contains blanks. Note that, if the operator presses FIELD EXIT through the selection field to get down to the desired record, the selection field is tagged as having been changed but the field has a blank in it. It is for this reason that we have accounted for this possibility by coding the program to ignore records where a blank selection is made.

If the selection made is determined to be in error, we set on the error indicator (42) so the SFLMSG keyword is activated and the error is displayed. We also load the relative record number of the subfile record (stored in the SFLRRN hidden field) that is incorrect into the SETPOS (SFLRCDNBR) field. This causes the cursor to be positioned on the error record and ensures that the appropriate page of the subfile is displayed.

Performing an UPDAT operation on the subfile record that is in error is done so the record is flagged as changed the next time the subfile control record is read. If we fail to do this and the operator does not correct or change the record that we found in error, the record is not read the next time the READC operation is performed. The record remains in an error condition and the record is not edited again.

ERROR HANDLING WITH A MESSAGE SUBFILE

The message subfile is unique; it has been designed specifically to present error messages to the screen. It allows us to present multiple error messages in a single output operation and easily lends itself to allowing us to pass variable information into the error messages themselves. And, for those of us who code a lot of subprograms, it also enables us to write an error message in one program and have it sent to the message queue of another.

In this next example, we look at an RPG program that prompts for and edits a customer number. If the customer number is deemed invalid, we use an API to send an error message to our program and output the message to our message subfile.

Figure 2.12 shows the DDS necessary to code an error message subfile. The SFLMSGRCD keyword tells the system on what line to display the error message. The SFLMSGKEY keyword tells the system if it is to display only messages with a certain message ID, or all messages in the message queue. The field identified by the SFLPGMQ keyword indicates which program message queue to display. In our example in Figure 2.13, we load this field with an asterisk (*) to indicate that the current program message queue is to be used.

Figure 2.12: DDS for a Message Subfile

```
     A              R MSGSFL                     SFL
     A                                           SFLMSGRCD(24)
     A                MSGKEY                      SFLMSGKEY
     A                PGMQ                        SFLPGMQ
     A              R MSGCTL                      SFLCTL(MSGSFL)
     A                                           OVERLAY
     A                                           SFLSIZ(3) SFLPAG(1)
     A                                           SFLDSP SFLINZ
     A 90                                         SFLEND
     A                PGMQ                        SFLPGMQ
     A              R FORMAT1
     A 40                                         OVERLAY
     A                                           CF03(03 'End of job')
     A                                    21  3'                         -
     A                                                      '            -
     A                                           DSPATR(UL)
     A                                    22  5'F3=Exit'
     A                                     9 21'Customer Number:'
     A                CUSTNO        10A  B  9 38
     A                                     1 27'Customer Inquiry'
     A                                           DSPATR(HI)
     A                                           DSPATR(UL)
```

Figure 2.13: RPG for a Message Subfile

```
FSFLMSGDSCF  E                    WORKSTN
IERROR       IDS
I                                 B   1    40BYTPRV
I                                 B   5    80BYTAVA
I                                     9  15 MSGID
I                                    16  16 ERR###
I                                    17 116 MSGDTA
I            DS
I                                 B   1    40MSGKY
I                                 B   5    80MSGDLN
I                                 B   9 120MSGQNB
I            'IS INVALID'         C         CONINV
C                   MOVEL'*'      PGMQ  10
C                   SETON                    90
C            *IN40  DOUNE*ON
C            *IN40  IFEQ *ON
C                   WRITEMSGCTL
C                   ENDIF
C                   EXFMTFORMAT1
C                   MOVE *OFF     *IN40
C            CUSTNO IFEQ *ALL'9'
C                   EXSR SNDERR
C                   MOVE *ON      *IN40
C                   ENDIF
C                   ENDDO
C                   SETON                    LR
C            SNDERR BEGSR
C                   MOVEL'CPF9898' MSGID
C            'QCPFMSG' CAT  'QSYS':3 MSGF
C            'CUSTOMER'CAT  CUSTNO:1 MDATA   P
C                   CAT  CONINV:1 MDATA
C                   Z-ADD50       MSGDLN
C                   CALL 'QMHSNDPM'          SEND ERROR MESSAGE
C                   PARM          MSGID  7
C                   PARM          MSGF  20
C                   PARM          MDATA 50
C                   PARM          MSGDLN
C                   PARM '*DIAG'  MSGTYP 10
C                   PARM '*'      MSGQ  10
C                   PARM 0        MSGQNB
C                   PARM          MSGKY
C                   PARM          ERROR      ERROR CODE
C                   ENDSR
```

Like all subfiles, the control record contains the required SFLSIZ, SFLPAG, SFLCTL, and SFLDSP keywords. Our SFLPAG is set to 1, so only one error message line appears at a time, but the user can position the cursor on that line and roll through any other messages that may be in the subfile. A plus sign (+) appears on the message line if there is more than one message.

We chose to use the SFLINZ keyword so that all messages could be written to the message queue in a single output operation. If we had not used the SFLINZ keyword, then only one message at a time could be written to the subfile message record.

The RPG code necessary to write an error message to a message queue and to display that message on the screen is shown in Figure 2.13. The field PGMQ (which is the field specified on the SFLPGMQ keyword) is loaded with an *. This indicates that the current program message queue is to be used.

Next, the format that contains the customer input field that is to be edited is displayed. If the customer number doesn't pass our edit, the SNDERR subroutine is executed where the API is executed to send an error to our program's message queue.

Substitution Variables in Error Messages

SNDERR uses the global message CPF9898, which is found in every system-supplied QCPFMSG message file. It has only one data field, which is a vacant space where you supply the error to be displayed. Using the Concatenate (CAT) op code, we construct an error message that contains the variable that we want included in the body of the message.

Our program then uses the QMHSNDPM API (Send Program Message) to send the message to the message queue. Again, the variable MSGQ contains an *, which means send it to this message queue. Message queue number (MSGQNB) indicates the number of invocation levels back you want the message sent. A 0 in this field indicates send it to the current program, a 1 means that you want it sent to the previous calling program, and so on.

Once the message is written to the message queue, the write to MSGCTL format displays the error message subfile records. The EXFMT to FORMAT1 redisplays the screen in error and waits for the correction from the user.

Note that FORMAT1 needs the OVERLAY keyword to be optioned on when an error is being displayed. The normal routine that the system employs when displaying a screen is to first remove everything currently on the screen and then display a new screen. Because this would erase the error message just displayed, we condition the OVERLAY keyword on the FORMAT1 screen, telling the system to leave the screen as it is and write over it with the new screen.

USING SEARCH FIELDS IN THE SUBFILE CONTROL RECORD FORMAT

Most of the time when you want to present a database file in a subfile, you want to allow the program operator the opportunity to search for or *lookup* a specific record. This is particularly true in the case of large database files that you present as page-at-a-time.

Obviously it is not productive for somebody to sit and scroll through page after page of data looking for the desired record. You may as well give them a printed list.

It is for this reason that search fields in the subfile control record format are so useful. The search field allows the program operator to key all or part of a search word/field. The keyed entry is used to reposition the database pointer so the subfile can be written with records that more closely match what the operator is looking for.

For our example of this technique (Figure 2.14), we have chosen a printer lookup window subfile program that could be inserted easily into any report or list request program. This window subfile presents the printer description records alphabetically on the screen (by printer description) and allows an end user to look up, or search for, the printer to which the printed output is sent. When a subfile record on the screen is selected (by keying the appropriate option), the printer ID is returned to the calling program in a parameter. If the operator does not see the desired record within the window, they may either press the page keys or key all or part of a printer description and press Enter to reposition the database file (and consequently the subfile) appropriately.

Figure 2.14: Lookup Window to Select a Printer

```
: Options: 1=Select                                      :
:                                                        :
: OR Key partial description: _____         :
:                                                        :
: Opt  Code          Description                         :
:  _   LASER6     ACCOUNTING - CHECKS                     :
:  _   LASER7     ACCOUNTING - INVOICES                   :
:  _   LASER3     ACCOUNTING - LASER PRINTER              :
:  _   PRT03      COMPUTER ROOM - INVOICE PRINTER         :
:  _   LASER1     COMPUTER ROOM - LASER PRINTER           :
:  _   PRT02      COMPUTER ROOM - LETTER QUALITY          :
:  _   LASER2     FRONT DESK - LASER PRINTER              :
:                                          More...  :
:  F3=Exit  F12=Previous                                 :
:                                                        :
```

For the purposes of our sample program (Figures 2.15 and 2.16), we created DDS for a physical file and a logical file that are used to describe the printers on your system. The physical file is called PRINTER, and the logical file that lets us view the file by description is called PRINTERS.

Figure 2.15: DDS for Physical File PRINTER

```
        R PRTREC                    TEXT('PRINTER DESCRIPTIONS')
          PRTRID       10A          TEXT('PRINTER I.D.')
                                    COLHDG('PRINTER' 'I.D.')
          PRTDSC       35A          TEXT('PRINTER DESCRIPTION')
                                    COLHDG('PRINTER' 'DESCRIPTION')
```

Figure 2.16: DDS for Logical File PRINTERS

```
        R PRTREC                    PFILE(PRINTER)
        K PRTDSC
```

The DDS for this application, seen in Figures 2.17 and 2.18, is very much the same as it would be for any window subfile you are coding. There are three basic ingredients required:

- The DDS window.

- The subfile record.

- The subfile control record.

Figure 2.17: DDS for Display File LOOKUPDS

```
A                                   DSPSIZ(24 80 *DS3)
A                                   PRINT(*LIBL/QSYSPRT)
A           R WINDOW
A                                 · WINDOW(3 4 16 56)
A                                   RMVWDW
A                              15  2'F3=Exit  F12=Previous'
A                                   DSPATR(HI)
A           R SFLRC1               SFL
A             HDNKY1     12A  H
A             SFLOPT      1A  B  7  2DSPATR(HI)
A                                   DSPATR(UL)
A             SFLCOD     10A  O  7  5
A             SFLDSC     40A  O  7 16
A           R SFLCT1               SFLCTL(SFLRC1)
A                                   SFLSIZ(0007)
A                                   SFLPAG(0007)
A                                   WINDOW(WINDOW)
A                                   ROLLUP(95)
A                                   ROLLDOWN(96)
A                                   CA03(03 'EOJ')
A                                   CA12(12 'PREVIOUS')
A                                   BLINK
A  40                               ALARM
A                                   OVERLAY
A                                   PUTOVR
A  21                               SFLDSP
```

```
A  22                                  SFLDSPCTL
A  23                                  SFLCLR
A  24                                  SFLEND(*MORE)
A                                 2  1'Options:'
A                                 2 10'1=Select'
A                                    DSPATR(HI)
A                                 4  1'OR'
A                                    DSPATR(RI)
A                                 4  4'Key partial description:'
A          SEARCH      15A  B     4 29DSPATR(HI)
A  76                               DSPATR(PC)
A                                    OVRATR
A                                 6  1'Opt    Code              Descrip-
A                                    tion                '
A                                    DSPATR(UL)
A        R DUMMY
A                                    KEEP
A                                    ASSUME
A                                 1  2' '
```

Figure 2.18: RPG Specifications for Program LOOKUP

```
FLOOKUPDSCF   E                    WORKSTN
F                                        RRN   KSFILE SFLRC1
FPRINTERSIF   E          K         DISK                       UC
  **
  ** Possible values of the return code (RTNCOD) are:
  **
  **     03 = End of Job Requested
  **     12 = Previous screen requested
  **     50 = Valid record was selected & record key is in the PASKEY field
  **
C           *ENTRY     PLIST
C                      PARM           RTNCOD  2    RETURN CODE
C                      PARM           FILCOD  4    FILE TO LOOKUP
C                      PARM           PASKEY 10    KEY VALUE TO RETURN
  *
B1 C        RTNCOD     DOUNE*BLANKS
B2 C        NXTFMT     CASEQ'FMT1 '   @FMT1
E2 C                   ENDCS
E1 C                   ENDDO
  **
C                      SETON                      LR
  *
  *****    SUBROUTINE: "*INZSR" ****************************************
  ***   PROCESS INITIALIZATION ROUTINE  ******************************
CSR         *INZSR     BEGSR
  *
B1 C                   SELEC
C        FILCOD        WHEQ 'PRT '                OPEN FILES
C                      OPEN PRINTERS
E1 C                   ENDSL
  *
C                      MOVE *BLANKS   RTNCOD
C                      MOVE *ON       RESET
C                      EXSR FILSET                SET FILE POINTERS
C                      EXSR LODSFL                LOAD SUBFILE
C                      MOVE 'FMT1 '   NXTFMT  5
  *
CSR                    ENDSR
```

```
      *****     SUBROUTINE: "@FMT1"   ****************************************
      ***   PROCESS SUBFILE FORMAT    ****************************************
      CSR           @FMT1     BEGSR
      *
      C  N95N96               WRITEWINDOW
      C                       MOVEA'10'       *IN,22
      C                       EXFMTSFLCT1
      C                       MOVEA'0000'     *IN,38
      *
B1    C           *IN96       IFEQ '1'                        ROLL BACKWARDS
      C                       EXSR ROLBAK
      C                       GOTO END1
E1    C                       END
      C                       SETOF                      97
      *
B1    C           *IN95       IFEQ '1'                        ROLL FORWARD
B2    C           *IN24       IFEQ '0'
      C                       EXSR LODSFL
E2    C                       END
      C                       GOTO END1
E1    C                       END
      *
B1    C           SEARCH      IFNE *BLANKS                    REPOSITION FILE
      C                       EXSR FILSET
      C                       EXSR LODSFL
      C                       GOTO END1
E1    C                       END
      *
B1    C           *IN03       IFEQ *ON                        EOJ REQUEST
      C                       MOVE '03'       RTNCOD
      C                       GOTO END1
E1    C                       ENDIF
      *
B1    C           *IN12       IFEQ *ON                        PREVIOUS
      C                       MOVE '12'       RTNCOD
      C                       GOTO END1
E1    C                       ENDIF
      *
B1    C           *IN47       DOUEQ'1'                        READ CHANGES LOOKING
      C                       READCSFLRC1               47 FOR RECORD SELECTED
B2    C           *IN47       IFEQ *OFF
B3    C           SFLOPT      IFNE '1'
      C           SFLOPT      ANDNE' '
      C                       MOVE *ON        *IN40           SOUND ALARM ON
      C                       UPDATSFLRC1                     ERR CONDITION
X3    C                       ELSE
B4    C           SFLOPT      IFEQ '1'                        SELECT RECORD...
      C                       MOVE HDNKY1     PASKEY          PASS FILE KEY BACK
      C                       MOVE '50'       RTNCOD          TO CALLING PROGRAM
      C                       LEAVE
E4    C                       ENDIF
E3    C                       ENDIF
E2    C                       ENDIF
E1    C  N40                  ENDDO
      CSR           END1      ENDSR
      *
      *****   SUBROUTINE: "LODSFL"  ****************************************
      ***   BUILD SUBFILE AND DISPLAY WITH SCREEN 1  *******************
      CSR           LODSFL    BEGSR
      *
      C                       Z-ADD*ZEROS     RRN       40
      C                       MOVEA'0010'     *IN,21          CLEAR SUBFILE
      C                       WRITESFLCT1
      *
```

```
B1  C           1           DO   7         X            READ RECORDS AND
    C                       EXSR REDFWD                 FILL THE SUBFILE
B2  C           *IN24       IFEQ '0'
    C                       ADD  1          RRN
    C                       SETON                   21
    C                       MOVE *BLANKS    SFLOPT
B3  C                       SELEC
    C           FILCOD      WHEQ 'PRT '                 PRINTERS
    C                       MOVELPRTRID     HDNKY1   P   SAVE KEY FIELDS
    C                       MOVELPRTRID     SFLCOD   P   CODE
    C                       MOVELPRTDSC     SFLDSC   P   DESCRIPTION
E3  C                       ENDSL
    C                       WRITESFLRC1
E2  C                       END
E1  C  N24                  END
    C                       MOVE *BLANKS    SEARCH
    CSR                     ENDSR
    *****    SUBROUTINE: "ROLBAK" *****************************************
    ***   ROLL DOWN PROCESSING FOR SUBFILE  ***************************
    CSR         ROLBAK      BEGSR
    C                       SETOF                   24
    C           8           ADD  RRN        Y     20
B1  C           1           DO   Y          X     20
    C                       EXSR REDBAK
B2  C           *IN24       IFEQ '1'
    C                       MOVE *ON         RESET
    C                       EXSR FILSET
E2  C                       END
E1  C  N24                  END
    C                       EXSR LODSFL
    CSR                     ENDSR
    *****    SUBROUTINE: "FILSET" *****************************************
    ***   SET READ POSITIONING FOR SUBFILE  ***************************
    CSR         FILSET      BEGSR
B1  C                       SELEC
    C           FILCOD      WHEQ 'PRT '
B2  C           RESET       IFEQ *ON                    RESET TO TOP OF
    C                       MOVE *BLANKS    SEARCH       THE FILE?
E2  C                       ENDIF
    C                       MOVELSEARCH     PRTDSC
    C           PRTDSC      SETLLPRTREC
E1  C                       ENDSL
    C                       MOVE *OFF        RESET  1
    CSR                     ENDSR
    *****    SUBROUTINE: "REDFWD" *****************************************
    ***   READ FORWARD THROUGH THE FILE   ***************************
    CSR         REDFWD      BEGSR
B1  C                       SELEC
    C           FILCOD      WHEQ 'PRT '
    C                       READ PRTREC              24
B2  C           *IN24       IFEQ *ON
    C           *HIVAL      SETGTPRTREC
E2  C                       ENDIF
E1  C                       ENDSL
    CSR                     ENDSR
    *****    SUBROUTINE: "REDBAK" *****************************************
    ***   READ BACKWARDS THROUGH THE FILE  ***************************
    CSR         REDBAK      BEGSR
B1  C                       SELEC
    C           FILCOD      WHEQ 'PRT '
    C                       READPPRTREC              24
E1  C                       ENDSL
    CSR                     ENDSR
```

Subfiles Over Database Files with Keys That Are Not Unique

Sometimes it is necessary to write a subfile program over a file path where there is no key or where the key is not unique. If you have written a page-at-a-time subfile and you need to reset the database pointer because the Page Up key has been pressed, you have a problem. You can not simply read backwards, because you probably do not know where the file pointer is currently unless you count how many times the Page Down key is pressed.

A file whose path is alphabetic by name is one instance where there may be more than one record with the same key. After all, there are a lot of people named Jones. This can present a problem when paging backwards and one of the duplicate keys is represented by the first record in the subfile, because the first thing the roll back subroutine must do is position the pointer of the database file. The question is, which of the duplicate database records is the correct record at which to position the read/write heads? If you do not position the read/write heads to the correct record, database records are skipped or duplicated when rolling backwards.

The solution to this problem is to keep track of the relative record number of the database record at the time it is written to subfile. We do not want to display this number on the screen, only to use it when rolling. This is accomplished by using a hidden field in the subfile.

The relative record number of the database file can be found in position 397 to 400 of the file information data structure. In the example in Figure 2.19, this field is named DBRRN in the data structure INFO. (The file information data structure is defined by the KINFDS line immediately following the file definition statement.) We then move this field into a hidden field in our subfile.

In the roll back subroutine, chain to the first subfile record and then establish a loop to read the database file until the hidden field relative record number equals the relative record number of the database record. The read/write heads are then positioned on the correct record.

Figure 2.19: Retrieving the Relative Record Number of a Database File

```
FDISPLAY CF   E                   WORKSTN
F                                       RRN   KSFILE SFLRCD
FFILENAMEIF   E         K         DISK
F                                       KINFDS INFO
IINFO         DS
I                                   B 397 4000DBRRN
```

HOORAY FOR SUBFILES!

As you read this chapter, you can not have helped but notice that subfiles are one of the most powerful tools in the AS/400 programmer's arsenal. They are both versatile and effective at addressing a variety of needs that we must contend with as programmers. We hope that this chapter has helped you to appreciate and value AS/400 subfiles as much as we do.

Chapter 3

We Do Windows (and Menu Bars Too)!

Surely you have noticed—the world has gone GUI (graphical user interface). You can not pick up a magazine or newspaper without seeing advertisements for personal computers that rely on Windows, OS/2, or Apple Macintosh operating systems. The reason for this, of course, is the overwhelming popularity of the graphical user interface operations that make these systems both intuitive and easy to use.

Let's face it. When it comes to ease of use, the point-and-click interface can not be beat. This does not mean, however, that the green screen is dead and gone. There are millions of green screen interactive programs that work just fine and will be doing the job for many years to come. But the principle reason for this projected longevity is that the cost of rewriting them for a new GUI interface simply can not be justified.

How to Write GUI Applications, without Getting "Gooey" Applications

Newly designed interactive programs can, and probably should, employ a graphical user interface. IBM has begun to offer us a path to get there with the last several releases of the OS/400 operating system. We have seen the announcement of a variety of DDS keywords that support DDS windows, menu bars, scroll bars, radio buttons, and so on. There is every indication that IBM will continue to lead us down the path toward creating programs that use the graphical user interface.

This chapter gives you a head start on this path. We demonstrate how to use a variety of the new DDS functions that have been announced over the last few years. A list of the topics we cover includes the following:

- **Hardware Configuration and Its Effect on GUI Applications**

  - What equipment you are using will determine what "look" you get

  - What options work with which equipment?

- **Pull-down Menu Bars**

  - Radio buttons

  - Choice options

  - Shortcut keys

  - Accelerator keys

  - Choice filters

  - Setting choice defaults

- **DDS Windows**

  - Borders and colors

  - Window placement

- Message lines

- Restoring the display

- Sample DDS window program

- **Scroll Bars**

- Using scroll bars on your subfiles

HARDWARE AND ITS EFFECT ON GUI-ENABLED APPLICATIONS

Before you begin writing GUI-enabled applications, you need to be aware that the actual format of the display presented to the user is dependent upon the hardware configuration. Older workstations and controllers were not designed or manufactured with a graphical user interface in mind.

When IBM began to employ the newer GUI functions in the operating system, they still had to make allowances for the millions of dollars worth of older equipment that was already in place. They were forced to consider the older workstations and workstation controllers attached to the two- or three-hundred thousand AS/400 systems already installed.

Consequently, the look and feel of the new GUI functions vary widely depending upon the equipment you happen to be running. We compiled a table of the equipment possibilities as of V3R1. Table 3.1 shows the possible configurations and how each function appears.

Table 3.1: Hardware Configurations and Workstations

Configuration	Selection Fields	Selection Lists
GUI-programmable Workstations [1]	GUI [2]	Bar selection cursor. Possible check boxes for multiple-choice lists. Possible radio buttons for single-choice lists.
InfoWindow II Display Stations [3] Attached to Enhanced Interface Controller [4]	Character-based GUI [5]	Bar selection cursor. Possible check boxes for multiple-choice lists. Possible radio buttons for single-choice lists.
3477 Display Station Attached to Enhanced Interface Controller [4]	Mnemonics (shortcut keys); bar selection cursor.	Bar selection cursor. Input field to left of list.
5250 Display Station Attached to Enhanced Interface Controller [4]	Bar selection cursor.	Bar selection cursor. Input field to left of list.
ASCII Display Station Attached to ASCII Controller Supporting Enhanced Interface [6]	Bar selection cursor.	Bar selection cursor. Input field to left of list.
Any Display Station Attached to Controller Not Supporting Enhanced Interface [7]	Entry field driven.	Input field to left of list.

> **NOTES:**
> [1] For example, RUMBA/400.
> [2] GUI shows as solid-line window borders.
> [3] InfoWindow II display stations: 3486, 3487, 3488.
> [4] Twinaxial controllers: 5494 Release 1.1, features 6050, 2661, 9146, and 9148.
> [5] Character-based GUI, except lines are created using characters.
> [6] ASCII controllers that support enhanced interface: features 6041, 6141, 2637, 9145, and 9147.
> [7] For example, 5250 display stations attached to 5294 and 5394 controllers or features 2638, 6040, and 6140. Another example: Client Access/400—PCs emulating a controller with an attached 5250 display station.

MY SCREEN STILL DOESN'T LOOK RIGHT

Normally, display files are created with the default for the ENHDSP, which is *YES. This means that, if the display station is capable of enhanced interfaces, they are used automatically. In other words, window borders and menu bar separators are presented graphically on a graphical display. This parameter can be overridden or changed with the OVRDSPF and CHGDSPF commands, respectively. Make sure this parameter is *YES.

If you are showing formats that use ENHDSP *YES and formats that use ENHDSP *NO, all formats display as if ENHDSP *NO is active (no graphics).

If you are using User Interface Manager (UIM) help with a file that has ENHDSP(*YES) specified, the display changes from graphical to character-based.

A window is always displayed as though ENHDSP(*NO) is specified if the window is placed in the first or last column on the screen.

Some PCs ignore the window border and menu bar separator keywords, even if they support the enhanced interface.

THE MENU BAR

A menu bar is a horizontal row of keywords found at the top of your screen, as shown in Figure 3.1. Pressing a function key or using a mouse pointer device draws the cursor to the top of the screen where an operator can *pull down* a menu of functions that are generally associated with the selected keyword on the menu bar. You can see an example of a pull-down menu in Figure 3.2.

Figure 3.1: Example of a GUI Menu Bar

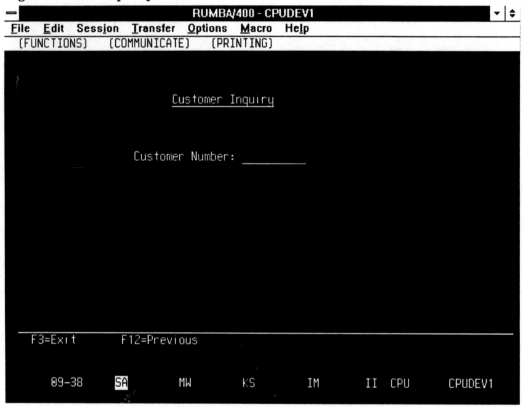

Figure 3.2: Example of a Pull-down Menu

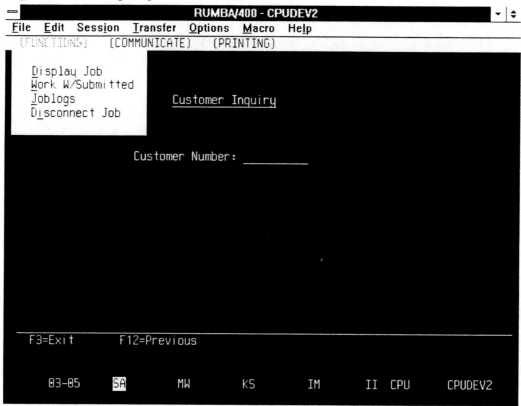

The row of text at the top of the screen with the menu keywords (FUNCTIONS), (COMMUNICATE), and (PRINTING) constitutes the menu bar in Figure 3.1. Positioning the cursor on one of these phrases (using a mouse pointer/mouse button or the F10 function key and pressing the Enter key) displays a pull-down menu of functions you can perform. An example of the result appears in Figure 3.2.

Functions on a pull-down menu usually are executed by positioning the cursor on one of the functions listed and pressing the Enter key or mouse button again (generally referred to as point and click). If you have done any work at all using GUI-enabled personal computer operating systems, you already know all about menu bars. If you haven't, it's time to move into the 20th century.

DDS KEYWORDS FOR CODING THE MENU BAR

Table 3.2 contains DDS keywords that are associated with menu bars. While we have included all of the keywords, only a few are necessary to produce a workable menu bar. The rest provide more functionality, but are not necessarily required.

Table 3.2: Menu Bar DDS Keywords

Keyword	Keyword Text	Description
CHCACCEL	Choice Accelerator Text	Specify text for accelerator function key.
CHCAVAIL	Choice Attribute Available	Specify the color or attribute when displaying choices.
CHCCTL	Choice Control	Control availability of the choices.
CHCSLT	Choice Selected Attribute	Specify the color or display attribute when a choice is selected.
CHCUNACAIL	Choice Unavailable	Specify the color or display attribute for unavailable choices.
CHOICE	Selection Field Choice	Define a field for a selection choice.
MLTCHCFLD	Multiple Choice Selection Field	Define a multiple-choice selection field.
MNUBAR	Menu Bar	Define a menu bar.
MNUBARCHC	Menu Bar Choice	Define a choice for a menu bar field.
MNUBARDSP	Menu Bar Display	Display a menu bar.

Keyword	Keyword Text	Description
MNUBARSEP	Menu Bar Separator	Specify the color, attribute, or character of the menu bar separator character.
MNUBARSW	Menu Bar Switch	Assign a function key to toggle between menu bar and user screen.
MNUCNL	Menu Cancel Key	Assign a function key to cancel the menu bar or pull-down menu.
PULLDOWN	Pull Down Menu	Define a format as a pull-down menu.
SNGCHCFLD	Single Choice Field	Define a single-choice selection field.

The DDS required to code the display file with the menu bar shown in Figures 3.1 and 3.2 is shown in Figure 3.3. We first coded a couple of file-level keywords that control access to the menu bar. MNUBARSW is a keyword that allows you to define a function key that, when pressed, toggles between your format and the menu bar.

Figure 3.3: Sample DDS for Menu Bar in Figures 3.1 and 3.2

```
*****************************************************************
*   TO COMPILE:
*     CRTDSPF FILE(XXXLIB/BAREXDSP)
*****************************************************************
A                                      DSPSIZ(24 80 *DS3)
A                                      MNUBARSW(CA10)
A                                      MNUCNL(CA12 12)
A          R FMTC
A                                      CF03(03 'End of job')
A                                      OVERLAY
A                                      MNUBARDSP(MENUBAR1 &MNUCHC &PULINP)
A                            21  3'                                        -
A                                        '                                 -
A                                      DSPATR(UL)
A                            22  5'F3=Exit'
A                            22 19'F12=Previous'
A                             9 21'Customer Number:'
A          CUST#     10A  B   9 38DSPATR(PC)
A                             5 27'Customer Inquiry'
A                                      DSPATR(HI)
```

```
A                                          DSPATR(UL)
A              MNUCHC        2Y 0H
A              PULINP        2S 0H
A      R MSGSFL                             SFL
A                                          SFLMSGRCD(24)
A              MSGKEY                       SFLMSGKEY
A              PGMQ                         SFLPGMQ
A      R MSGCTL                            SFLCTL(MSGSFL)
A                                          OVERLAY
A                                          SFLSIZ(3) SFLPAG(1)
A                                          SFLDSP SFLINZ
A  90                                      SFLEND
A              PGMQ                         SFLPGMQ
A      R MENUBAR1
A                                          MNUBAR
A              MNUFLD        2Y 0B  1  2CHCSLT((*COLOR TRQ))
A                                          MNUBARCHC(1 SYSREC '(FUNCTIONS)')
A                                          MNUBARCHC(2 COMREC '(COMMUNICATE)')
A                                          MNUBARCHC(3 PRTREC '(PRINTING)')
A      R SYSREC
A                                          PULLDOWN(*NOSLTIND)
A                                          WDWBORDER((*COLOR GRN) (*DSPATR RI)-
A                                          (*CHAR '          '))
A              SYSFLD        2Y 0B  1  2SNGCHCFLD
A                                          CHECK(ER)
A                                          CHOICE(1 '>Display Job')
A                                          CHOICE(2 '>Work W/Submitted')
A                                          CHOICE(3 '>Joblogs')
A                                          CHOICE(4 'D>isconnect Job')
A      R COMREC
A                                          PULLDOWN
A              COMFLD        2Y 0B  1  3MLTCHCFLD
A                                          CHOICE(1 '>Passthrough')
A                                          CHOICE(2 '>Establish Communication')
A                                          CHOICE(3 '>Send Message')
A                                          CHOICE(4 '>Delete Communication')
A                                          CHCCTL(1 &CFLD1)
A                                          CHCCTL(2 &CFLD2)
A                                          CHCCTL(3 &CFLD3)
A                                          CHCCTL(4 &CFLD4)
A              CFLD1         1Y 0H
A              CFLD2         1Y 0H
A              CFLD3         1Y 0H
A              CFLD4         1Y 0H
A      R PRTREC
A                                          PULLDOWN(*NOSLTIND)
A                                          WDWBORDER((*COLOR GRN) (*DSPATR RI)-
A                                          (*CHAR '          '))
A              PRTFLD        2Y 0B  1  2SNGCHCFLD
A                                          CHECK(ER)
A                                          CHOICE(1 '>Work Writers')
A                                          CHOICE(2 'Work >Spool Files')
A                                          CHOICE(3 'Work >Outqueues')
```

In our example, if the cursor is positioned on the customer number field and F10 is pressed, the cursor automatically moves to the first phrase in the menu bar— (FUNCTIONS). On the other hand, if the cursor is on the menu bar and F10 is pressed, it moves to the customer number field.

The MNUCNL keyword provides a function key that cancels a pull-down menu. In our example, pressing F12 cancels the pull-down menu request.

Next, we need to name the format on which we are going to place the menu bar. The keyword for that is MNUBARDSP. This keyword has two possible formats: one for records that have the MNUBAR keyword and one for records that do not have the MNUBAR keyword. We have chosen to define the menu bar as a separate record with the MNUBAR keyword on another format, so we use the second format of the MNUBARDSP keyword:

```
MNUBARDSP(Menu bar record &Choice field &Pull down input)
```

—or—

```
MNUBARDSP(&Pull down input)
```

Parameter Definitions:

Menu bar record: The name of the menu bar format to be displayed when this record is written to the screen.

Choice field: Field name that our RPG program can use to determine which option the user selected. This field must be defined on the format as a two-digit hidden field with a Y in position 35 and zero decimal positions.

Pull down input: Optional. If used, must be defined as a two-digit, zoned numeric hidden field. It can be used to retrieve which option was selected on the pull-down menu when the pull-down menu contains only a single-choice selection field.

You designate a format as a menu bar by using the keyword MNUBAR. A format with the MNUBAR keyword specified must also contain a field with at least one MNUBARCHC keyword:

```
MNUBAR(*Separator OR *Noseparator)
```

Parameter Definitions:

*Separator/*Noseparator: An optional parameter is available with this keyword to indicate whether or not a separator line should be placed below the last line of the menu bar choices. *Separator is the default.

The MNUBARCHC keyword does most of the work. The format for this keyword is:

```
MNUBARCHC(choice field, PullDown format name, choice text, return field)
```

Parameter Definitions:

Choice field: Provides a number that is returned to the program (in the choice field) to indicate which option was selected.

PullDown format name: Names the window format that is presented if the user selects this choice.

Choice text: The phrase that is displayed to represent this choice.

Return field: Optional parameter. Specifies whether or not control is returned to the application when a menu bar choice is selected (instead of automatically presenting the pull-down format). Field must be defined as two-digit, zero-decimal, zoned, and hidden. Possible values are:

- 0 - No selection made.

- n - Choice number in the pull-down menu.

- -1 - Pull-down record contains something other than a single-choice selection field. Read the pull-down format to determine the actual selection made.

The actual pull-down menu that appears is a record format that has been coded with the keyword PULLDOWN.

```
PULLDOWN(*SLTIND OR *NOSLTIND *NORSTCSR OR *RSTCSR)
```

Parameter Definitions:

*SLTIND/*NOSLTIND: Specifies whether or not selection indicators (such as radio buttons) should be displayed. *SLTIND is the default.

*NORSTCSR/*RSTCSR: Specifies whether or not functions should be restricted when the cursor is outside the window. If *NORSTCSR is specified, the window function keys will operate regardless of where the cursor is located. If *RSTCSR is specified and a function key is pressed while the cursor is outside of the window, you hear a beep and the cursor is placed inside the window. Control is not returned to the program at this time.

CODING RPG FOR MENU BARS AND PULL-DOWN MENUS

The RPG for processing a menu bar is straightforward, as you can see in Figure 3.4. The field we named MNUCHC is checked to determine which format to read. Each format has a different choice field that is checked to determine which option was selected.

Figure 3.4: The BAREX RPG Program to Present a Menu Bar

```
***********************************************************************
      *   TO COMPILE:
      *      CRTRPGPGM PGM(XXXLIB/BAREX)
      ***********************************************************************
      FBAREXDSPCF   E                   WORKSTN
      C                         Z-ADD0       CFLD1
      C                         Z-ADD0       CFLD2
      C                         Z-ADD0       CFLD3
      C                         EXFMTFMTC
      C                         EXSR MENUSL
      C                         SETON                          LR
      C           MENUSL        BEGSR
B1    C                         SELEC
      C           MNUCHC        WHEQ 1                    SYSTEM FUNCTIONS
      C                         READ SYSREC              68
B2    C           SYSFLD        IFEQ 1
      C                         CALL 'SYSJOB'             DISPLAY JOB
      C                         PARM '1'      ONE      1
E2    C                         ENDIF
B2    C           SYSFLD        IFEQ 2
      C                         CALL 'SYSJOB'             WORK SUBMITTED JOBS
      C                         PARM '2'      ONE
E2    C                         ENDIF
B2    C           SYSFLD        IFEQ 3
      C                         CALL 'SYSJOB'             WORK JOBLOGS
      C                         PARM '3'      ONE
E2    C                         ENDIF
B2    C           SYSFLD        IFEQ 4
      C                         CALL 'SYSJOB'             DISCONNECT JOB
      C                         PARM '4'      ONE
E2    C                         ENDIF
      C           MNUCHC        WHEQ 2                    COMMUNICATIONS
      C                         READ COMREC              68
B2    C           CFLD1         IFEQ 1
      C                         CALL 'COMJOB'             PASSTHROUGH
      C                         PARM '1'      ONE
E2    C                         ENDIF
B2    C           CFLD2         IFEQ 2
      C                         CALL 'COMJOB'             ESTABLISH COMMUNIC
      C                         PARM '2'      ONE
E2    C                         ENDIF
B2    C           CFLD3         IFEQ 3
      C                         CALL 'COMJOB'             SEND MESSAGE
      C                         PARM '3'      ONE
```

```
E2   C                    ENDIF
B2   C         CFLD4      IFEQ 4
     C                    CALL 'COMJOB'                     DELETE COMM STUFF
     C                    PARM '4'        ONE
E2   C                    ENDIF
     C         MNUCHC     WHEQ 3                            PRINTING
     C                    READ PRTREC                  68
B2   C         PRTFLD     IFEQ 1
     C                    CALL 'PRTJOB'                     WORK WRITERS
     C                    PARM '1'        ONE
E2   C                    ENDIF
B2   C         PRTFLD     IFEQ 2
     C                    CALL 'PRTJOB'                     WORK SPOOL FILES
     C                    PARM '2'        ONE
E2   C                    ENDIF
B2   C         PRTFLD     IFEQ 3
     C                    CALL 'PRTJOB'                     WORK OUTQUEUE
     C                    PARM '3'        ONE
E2   C                    ENDIF
     C                    ENDSL
     C                    ENDSR
```

This program is presented for example only. The CL programs to actually provide the functions on the pull-down windows are not shown.

SINGLE-CHOICE, PULL-DOWN MENUS

A single-choice selection screen is a screen that contains a fixed number of choices from which only one choice or option is allowed. The choices appear as a vertical list. You indicate a single-choice field by using the SNGCHCFLD keyword. The format is shown below:

```
SNGCHCFLD((*RSTCST OR *NORSTCSR) (*NOAUTOSLT OR *AUTOSLT OR *AUTOSLTENH)
(*NOSLTIND OR *SLTIND) (*NOAUTOENT OR *AUTOENT OR *AUTOENTNN) (*NUMCOL
NUMBER OF COLUMNS) (*NUMROW NUMBER OF ROWS) (*GUTTER GUTTER WIDTH))
```

Parameter Definitions:

*RSTCST/*NORSTCSR: Optional parameter that indicates whether or not the arrow keys are allowed to move the cursor outside of the selection field. The default is *NORSTCSR. This parameter is ignored if the display is attached to a controller that does not support an enhanced interface.

An exception to the restrictions imposed by this keyword occurs if the selection field is the only field contained in the pull-down window. If this is true, when the cursor is within the left-most or right-most columns, the respective arrow key closes the current window and opens the pull-down window associated with the menu bar choice to the left or right of the current menu bar choice.

*NOAUTOSLT: Optional parameter indicating whether or not the Enter key is allowed to select the current choice automatically, as determined by the cursor position. *NOAUTOSLT means the users must select the choice. *AUTOSLTENH means that autoselect is only in effect if the display is attached to an enhanced controller.

*NOSLTIND/*SLTIND: Optional parameter indicating whether or not selection indicators (push buttons, check boxes) should be displayed. *SLTIND is the default.

*NOAUTOENT: This parameter indicates to what extent to enable the autoenter feature. The autoenter feature causes the record to be returned to the program as soon as a choice is selected, without the user having to press the Enter key. *Noautoent disables the feature. *AUTOENT enables the feature. *AUTOENTNN enables the feature only if numeric selection of the choices is not required.

*NUMCOL: Optional parameter indicating that the selection field should be displayed in multiple columns sequenced from left to right across the columns as shown below:

        choice1   choice2   choice3
        choice4   choice5   choice6

*Numrow: Optional parameter indicating that the selection field should be displayed in multiple rows sequenced from top to bottom as shown below:

        choice1   choice3   choice5
        choice2   choice4   choice6

*Gutter: Optional parameter used to control the number of spaces between the columns of multiple-choice selection fields. Must have a minimum value of at least 2; default spacing is three characters.

The choices that appear on the pull-down format are defined with the CHOICE keyword. Similar to the MNUBARCHC keyword, it allows for a choice number to be keyed to select the option and displays the phrase on the pull-down menu. On nongraphical displays, the choice number is displayed next to the choice text.

```
CHOICE(Choice number Choice text *SPACEB)
```

Parameter Definitions:

Choice number: Indicates an identification number representing this choice. Valid values are from 1 to 99. Duplicate values within a selection field are not allowed.

Choice text: Defines the text that appears representing this choice. May be defined as a character string, or as a program-to-system field.

*SPACEB: Optional parameter that inserts a blank line before this choice on the menu bar. Should be used to logically group choices that are numbered consecutively. If the choices are not numbered consecutively and you are using vertical selection fields (single column), a blank line is automatically placed between nonconsecutive choices.

RADIO PUSH BUTTONS

Before the advent of electronic switches and remote-controlled radios for cars, car radios were controlled by pushing a button (we are not making this up). When you wanted to change the station, you pushed a button, which stayed depressed while that station was being selected. The computer industry borrowed this phrase and coupled it with a GUI interface so that, when a user selects an option, it appears as if a button is pushed.

The PULLDOWN keyword accepts a parameter that can be either *SLTIND (which is the default) or *NOSLTIND. If you use the *SLTIND option, when a user selects an option, a box is placed around the option, giving the illusion that a button is being pushed.

MULTIPLE-CHOICE, PULL-DOWN MENUS

Note in Figure 3.3 that format COMREC contained the keyword MLTCHCFLD while the other formats contained the SNGCHCFLD keyword. The single-choice keyword SNGCHCFLD indicates that only one selection at a time is allowed from the pull-down window. The MLTCHCFLD keyword is used to indicate that more than one item can be selected. For example, you may need an application with which to establish communications and pass-through at the same time. The format for the MLTCHFLD keyword is as follows:

```
MLTCHCFLD((*RSTCSR OR *NORSTCSR) (*NOSLTIND OR *SLTIND) (*NUMCOL NUMBER
OF COLUMNS) (*NUMROW NUMBER OF ROWS) (*GUTTER GUTTER WIDTH))
```

Parameter Definitions:

*RSTCSR/*NORSTCSR: Optional parameter that indicates whether or not the arrow keys are allowed to move the cursor outside of the selection field. The default is *NORSTCSR. This parameter is ignored if the display is attached to a controller that does not support an enhanced interface.

An exception to the restrictions imposed by this keyword occurs if the selection field is the only field contained in the pull-down window. If this is true, when the cursor is within the left-most or right-most columns, the respective arrow key closes the current window and opens the pull-down window associated with the menu bar choice to the left or right of the current menu bar choice.

*NOSLTIND/*SLTIND: Optional parameter indicating whether or not selection indicators (e.g., push buttons, check boxes) should be displayed. *SLTIND is the default.

*NUMCOL: Optional parameter indicating that the selection field should be displayed in multiple columns sequenced from left to right across the columns as shown below:

       choice1   choice2   choice3
       choice4   choice5   choice6

*NUMROW: Optional parameter indicating that the selection field should be displayed in multiple rows sequenced from top to bottom as shown below:

       choice1   choice3   choice5
       choice2   choice4   choice6

*GUTTER: Optional parameter used to control the number of spaces between the columns of multiple-choice selection fields. Must have a minimum value of at least 2, but the default spacing is three characters.

On a multiple-choice format, there must be one CHCCTL keyword for every CHOICE keyword used. The CHCCTL keyword contains the name of the field that the program will use to determine if the choice was selected. As with the single-choice field, a 1 in the field on input indicates it was selected.

On output, you must load the field associated with each CHCCTL field with a 0, 1, or 2. A 0 in the field indicates the selection is available to be selected. A 1 indicates that the selection is available and is also the default selection. A 2 in the corresponding field indicates the selection is not available at this time.

The CHCCTL keyword optionally controls error handling when the user selects an invalid option. You can specify the error message number and the file where it resides. The specified message is displayed if the user selects an invalid option. You can also hard code the message. A third option is to load the error message into a field in your program and display that field.

```
CHCCTL(Choice number &Control field Msgid Msglib Msgfile)
```

Parameter Definitions:

Choice number: Required parameter that specifies the choice to which this keyword applies.

Control field: Required parameter that is the name of a 1-byte, numeric hidden field. On output, your program outputs the control value to indicate whether or not the field is available. On input, the field indicates if the field was selected. Possible values and their meanings are:

- 0 - Available.

- 1 - Selected.

- 2 - Unavailable; cursor not allowed here unless help is available for choice.

- 3 - Unavailable; placing cursor on choice is allowed.

- 4 - Unavailable; can not place cursor on choice even if help is available.

<u>Msgid</u>: Message number to display if the user selects an unavailable choice. This field is optional and, if not specified, the default message CPD919B is issued. This parameter can also be a program-to-system field, in which case it must be a 7-byte, alphanumeric field with a data type of P and the field must exist in the record format you are defining.

<u>Msglib</u>: Library name containing the message file that contains the message displayed when the user selects an unavailable choice.

<u>Msgfile</u>: Name of the message file containing the message that is displayed when the user selects an unavailable choice.

PULL-DOWN MENU SHORTCUT KEYS

You may have noticed the right angle bracket (>) symbol embedded in the functions displayed in the pull-down menu. This symbol designates a shortcut key that can be used to select the option. The character following the symbol is the shortcut key and is highlighted on the display. Pressing the designated shortcut key while the cursor is positioned on the menu bar also selects the option.

> **Note**: Shortcut keys only work on character-based graphical displays attached to a controller that supports an enhanced interface for nonprogrammable workstations.

PULL-DOWN MENU ACCELERATOR KEYS

An accelerator key is a function key that performs the same function as the selected phrase. It is displayed next to the pull-down menu choice (three spaces after the length of the longest choice text), but the pull-down menu does not have to be displayed for the accelerator key to be active. You define the key just as you define any other function key, at either the file or field level.

After you have defined the function key, you define the text that is displayed with the choice. Use the CHCACCEL keyword to accomplish this. It is up to you to code the program to operate correctly if the function key is pressed, just as you would with any other function key. All the CHCACCEL keyword does is provide a way to enter the text for the accelerator key to be displayed with the choice text.

```
CHCACCEL (Choice number Accelerator text)
```

Parameter Definitions:

<u>Choice number</u>: Specifies the number of the choice to which this keyword applies. Valid values are from 1 to 99.

<u>Accelerator text</u>: Specifies the text displayed to identify the accelerator key. This parameter may be entered in two ways:

- As a quoted character string.

- As a program-to-system field.

This text is placed three columns to the right of the longest choice text. The actual display length of the accelerator text is also determined by the length of the longest choice text in that the combination of the two can not exceed the width of the smallest display size for the file.

CONTROLLING THE ATTRIBUTES OF AVAILABLE/UNAVAILABLE CHOICES

We have already seen that the CHCCTL keyword controls whether or not a field is available when the pull-down menu appears. The CHCAVAIL keyword controls the color or display attribute of available selections in a menu bar or selection field. The CHCUNAVAIL does the same thing for unavailable choices. The CHCSLT keyword specifies the color and display attributes of a selected choice.

```
CHCAVAIL (Color  Display attributes)
```

Parameter Definitions:

<u>Color</u>: Specifies the color of the choice text. It is expressed in the form *COLOR XXX where *XXX* is:

BLU	Blue
GRN	Green
PNK	Pink
RED	Red
TRQ	Turquoise
YLW	Yellow
WHT	White

<u>Display attributes</u>: Specifies the display attribute of the choice text. It is expressed in the form (*DSPATR (value1) (value2)...) where *value* is:

BL	Blink
CS	Column separator
HI	High intensity
ND	Nondisplay
RI	Reverse image
UL	Underline

SETTING PULL-DOWN MENU DEFAULTS

If your program outputs a valid choice in the option field when the format is displayed, that choice becomes the default. If the user simply presses the Enter key without actually making a selection, the choice number in that field is executed. On output, regardless of how the user selects the option (i.e., entering a number, positioning the cursor, or using the shortcut key) this field is filled with the number corresponding to the option selected.

TO MENU BAR OR NOT TO MENU BAR

Using menu bars can give you the look and feel of a graphical user interface if you are on an enhanced controller. If you are not, the look is undesirable and the feel is anything but good. If the software you develop runs on systems with the enhanced controllers (as all newer systems do), menu bars provide a nice and easy interim interface, even for workstations that do not have a mouse.

WE DO WINDOWS

Windows have been with us for a long time. Clever prehistoric programmers (more commonly referred to as System/36 programmers) were able to code pop-up windows in their applications, but it took an extraordinary amount of effort to achieve and maintain these results.

Today's more contemporary programmers (which we of course define as AS/400 RPG programmers) are able to code windows with just a couple of simple DDS keywords. We can put subfiles in windows, move windows around on the fly, control the window border characteristics, put titles on the window, and much more. All of this functionality is achieved simply by using the correct keyword on the file format definition. We've come a long way, baby!

In case you have lived all of your life on the dark side of the moon and still think that a window is a portal you look out of or open for fresh air, let's define terms. Simply put, a *window* is information that overlays an existing screen, with some form of border (or window) around the information to make it stand out. You can view both the information inside the window and the information outside the window so that you do not lose your point of reference. However, only the information inside the window is active; you can not work with the underlying display while the window is active.

WHO NEEDS WINDOWS?

In addition to the dozen reasons any slightly paranoid claustrophobic could come up with, windows can do a lot to enhance the visual appeal and functionality of your programs. One of the most obvious uses for windows is to provide field-level help. Program operators should be able to place the cursor on a field, press the HELP key, and have a pop-up window appear telling them all about the field. You can see this application throughout the OS/400 operating system.

Another good use for a window interface is to provide a *subfile* list of records from which the user can choose. Let's say an operator needs to enter a salesperson's number in a field, but they only know the salesperson's name. You could set up your program so that placing the cursor in the salesperson number field and pressing a function key cause a pop-up window to appear with an alphabetical list of all salespeople. A subfile selection field allows the operator to select the salesperson they want, and the number is entered into the field automatically.

Another good example (demonstrated in this chapter) is to present a subfile of commands that the user can execute by selecting a subfile record from the window. It's a very user-friendly interface to the operating system, similar in function to the assist window, but with the ability to customize the options presented to each user.

These are just a few of the many uses for windows. We are sure you can come up with many more once you see how easy they are to code. The chart shown in Table 3.3 lists the five keywords that allow you to create and work with windows.

Table 3.3: DDS Window Keywords

Keyword	Description
WINDOW	Defines a window, changes the contents of a window, or activates an inactive window.
WDWBORDER	Specifies the color, display attributes, and characters of the border around the window.
WDWTITLE	Specifies the text, color, and display attributes of the title of the window, which is embedded in the top or bottom border.
RMVWDW	Removes other windows from the display.
USRRSTDSP	Prevents the system from automatically saving and restoring the underlying display when a window is written or removed.

THE WINDOW KEYWORD

The WINDOW keyword has two different formats, as shown in the following examples. The first format defines a window, while the second format indicates that the system is to place the record format into a window already defined in another record format.

In the first format, you tell the system where to put the window and how big it's going to be. The beginning line number and column fields control where the window is placed on the screen at execution time. For instance, if you are trying to present help text on a particular field, you can retrieve the cursor position and have the window appear one line below it.

But what if the cursor was on the last line, or last column, of the screen? Where would you put the window? What if it was on the second-to-the-last line? You could, with a lot of code, determine the correct placement of the window based upon how close the cursor is to the bottom or edge of the screen. But it would be rather tedious to code and very difficult to maintain if you had to change the screen later.

Wouldn't it be nice if the system could determine the best position of the window? Well it can! (You knew we were leading up to that, didn't you?) Take a look at the special option *DFT. Instead of the beginning line and column number parameters, you code the keyword *DFT and the system decides where to place the window.

To display a window, the first window record written must contain the window size and location parameters (or you can specify *DFT to let the system do it for you). A window containing the size and location information is called a window definition record. It is the record that actually creates the window and makes it visible. It is all you need to display a window.

It is possible to display the same window on a screen more than once. The second edition of the window becomes the active window and has the same name as the first window. If you want to move the window, write the same window a second time with the keyword RMVWDW keyword active. This keyword removes the first edition of the window from the screen and gives the appearance of moving the window from one location to another.

Here are two different examples of how you may use the WINDOW keyword:

```
WINDOW(Beginning line # OR Field containing beginning line # Beginning
column OR Field containing beginning column Number of lines Number of
columns *MSGLIN OR *NOMSGLIN *RSTCSR OR *NORSTCSR)
```

—or—

```
WINDOW(*DFT Number of lines Number of columns *MSGLIN OR *NOMSGLIN
       *RSTCSR *OR *NORSTCSR)
```

Parameter Definitions:

Beginning line #: The line number at which to place the top of the window, —or— field name containing the line number at which to place the top of the window. If a field name is used, it must exist in the record format as a signed numeric, program-to-system field, with length no greater than 3.

Beginning column: The position of the uppermost left corner of the window, —or— field name containing the position of the uppermost left corner of the window. If a field name is used, it must exist in the record format as a signed numeric, program-to-system field, with length no greater than 3.

*DFT: Let the system decide where the starting line number and column number should be. The system uses a set order of rules when determining where to position the window. See the note following these definitions for the rules.

Number of lines: The total number of lines the window spans. Must be no greater than the number of lines in the display minus 2. The last line in a window is used for messages and can not contain any fields.

Number of columns: The number of columns within the window. Can not exceed four less than the available positions for the display.

*MSGLIN: Message line, indicates that the message line is contained within the window. *MSGLIN is the default. *NOMSGLIN moves the message line out of the window and to the bottom of the screen (or wherever the MSGLOC keyword specifies).

*RSTCSR: Restricted cursor, indicates that the user is limited in functions when the cursor is outside the window. *NORSTCSR indicates that, when the cursor is outside the window, all the function keys are still available as if the cursor is within the window.

SYSTEM RULES FOR AUTOMATIC WINDOW PLACEMENT

If you use the *DFT parameter and let the system decide where to place the window, it uses a set of rules in making that determination. These rules are as follows:

1. If it fits below the cursor, with the top row of the window being one line below the cursor position, place it there. If the window fits on the screen, beginning in the same column as the cursor, place it there. If it does not fit, place it as far to the left of the column as necessary to fit the complete window on the screen.

2. If it does not fit below the cursor, see if it fits above. If it can, place it there. The bottom of the window will be one line above the cursor. Position the window left to right according to the same criteria as rule 1.

3. If the window fits to the right of the cursor, place it there. The right border of the window is placed in the next-to-the-last column of the display. Position the top row of the window on the same line as the cursor, if possible; otherwise position the window only as far above as necessary to fit the window on the screen.

4. If the window fits to the left of the cursor, place it there. Position the right border of the window two columns to the left of the cursor. Position it vertically as described above.

5. Position the window in the lower, right-hand corner of the display if it does not fit anywhere else.

WINDOW BORDER KEYWORD

The Window Border keyword allows you to control the color, attributes, and characters used to create the border of the window. If you specify this keyword, at least one of the parameters also must be specified.

The Window Border keyword has the following format:

```
WDWDORDER((COLOR) (DISPLAY ATTRIBUTE) (CHARACTERS))
```

Parameter Definitions:

COLOR: Specify the color of the border. The default color is blue. The parameter is ignored on a monochrome display.

DISPLAY ATTRIBUTE: Specify the display attribute of the border. Use the form (*DSPATR (value 1 (value 2...))). If more than one attribute is coded, they are combined to form one attribute for the entire border.

 CHARACTERS: Specify the characters that make up the border. Use the form (*CHAR 'characters'). This parameter must be an eight-character string, with each character specifying a different position of the window. The order is as follows:

*   Position 1 - Top left corner.

*   Position 2 - Top border.

*   Position 3 - Top right corner.

*   Position 4 - Left border.

- Position 5 - Right border.

- Position 6 - Bottom left corner.

- Position 7 - Bottom border.

- Position 8 - Bottom right corner.

WINDOW TITLE KEYWORD

The Window Title (WDWTITLE) keyword is used to assign a title that appears in the header of the window. The Window Title keyword format is as follows:

```
WDWTITLE((Title text) (color) (display attribute) (*CENTER or *RIGHT or
*LEFT or *TOP or *BOTTOM))
```

Parameter Definitions:

Title text: Optional parameter specifying the text to be placed in the border. Use the form (*TEXT value) where value can be either hard coded or a program-to-system field. If the title characters are blanks, a blank title is displayed. If the characters are nulls, then no title is displayed.

Color: Specify the color of the text title. Use the form (*COLOR value). If no color is specified, it defaults to the color of the border. It is ignored on a monochrome display.

*CENTER, *LEFT, *RIGHT: Specify the alignment of the text field.

REMOVE WINDOW KEYWORD

There are no parameters for the RMVWDW keyword. When you write to a format that has this keyword, all other windows currently on the display are removed. If there are no other windows on the display, the keyword is ignored.

If you only want to remove some of the windows on the screen that are overlaying the window you want to activate, read or write to the window to be activated. This causes the new window to display, and any windows overlaying it to be removed.

USER RESTORE DISPLAY KEYWORD

There are no parameters for the User Restore Display (USRRSTDSP) keyword. Writing to a format with this keyword, in effect, causes the system to bypass the normal window save and restore processing. It shuts off the save operation beginning with the screen prior to the current one with USRRSTDSP specified and all subsequent screens.

Normal window processing by the system creates a situation where, before any window is displayed, the current display is saved (including any windows not being removed). When a window is then removed, the system restores the display from its saved version. Normal window processing is a resource-intensive function and, therefore, use of the USRRSTDSP keyword is greatly encouraged. In fact, under the following conditions, the system actually performs *two* saves of the screen:

- You are displaying only one window at a time.

- The current display file is compiled with RSTDSP(*YES).

- The window record that is to overlay the current display is in a different file.

The first save operation is performed because the display file is compiled with RSTDSP(*YES) and the second save is performed because of normal window processing. Use of USRRSTDSP eliminates the second save operation. Be sure to specify the keyword on the window following the first window you do not want the system to save. The USRRSTDSP keyword is only allowed on records containing the window keyword. It is ignored on the window reference record.

Although option indicators are allowed on the USRRSTDSP keyword, once the keyword is in effect, it remains in effect (even if the option indicator is set off) until you perform I/O on either the initial display screen or the window that is two windows before the window on which the USRRSTDSP is specified.

Although the rules governing USRRSTDSP sound complicated, the reward is worth the effort. The AS/400 sometimes takes an undeserved beating when talking about response time. More often than not, it's programming and operation techniques that cause response problems, not the system itself.

WINDOWS AND RESPONSE TIME

Response time, as it pertains to windows, is dependent upon your communications setup and on the complexity of the window being displayed. For our purposes, complexity is defined as the amount of information that must be saved and restored. The slowest response time occurs when the first window is added to a display and the system must perform the read and save operations.

A window of average size and complexity, on a terminal attached to the AS/400 by twinaxial, local area network (LAN), or other high-speed communications line, should have approximately a 1-second response time. If you are attached to a 9600-baud line, expect about 2.5 seconds to perform the read and save operations and display the window. If you are on a 2400-baud line, well, you're probably not reading this section anyway because you obviously do not care about response time (but figure about 10 seconds to display a window).

THE SYSTEM REQUEST WINDOW PROGRAM

Now let's look at a sample window program that may be used to provide some sizzle to your system. The AS/400 operating system is touted as one of the easiest operating systems to use (not as easy as a graphical user interface, but easy nevertheless). The AS/400 has a consistent command interface: All commands conform to the same naming conventions. Once you learn the convention, it is relatively easy to find commands. But we think that it can be made even easier!

We have put together a System Request Window program that allows you to put all system operation functions at the fingertips of your users. All system operations and special system-wide functions are made available by simply pressing the System Request key (Figure 3.5).

Power RPG III

Figure 3.5: System Request Window Program

```
.............................................................
:                                                           :
:   Options: 1=Select or press F12 to cancel                :
:                                                           :
:   Option   Request                                        :
:     _    DISPLAY JOB                                       :
:     _    WORK WITH SPOOLED FILES                           :
:     _    WORK WITH PRINTERS                                :
:     _    GET COMMAND ENTRY LINE                            :
:     _    WORK WITH SUBMITTED JOBS                          :
:     _    SEND A MESSAGE                                    :
:     _    SEND A BREAK MESSAGE                              :
:                                           More...         :
:                                                           :
:...........................................................:
```

This program also allows you to customize the list of options each user should have available. You can establish a default template of options that is available to all users, or you can specify options per User ID for those users you want to make exceptions to the norm.

Figure 3.6 shows the DDS to a physical file that we have named REQUEST. This file holds a display field, a command to be executed, a user name, and a sequence number. A subfile program (shown in Figure 3.7) displays this file in a window. The DDS for the window is shown in Figure 3.8.

Figure 3.6: DDS for File REQUEST

```
         R REQREC
           USERNM          10             COLHDG('USER NAME')
           DSPFLD          45             COLHDG('DISPLAY FIELD')
           SEQ#             5   0          COLHDG('SEQUENCE #')
           COMAND         256             COLHDG('COMMAND')
         K USERNM
         K SEQ#
```

Figure 3.7: REQ001RG RPG Attention Window Program

```
 *************************************************************************
 *   TO COMPILE:
 *     CRTRPGPGM PGM(XXXLIB/REQ001RG)
 *************************************************************************
FREQ001DSCF E                    WORKSTN
F                                          SFLRRNKSFILE SFLRCD
FREQUEST IF  E           K        DISK
I            SDS
I                                    254 263 USER
I                              *PARMS    PARMS
```

92

```
        C           *ENTRY    PLIST
        C                     PARM                RTNCOD  2
        C                     MOVE *BLANKS  SFLSEL
        C                     Z-ADD1        SETPOS
        C           USER      SETLLREQUEST                    24
B1      C           *IN24     IFEQ *OFF
        C                     MOVE *BLANKS  USER
        C           USER      SETLLREQUEST
E1      C                     ENDIF
B1      C           *IN24     DOUEQ*ON
        C           USER      READEREQUEST                    24
B2      C           *IN24     IFEQ *OFF
        C                     MOVE DSPFLD   SFDESC
        C                     MOVE SEQ#     HDSEQ#
        C                     MOVE COMAND   HDCOMD
        C                     ADD  1        SFLRRN
        C                     WRITESFLRCD
E2      C                     ENDIF
E1      C                     ENDDO
        *
B1      C           SFLRRN    IFNE *ZEROS
        C                     SETON                       21
E1      C                     ENDIF
B1      C           *IN12     DOUEQ*ON
        C           *IN03     OREQ *ON
        C                     WRITEWINDOW
        C                     EXFMTSFLCTL                 DISPLAY/READ SUBFILE
B2      C           *IN12     IFEQ *OFF
        C           *IN03     ANDEQ*OFF
        C                     MOVE *OFF     *IN42
        C                     MOVE CURPOS   SETPOS        SET CURSOR
B3      C           *IN41     DOUEQ*ON                    READ CHANGES LOOKING
        C                     READCSFLRCD             41 FOR SELECT REQUEST
B4      C           *IN41     IFEQ *OFF
B5      C                     SELEC
        C           SFLSEL    WHEQ '1'                  GET OUT IF RECORD
        C                     CALL 'QCMDEXC'         99 SELECTED
        C                     PARM          HDCOMD
        C                     PARM 256      LENGTH 155
        C                     MOVE *BLANKS  SFLSEL
        C                     UPDATSFLRCD
        C           SFLSEL    WHNE *BLANKS
        C                     MOVE *ON      *IN42         FALL THRU TO ERROR
        C                     MOVE SFLRRN   SETPOS
        C                     UPDATSFLRCD
        C                     LEAVE
        C                     OTHER
        C                     ITER
E5      C                     ENDSL
E4      C                     ENDIF
E3      C                     ENDDO
E2      C                     ENDIF
E1      C                     ENDDO
        *
        C                     MOVE *ON      *INLR
```

Figure 3.8: DDS for the REQ001DS System Request Window

```
A*****************************************************************
A*   TO COMPILE:
A*      CRTDSPF FILE(XXXLIB/REQ001DS)
A*****************************************************************
A                                        DSPSIZ(24 80 *DS3)
A                                        CA12(12)
A                                        CA03(03)
A            R WINDOW
A                                        WINDOW(*DFT 15 53 *NORSTCSR)
A                                        RMVWDW
A                                    14  2'F3=Exit'
A                                        COLOR(BLU)
A                                    14 11'F12=Cancel'
A                                        COLOR(BLU)
A            R SFLRCD                     SFL
A   42                                   SFLNXTCHG
A              SFLSEL      1A  B  6  4
A              SFDESC     45A  O  6  8
A              SFLRRN      4S 0H
A              HDSEQ#      5S 0H
A              HDCOMD    256A  H
A            R SFLCTL                     SFLCTL(SFLRCD)
A                                        SFLSIZ(0050)
A                                        SFLPAG(0007)
A                                        WINDOW(WINDOW)
A   21                                   SFLDSP
A                                        SFLDSPCTL
A   24                                   SFLEND(*MORE)
A   42                                   SFLMSG('Invalid Selection Entry')
A                                        OVERLAY
A                                        USRRSTDSP
A              SETPOS      4S 0H          SFLRCDNBR(*TOP)
A              CURPOS      5S 0H          SFLSCROLL
A                                     2  2'Type options, press Enter.'
A                                        COLOR(BLU)
A                                     3  4'1=Select'
A                                        DSPATR(HI)
A                                        COLOR(BLU)
A                                     5  3'Opt  Request'
A                                        DSPATR(HI)
A            R DUMMY
A                                        KEEP
A                                        ASSUME
A                                     1  2' '
```

This program allows a user to run commands by selecting a subfile record from within a
window. The command to be run is stored in the REQUEST file, keyed by user name and
sequence number. When the user selects a subfile record, the command is executed via
QCMDEXC. What could be easier? No commands or parameters to memorize. Just read
the screen, select a record based on a description of what the function is, and the
command is executed.

To make our program even easier to use, our program may be called when the Attention key is pressed. Assuming that you have compiled the program shown in Figure 3.7 as REQ001RG, you change the user profile by entering the following command:

```
CHGUSRPRF USRPRF(XXX) ATNPGM(REQ001RG)
```

Thereafter, whenever user XXX presses the Attention key, the window shown in Figure 3.8 appears. The actual functions that appear in the window are dependent upon the records entered into the REQUEST file. We have not provided a file maintenance program for this file. You can either write your own, or use a product like the Data File Utility (DFU). Key the default records you want to make available to all users and leave the User ID field blank. Only specify the User ID for those users whom you want to set up as exceptions.

The code for the RPG subfile program is rather simple. We assume that there will not be many records per user in the REQUEST file, so we use the fill-'er-up technique of subfile processing to load the subfile. Because of this, we do not have to code any rolling routines; the system handles rolling for us.

First check to see if this user (taken from the Program Status Data Structure) has any records in the REQUEST file. If not, then we use the default records, which are those with a blank user name. In addition to the fields being displayed in the subfile, we load the command to be run into a hidden field so that we can execute the hidden command when the user makes a selection.

After displaying the subfile, set up a loop and read all changed subfile records looking for a 1 in the selection field. Once one is found, the process subroutine retrieves the correct REQUEST file record and passes the command field to the QCMDEXC API (see Chapter 6) to execute the command. All of the normal prompting characters (e.g., ?? and ?*) can be used in the command field to prompt for the command.

SCROLL BARS AND SUBFILES

The ability to put subfiles into DDS windows was a welcome announcement with the release of V2R3. At long last, we were able to add graphically oriented lookup capabilities to our interactive programs. Subfiles could be presented that would not wipe out the entire displayed screen.

And along with V3R1 came the ability to employ a scroll bar with our subfiles. The AS/400 scroll bar works much as it would with other graphical interfaces in that it has a scroll block to indicate how big the subfile is, and where you are within it. The scroll block can be moved with the pointing device (provided that you are on a graphical workstation) and the subfile is repositioned accordingly.

The scroll bar may be employed by using a keyword option on the Subfile End (SFLEND) DDS keyword. We cover this option in detail in Chapter 2 on subfiles.

GUI This, and GUI That

Sizzle, pizzazz, function, and ease of use. That is what the graphical user interface craze is all about. So why shouldn't AS/400 programmers join the fray?

As you have seen, some of the GUI elements are so easy to code that they are actually irresistible! We've been coding windows in programs for more years than we care to admit, and the hoops we had to jump through to do it were numerous—PUTOVR, OVRDTA, OVERLAY, RSTDSP, etc., etc., etc. If you wanted a subfile in a window (and this was a very common request), you had to fake it. If you wanted a pull-down menu, just forget it!

Now, there are just five keywords to control a window and you don't even have to know where the window is going to appear—the system decides for you! Want a subfile in a window? No problem. The system does it. Want a scroll bar displayed on that subfile? Piece of cake!

If you have not added GUI features to your applications yet, **WHAT IN THE WORLD ARE YOU WAITING FOR?**

Chapter 4

Information Data Structures
and Error Handling

While it's true that the AS/400 operating system communicates mainly via messages, it is equally true that it communicates a wealth of information via special data structures. Two such data structures are the File Information Data Structure and the Program Status Data Structure.

In this chapter, we explain the information that is contained in these two very special data structures, as well as show you how to access them in your RPG programs. We also show you how to handle file and program errors by using the plethora of information that can be found in these data structures.

FILE INFORMATION DATA STRUCTURE

The first thing you should know about the data found in the File Information Data Structure is that it varies depending upon the type of file you are processing. You can get detailed information on every I/O operation you perform in your program—if you know how to get to it.

A File Information Data Structure is maintained for every file that your program uses, regardless of whether or not you code the data structure in your program. It is up to you to decide if you want to access the information. As you will see, it is not difficult to code and can be very advantageous in certain situations. Making the File Information Data Structure for one of the files in your program available, it is as simple as adding a continuation line to the File Description Specification describing the file in question. You can see two examples of this in Figure 4.1.

Figure 4.1: Specifying the File Information Data Structure

```
FFILE1    IF  E        K       DISK
F                                        KINFDS  FILE1DS
FFILE2    IF  E        K       DISK
F                                        KINFDS  FILE2DS
IFILE1DS      DS
I                                    1    8 F1NAME
I                                   11  150F1STAT
IFILE2DS      DS
I                                    1    8 F2NAME
I                                   11  150F2STAT
```

The File Description Specification continuation line must have the INFDS keyword (in positions 54 to 58) followed by the name of an associated data structure (in positions 60 to 67). In Figure 4.1, we see a continuation line directly following the File Description Specification line describing the database file named FILE1. You can see that the name of the File Information Data Structure for database file FILE1 is named FILE1DS.

After any I/O operation to FILE1 (including opening the file), the data structure FILE1DS contains the requested information that is coded in the data structure. For our example in Figure 4.1, the file name (F1NAME) and the status code (F1STAT) are coded into our data structure. We could name the fields anything because the fields are stored positionally in the data structure. It is the From and To positions of the field that determine what information is in the field.

For the example in Figure 4.1, we also created a File Information Data Structure for the FILE2 database file, named FILE2DS. The naming conventions are totally arbitrary, but you can not have the same field defined in two different data structures, so we named them differently. We believe it is good practice to establish some kind of naming convention to help make the names easy to remember.

The File Information Data Structure is segregated positionally into several primary areas. Note that there is an overlap in positions 367 to 499. Information in this area is dependent upon the type of file being described. Basically, data is segmented into sections (Table 4.1).

Table 4.1: Contents of the File Information Data Structure

Type of Feedback	Positions in the Data Structure
File Feedback Information	1 to 76
Open Feedback	81 to 240
Common I/O Feedback	241 to 286
Device-dependent Feedback—ICF, DSP	367 to 446
Device-dependent Feedback—Printers	367 to 404
Device-dependent Feedback—Database	367 to 499

Special Keywords

IBM has determined that certain fields in the Information Data Structures are more likely to be requested by a program than others. Because of this, these fields have been assigned special keywords that you may use to reference the information. The idea is to free you from the hassle of having to remember the From and To positions in the Information Data Structures. The need for this feature could be ruled as questionable because you still have to remember the special keywords.

Table 4.2 contains a list of the special keywords in the File Information Data Structure. You code the keyword in the Input Specification for the data structure subfield in positions 44 to 51 in lieu of the field positions. Figure 4.2 shows an example of how to code a File Information Data Structure using one of the special keywords.

Table 4.2: Special Keywords

Keyword	From Position	To Position	Decimal Positions	Description
*FILE	1	8	—	File name used by the RPG program associated with this data structure.
*INP	71	72	0	For workstation device files, this is the national language input capability.
*OUT	73	74	0	For workstation device files, this is the national language output capability.
*OPCODE	16	21	—	RPG operation code last used to access the file.
*SIZE	67	70	0	Total number of characters that can fit on the workstation device.
*STATUS	11	15	0	Status codes (defined later in this chapter).
*RECORD	38	45	—	Format name being processed.
*ROUTINE	22	29	—	RPG routine that was processing the file.

Figure 4.2: Coding Special Keywords

```
FFILE1   IF  E           K        DISK
F                                           KINFDS FILE1DS
IFILE1DS    DS
I                                    1    8 F1NAME
I                                *STATUS  F1STAT
```

FIELD DEFINITIONS

Now that you have seen two ways to code a File Information Data Structure, let's take a look at all of the common fields in the File Information Data. Figure 4.3 shows a sample data structure for all of the common fields that may be accessed, and field definitions. These fields are in the same positions, regardless of the file type. (Remember, some other portions of the data structure change based upon the type of file being described.)

Figure 4.3: Common Fields in File Information Data Structure

```
IFILE1DS    DS
I                                    1    8 F1NAME
I                                    9    9 F1OPEN
I                                   10   10 F1EOF
I                                   11  150F1STAT
I                                   16   21 F1OPCO
I                                   22   29 F1ROUT
I                                   30   37 F1STMT
I                                   38  420F1RESN
I                                   38   45 F1RECD
I                                   46   52 F1MSGI
I                                   53   66 F1UNUS
I                                   67  700F1SIZE
I                                   71  720F1INP
I                                   73  740F1OUT
I                                   75  760F1MODE
```

Field Definitions of the Common Fields in the File Information Data Structure:

Field Name	Description
F1NAME	First eight characters of the file name (as used by the RPG program).
F1OPN	File open indicator (1 = Open).
F1EOF	File at end of file indicator (1 = End of File).

Field Name	Description
F1STAT	Status codes. Very useful for error determination and handling (see Table 4.3 for complete list).
F1OPCO	RPG operation code last used to access the file. The first five characters specify the code while the sixth position is itself a code, where: F = Op code specified on a file name. R = Op code specified on a record format name. I = Last operation was implicit.
F1ROUT	Name of the RPG routine that was processing the file. Possible values are: *INIT - Program initialization. *GETIN - Read a record. *DETC - Detail calculations. *DETL - Detail output. *TOTC - Total calculation time (Level Break). *TOTL - Total time output. *OFL - Overflow output. *TERM - Program termination. PGMNAME - Name of a called program (for SPECIAL files).
F1STMT	RPG source statement number.
F1RESN	User-specified return code for SPECIAL files.
F1RECD	For an externally described file, the first eight characters of the name of the record format being processed when the error occurred. For internally described files, the record format indicator is left-justified into the field.
F1MSGI	System message ID of the error, i.e., CPF9801.
F1SIZE	Total number of characters that fit on the workstation display.

Field Name	Description
F1INP	National language input capability.
F1OUT	National language output capability.
F1MODE	National language preferred mode.

In Table 4.3, we list the possible status codes that may be contained in positions 11 to 15 of the File Information Data Structure. As previously noted, the *STATUS keyword may be used to access the status codes too.

Table 4.3: Status Codes

Code	Condition
00000	No exception/error occurred.
00002	Function key used to end display.
00011	Read to end of file.
00012	No record found on a CHAIN, SETLL, or SETGT operation.
00013	Subfile is full; trying to write another record.
01011	Undefined record type.
01021	Attempted to write duplicate record (either database or subfile).
01031	Matching records out of sequence.
01041	Array or table load sequence error.
01051	Too many entries in table or array.

Code	Condition
01071	Numeric sequence error.
01121	Print key pressed, but no indicator specified in DDS for print.
01122	Rollup pressed, but no indicator specified in DDS.
01123	Rolldown pressed, but no indicator specified in DDS.
01124	Clear key pressed, but no indicator specified in DDS.
01125	Help key pressed, but no indicator specified in DDS.
01126	Home key pressed, but no indicator specified in DDS.
01201	Record mismatch detected on input.
01211	I/O operation to a closed file.
01215	Open issued to a file already opened.
01216	Error on an implicit OPEN/CLOSE operation.
01217	Error on an explicit OPEN/CLOSE operation.
01218	Record locked; unable to allocate.
01221	Update without prior read or chain.
01231	Error on SPECIAL file.
01235	Error in PRTCTL space or skip entries.
01241	Record number not found in ADDROUT file.
01251	Permanent I/O error.

Code	Condition
01261	Attempted to exceed maximum number of acquired devices.
01271	Attempted to acquire unavailable device.
01281	Operation to device not yet acquired.
01282	Job ending with controlled option.
01285	Attempted to acquire a device that was already acquired.
01286	Attempted to open shared file with SAVDS or IND file options.
01287	Response indicators overlap IND indicators.
01299	Other I/O error detected.
01331	Wait time exceeded for READ from WORKSTN file.

Open Feedback Information

By now you may be feeling overwhelmed by the sheer volume of information available to you that is stored in the File Information Data Structure. But wait! There's more! Remember, the data structure varies, depending upon the file type.

The open feedback area resides in positions 81 to 240. RPG copies the contents of the file Open Feedback area to the Information Data Structure whenever the associated file is opened (hence the name). Members in a multimembered file opened as a result of a read operation to a member are copied into this area as well.

The Data Management Guide contains a layout of all these fields, but if you go there, be prepared to do a little math. The fields are laid out in this book by giving you the length, data type, and offset of each. You must calculate the actual From and To positions. To do so, you will need to use the following formula:

From = 81 + Offset
To = From -1 + Character Length (in bytes)

We have done the math for you, and you can see the results in Figure 4.4.

Figure 4.4: Open Feedback Area

```
IOPENFBDS     DS
I                              81   82 F1ODPT
I                              83   92 F1FNAM
I                              93  102 F1FLIB
I                             103  112 F1SNAM
I                             113  122 F1SLIB
I                           B 123 1240F1SNBR
I                           B 125 1260F1RCDL
I                           B 127 1280F1MAXK
I                             129  138 F1FMBR
I                           B 147 1480F1FTYP
I                           B 152 1530F1LINE
I                           B 154 1550F1COLS
I                           B 156 1590F1RCNT
I                             160  161 F1ACCT
I                             162  162 F1DUPK
I                             163  163 F1SRC
I                             164  173 F1UFCP
I                             174  183 F1UFCO
I                           B 184 1850F1VOLI
I                           B 186 1870F1BLKL
I                           B 188 1890F1OVRF
I                           B 190 1910F1BLKI
I                             197  206 F1REQR
I                           B 207 2080F1OPNC
I                           B 211 2120F1BASD
I                             214  215 F1OPNI
I                           B 216 2170F1FMTL
I                           B 218 2190F1CCSI
I                           B 227  229 F1NUMD
```

Field Definitions of the Open Feedback Area:

Field Name	Description
F1ODPT	Open data path type. Possible values are: DB = Database. DS = Display device. SP = Spooled file.

Field Name	Description
F1FNAM	File name as it is known to the system (which may be different from the way the RPG program knows it).
F1FLIB	Library name in which the file resides.
F1SNAM	Spooled file name.
F1SLIB	Library name in which the spooled file resides.
F1SNBR	Spooled file number.
F1RCDL	Record length of the file associated with this data structure.
F1MAXK	Maximum key length.
F1MBR	Member name.
F1MTYP	Type of file subtype code.
F1LINE	Number of lines on the workstation display.
F1COL	Number of columns on the workstation display.
F1RCDC	Number of records in the file when the file was opened.
F1ACCT	Type of data-file access. Possible values are: AR = Arrival sequence. KF = Keyed FIFO; duplicate keys allowed. KL = Keyed LIFO; duplicate keys allowed. KU = Keyed unique.
F1DUPK	Duplicate keys indicator. Possible values are: D = Duplicate keys are valid. U = Unique keys only.
F1SRC	Source file indicator (Y = This is a source file).

Field Name	Description
F1UFCP	User-file control block parameters.
F1UFCO	User-file control block parameter overrides.
F1VOLI	Offset to the location of the volume ID on the tape.
F1BLKL	Blocked input/output limit.
F1OVRF	Overflow line number.
F1BLKI	Blocked input/output offset. The offset from this record to the next record.
F1REQR	Requester name.
F1OPNC	Open count.
F1BASD	Number of members based on file.
F1OPNI	Open identifier.
F1FMTL	Maximum record format length.
F1CCSI	Database CCSID
F1NUMD	Number of devices defined.

I/O Feedback Area

Positions 241 through 366 are used for the I/O feedback information area. The content of this area is copied by RPG to the File Information Data Structure:

- On every I/O operation if a POST operation for the file is not specified anywhere in your program.

- Only after a POST for the file, if a POST operation for the file is specified anywhere in your program.

Again, you must go to the Data Management Guide to get a breakdown of the information in the data structure. Use the same calculations to figure From and To positions for this area of the File Information Data Structure as you do for the open feedback area, (using an offset position of 241 instead of 81), or refer to Figure 4.5 where we have, once again, done the math for you.

Figure 4.5: I/O Feedback Area

```
IINOUTFD      DS
I                                  B 243 2460F1WRTC
I                                  B 247 2500F1REDC
I                                  B 251 2540F1WRTR
I                                  B 255 2580F1OTHC
I                                    260 260 F1OPER
I                                    261 270 F1IFMT
I                                    271 272 F1CLAS
I                                    273 282 F1DEVN
I                                  B 283 2860F1IRLN
```

Field Definitions of the I/O Feedback Area:

Field Name	Description
F1WRTC	Number of writes performed.
F1REDC	Number of reads performed.
F1WRTR	Number of writes and reads performed.
F1OTHC	Number of other I/Os performed.
F1OPER	Current operation.
F1IFMT	Record format name.
F1CLAS	Device class.
F1DEVN	Device name.
F1IRLN	Record length.

Device-specific Feedback Area

The device-specific feedback area begins in position 367 and its length is dependent on two factors: The device type and whether or not DISK files are keyed. The minimum length of the data area when device-specific feedback is used is 528 bytes:

- On every I/O operation if a POST operation for the file is not specified anywhere in your program.

- Only after a POST for the file, if a POST operation for the file is specified anywhere in your program.

For the device-specific feedback areas, the offset position begins in 367 (if you want to go to the Data Management Guide). We went ahead and did the math for you in Figures 4.6, 4.7, and 4.8.

Figure 4.6: Device-specific Feedback Area—Printers

```
     IPRINTDS      DS
     I                                      B 367 3680F1CURL
     I                                      B 369 3720F1CURP
     I                                        401 402 F1MAJR
     I                                        403 404 F1MINR
```

Field Definitions of the Printer Device-specific Feedback Area:

Field Name	Description
F1CURL	Current line number.
F1CURP	Current page number.
F1MAJR	Major return code.
F1MINR	Minor return code.

Figure 4.7: Device-specific Feedback Area—Database File

```
     IFILEDS       DS
     I                                      B 367 3700F1SIZB
     I                                        371 374 F1JFIL
     I                                      B 377 3780F1LOK#
     I                                      B 379 3800F1MAXF
     I                                      B 381 3840F10ERR
     I                                      B 385 385 F1POSB
     I                                      B 386 386 F1DELB
     I                                      B 387 3880F1KEY#
     I                                      B 393 3940F1KEYL
     I                                      B 395 3960F1MBR#
     I                                      B 397 4000F1RRN
     I                                        4012400 F1KEYV
```

Field Definitions of the Database File Device-specific Feedback Area:

Field Name	Description
F1SIZB	Size of database feedback area.
F1JFIL	Joined file indicator.

Field Name	Description
F1LOK#	Number of locked records.
F1MAXF	Maximum number of fields.
F1OERR	Offset to error bit map.
F1POSB	File position bits.
F1DELB	Current record deleted indicator.
F1KEY#	Number of keys.
F1KEYL	Length of keys
F1MBR#	Member number.
F1RRN	Relative record number.
F1KEYV	Key value (maximum length 2,000 characters).

Figure 4.8: Device-specific Feedback Area—Workstation File

```
     IWORKSTDS    DS
     I                              367 368 F1FLAG
     I                              369 369 F1AID
     I                              370 371 F1CSRL
     I                          B 372 3750F1DATL
     I                          B 376 3770F1SRRN
     I                          B 378 3790F1SFLM
     I                          B 380 3810F1SFL#
     I                              382 383 F1WCSR
     I                              401 402 F1MAJR
     I                              403 404 F1MINR
```

Field Definitions of the Workstation File Device-specific Feedback Area:

Field Name	Description
F1FLAG	Display flags.
F1AID	AID byte.
F1CSRL	Cursor location.
F1DATL	Actual data length.
F1SRRN	Subfile relative record number.
F1SFLM	Subfile minimum relative record number.
F1SFL#	Number of records in the subfile.
F1WCSR	Active window cursor location.
F1MAJR	Major return code.
F1MINR	Minor return code.

Figure 4.6 shows this portion of the data structure for a printer file, Figure 4.7 reflects the data structure for a database file, and Figure 4.8 shows a breakdown of this part of the data structure for a workstation file.

PROGRAM STATUS DATA STRUCTURE

The Program Status Data Structure is similar to the File Information Data Structure, except that its purpose is to provide exception/error information about an RPG program. While a File Information Data Structure can be defined for each file, a Program Status Data Structure is defined once per program. Even though we show all of the fields in our example, you only need to code the elements that you need for your purposes. As you can see in Figure 4.9, the data structure is extremely easy to define.

Figure 4.9: Defining a Program Status Data Structure

```
I          SDS
I                          1  10 PGMNAM
I                         11  15 STATUS
I                         16  20 PRVSTS
I                         21  28 SRCSTM
I                         29  36 ROUTIN
I                         37  390PARMS
I                         40  42 EXCTYP
I                         43  46 EXCNBR
I                         47  50 MIODT
I                         51  80 WRKARA
I                         81  90 LIBNAM
I                         91 170 MSGDTA
I                        171 174 PRVMID
I                        175 198 UNUSED
I                        199 2000CENTR2
I                        201 208 FILENM
I                        209 243 FILSTS
I                        244 253 JOBNAM
I                        254 263 USRNAM
I                        264 2690JOBNBR
I                        270 2750RUNDAT
I                        276 2810SYSDAT
I                        282 2870RUNTIM
I                        288 293 CMPDAT
I                        294 299 CMPTIM
I                        300 303 CMPLVL
I                        304 313 SRCFIL
I                        314 323 SRCLIB
I                        324 333 SRCMBR
I                        334 429 UNUSE2
```

Field Definitions:

Field Name	Description
PGMNAM	Program name.
STATUS	Status codes. See Figure 4.10.
PRVSTS	Previous status code.
SRCSTM	RPG Source statement sequence number.
ROUTIN	RPG routine in which the exception/error occurred.
PARMS	Number of parms passed to this program.
EXCTYP	Exception type (CPF or MCH).

Field Name	Description
EXCNBR	Exception number.
MIODT	Machine instruction object definition template number.
WRKARA	Work area for messages. Used internally by the compiler.
LIBNAM	Library name in which the program resides.
MSGDTA	Error message data. CPF messages are placed here when status contains 09999.
PRVMID	Previous message ID. Identifies the exception that caused RPG9001 (the called program failed) to be signaled.
CENTR2	First two digits of four-digit year.
FILNAM	File name on which the last file operation occurred. Updated only when error occurs.
FILSTS	File status on the last file used. Includes status code, routine name, statement number, and record name. Updated only when error occurs.
JOBNAM	Job name.
USRNAM	User profile name.
JOBNBR	Job number.
RUNDAT	Date program started running in the system. UDATE is derived from this date.
SYSDAT	System date.
RUNTIM	Time of program running.
CMPDAT	Date program was compiled.
CMPTIM	Time program was compiled.

Field Name	Description
CMPLVL	Level of the compiler.
SRCFIL	Source file name used to compile the program.
SRCLIB	Source library name.
SRCMBR	Source file member name used to compile the program.

All you need to do to define the Program Status Data Structure is code an S in position 18 followed by DS in positions 19 and 20, then define the subfields you want to make accessible to your program. The Program Status Data Structure and all of the possible subfields are shown in Figure 4.9.

Just as the File Information Data Structure has predefined keywords for frequently used fields, the Program Status Data Structure does also. You can access these fields either by providing the From and To positions in the data structure, or by coding the special keyword in the From and To positions.

Figure 4.10 shows examples of both methods. Table 4.4 shows all of the special keywords in the Program Status Data Structure.

Figure 4.10: Defining Subfields with Special Keywords

```
I          SDS
I                            *PROGRAM PGMNAM
I                            11   15 STATUS
I                            16   20 PRVSTS
```

Table 4.4: Special Keywords

Keyword	From Position	To Position	Decimal Positions	Description
*PROGRAM	1	10	—	Name of this program. [1]
*STATUS	11	15	—	Status codes.

Keyword	From Position	To Position	Decimal Positions	Description
*ROUTINE	29	36	—	Error routine. [2]
*PARMS	37	39	—	Number of parameters passed to this program. [3]

Notes:

[1] If the program is running and someone compiles it, the program is renamed and put in library QRPLLIB. This parameter maintains the original name of the program.

[2] Possible error routines:

*INIT	Program initialization
*DETL	Detail lines
*GETIN	Get an input record
*TOTC	Total calculations
*DETC	Detail calculations
*OFL	Overflow lines
*TERM	Program ending

[3] Parameters expected by the program, but not passed by the calling program do not cause a problem until the program attempts to access the field. If you first check the number of parameters passed to the program and do not use the field if it was not passed, you can have a variable number of parameters.

Error Handling

If you have been programming on the AS/400 for longer than, say, a day, then you undoubtedly have experienced the frustration of having a program blow up. It's bad enough that some user has figured out a way to use a perfectly good program that you wrote in some totally weird and unexpected fashion that causes it to crash. And then, the system takes over and issues a totally useless and confusing message that only means something to someone buried deep within the halls of IBM.

Adding insult to injury, the user is sometimes given options to continue! Now when was the last time you met a user who, when presented with a choice of options, would choose the correct one? (Does option C mean Continue or Cancel?)

Wouldn't it be nice if you could tell the system what to do anytime it encounters an error, even if you hadn't thought of the error when you wrote the program? Well, this method of error prevention is called a *PSSR subroutine.

IMPLEMENTING THE *PSSR SUBROUTINE

A *PSSR subroutine is a user-written subroutine that receives control when the system detects an error in a program. You identify the subroutine by coding (surprise) *PSSR in factor one of the BEGSR statement.

You can access a *PSSR subroutine in three different ways:

- When you code a file access statement, such as CHAIN, and you do not specify an error indicator in positions 56 and 57, control is transferred by the system to this subroutine when an error occurs.

- You can code an error indicator in positions 56 and 57 and when this error indicator comes on, execute the subroutine by coding *PSSR in Factor 2 of the EXSR statement.

- Name it (*PSSR) in positions 60 through 64 on the File Definition Specification continuation line, with INFSR in positions 54 through 59.

The first thing you should be aware of when coding this type of subroutine is the possibility of creating an endless loop, which tends to slow other users' response time and totally destroy yours.

This subroutine is called by the system whenever an error occurs, so if an error occurs while you are in the subroutine, the subroutine gets called again, which could cause the error again, which again calls the subroutine, which again causes the error... Well, you get the picture.

So, to make sure this does not occur, the first thing to do in the *PSSR subroutine is to check and make sure that you have not come from an error inside the subroutine itself. This is done very simply by checking a field for blanks. If it's not blank, let the system take over and display its own error messages. If it is blank, continue with the subroutine and make the field nonblank. This flagging routine is very basic coding that must be done in every *PSSR subroutine that you write. The program compiles and runs without this code, but if you leave it out you pay the price.

So, now you are down inside the *PSSR subroutine, past the endless loop check so you know an error has occurred in your program. But, *what* happened? You can interrogate the *STATUS field of the File Information Data Structure or the MSGDTA field of the Program Status Data Structure to find out.

Another thing you could do at this point is call a generic error handling program and pass it the File Information Data Structure and the Program Status Data Structure. This program could then log the error information to a database file and present an error screen with a message like "An error has occurred - CALL Ron or Doug at 123-4567." This is a very nice technique that eliminates IBM's cryptic messages and also provides a log of all errors that occur.

Return Points

Regardless of what you do inside the subroutine, you have some options as to where to return control of the program. Factor 2 of the ENDSR statement of a *PSSR subroutine can be a field name that contains the control return point. Table 4.5 lists the valid values and their meanings. If the field contains an invalid entry, no error is indicated and the system acts as if the field is blank.

Table 4.5: Error Return Points

Value	Description
*CANCL	Cancel program.
*DETC	Detail calculations.
*DETL	Detail lines.
*GETIN	Get an input record.
*OFL	Overflow lines.
*TOTC	Continue at beginning of total calculations.
*TOTL	Continue at beginning of total lines.

Value	Description
Blanks	Return control to the system. This is true if field is blanks or not specified, or if field contains an invalid entry. If routine was called explicitly, control returns to the next sequential statement.

If the *PSSR subroutine is called explicitly via the EXSR statement and no return point is indicated, control returns to the next sequential statement after the EXSR statement.

If the subroutine is called implicitly (via INFSR on an F-Specification or no indicator on a CHAIN op code), a system error message is probably issued. An error message is not issued if the status code is from 1121 to 1126 because these error codes indicate that some invalid key was pressed on the keyboard (e.g., print or rollup). In this case, control returns to the next sequential statement.

Points to Remember

After the *PSSR subroutine is run, the system resets the field specified in Factor 2 of the ENDSR statement to blanks. This means that your program should set the value of the field each time the subroutine is executed. If an error occurs during the start or end of the program, control passes to the system and not to the *PSSR subroutine.

Record Locks

Every good programmer knows the proper way to code the functions of accessing a file so that the system does not maintain a lock on the record until you actually need the record (and every programmer has a different "proper" way to do it). But what about all those other "bad guys" who access the record and keep it locked so your program can't get at it?

Wouldn't it be nice if, when you chained to a file to get a record and some other program had that record locked, you could send a message to your user giving them the name of the bonehead who is keeping your program from running? The File Information Data Structure can tell you that you had a record lock on the file and the Program Status Data Structure can tell you the name of the job that has the lock! The sample programs in Figures 4.11 and 4.12 demonstrate this technique.

Figure 4.11: DDS for Sample Record Lock Program

```
A                                         DSPSIZ(24 80 *DS3)
A          R FMTC
A                                         CF03(03 'End of job')
A                                         CF12(12 'Return to Previous')
A                                         OVERLAY
A                               21  3'                              -
A                                    '
A                                         DSPATR(UL)
A                               22  5'F3=Exit'
A                               22 19'F12=Previous'
A                                9 21'Customer Number:'
A  99      FLD001        10A  B  9 38
A                                         ERRMSGID(CPF9898 QSYS/QCPFMSG 99 &M-
A                                         SGHLD)
A                                1 27'Customer Update'
A                                         DSPATR(HI)
A                                         DSPATR(UL)
A          MSGHLD        80A  P
```

Figure 4.12: Sample RPG Program for Record Locks

```
FRCDLCKDSCF  E                  WORKSTN
FCUSTOMERUF  E        K         DISK
F                                       KINFDS INFO
IINFO        DS
I                               *STATUS  STATUS
I            SDS
I                               91 170 MSGDTA
 *
C          *IN99    DOUEQ*OFF
C                   EXFMTFMTC
C          FLD001   CHAINCUSTOMER          6899
C          *IN99    IFEQ *ON
C                   EXSR *PSSR
C                   ENDIF
C                   ENDDO
C                   SETON                  LR
CSR        *PSSR    BEGSR
C          INB4     IFEQ *ON
C                   SETON                  LR
C                   RETRN
C                   ELSE
C                   MOVE *ON     INB4
C          STATUS   IFEQ 01218                  RECORD LOCK
C                   MOVELMSGDTA  MSGHLD 80
C                   ENDIF
C                   ENDIF
C                   MOVE *OFF    INB4   1
CSR                 ENDSR
CSR        NOCALL   BEGSR
C                   UPDATCUSREC
CSR                 ENDSR
```

The program in our example first brings up a screen asking for a customer number. It then attempts to get the record via the CHAIN op code. Because the file is coded as an update file in the File Specification, the system checks to see that the record is not being held for update elsewhere. If some other job (or even a previous job step within your job) has a lock on the record, indicator 99 comes on. Be aware that the amount of time the system waits for a record is determined by the RCDWAIT parameter on the CRTPF or CHGPF commands. The normal default is 60 seconds, but, if this is changed to *NOMAX, you could be waiting until you are old and gray.

When indicator 99 comes on, the *PSSR subroutine is called explicitly. The first thing it does is make sure that it is not taking part in an endless loop, by checking the INB4 field. If it is, it terminates. If it's not, it interrogates the status field for code 1218—record locked, unable to allocate.

If a record lock problem exists, it moves the message data field from the Program Status Data Structure into the program-to-system field MSGHLD. This field is defined on an ERRMSGID keyword, so the message data from the Program Status Data Structure is displayed as an error message at the bottom of the screen when the record format is output.

We then fall out of the *PSSR subroutine (after blanking out our endless loop protection field). We have not coded a return point in Factor 2 of the ENDSR statement and the subroutine was called explicitly, so control returns to the next sequential statement after the EXSR statement. Because indicator 99 is still on, we loop back up and redisplay the format with the error message indicating which job has the record locked.

The NOCALL subroutine is provided simply so this sample program will compile for demonstration purposes.

INFORMATION IS POWER

The File Information Data Structure and the Program Status Data Structure can provide a wealth of information to your programs. The special keywords provided in each structure make accessing the essential information a very easy task.

You can use the information, such as program name, rather than hard coding the data in your program. The obvious advantage is that, when the information changes (such as the program being renamed or cloned), the program does not have to be changed.

When combined with the *PSSR subroutine, these information data structures provide your program with a great deal of flexibility when handling errors. You can elect to present your own global error screen whenever an unexpected error occurs. You can monitor for particular errors, take appropriate action on them, and let the system handle any other unexpected errors.

The bottom line is: The choice is yours. Information is power!

Chapter 5

Tips and Techniques for the RPG/400 Programmer

The fact that you bought this book and are reading this chapter indicates one of three things:

    A. You are an experienced programmer who is always looking for ways to improve.

    B. You are a beginning programmer who is always looking for ways to improve.

    C. You are a family member or close friend.

If you are reading this book for reasons A or B, we trust you will find something to add to your toolbox. If you are reading this for reason C, thank you. Your obligation has been met and you may stop reading now.

In this chapter, we cover a little something for everyone. We start off by reviewing some basic RPG operation codes to perform routine tasks. For instance, did you know you can left-justify a field with only two statements of code? CHECK it out! There are a couple of ways we know of to translate lowercase to uppercase. We demonstrate how to do it using the Translate (XLATE) operation code.

The BITON/BITOF operation codes have been around for a long time and still make a very useful tool to have around, although they can be a "bit" cumbersome to use. Our example shows how they are used to control the display attributes of embedded fields. This can be a useful technique if you need to highlight or reverse image a key word or phrase within a line of text.

We follow this information with some techniques to make routine file maintenance tasks a little easier. Did you know that, with the proper use of the RTNDTA keyword, you can eliminate all of the tedious MOVE statements that are usually coded to move fields from a database file to a display file? We not only demonstrate this technique, we cover how to use multiple views of the same file in a program.

Parameters. To pass or not to pass, that is the question (please forgive us William Shakespeare). And the answer is... Who cares? If you code the receiving program correctly, it will not blow up, even if the calling program does not pass the parameters it expects.

REMOVING LEADING BLANKS (LEFT JUSTIFY)

The CHECK op code is very useful for removing leading blanks. When used in conjunction with the Substring (SUBST) op code, leading blanks can be removed from a field with two simple statements (Figure 5.1).

Figure 5.1: Using CHECK to Remove Leading Blanks

```
FMT C  .....CLON01N02N03Factor1+++OpcdeFactor2+++ResultLenDHHiLoEqComments++++++
     C          ' '         CHECKNAME      X        20
     C                      SUBSTNAME:X    NAME      P
```

The example in Figure 5.1 uses the CHECK op code to find the first nonblank character in the NAME field and stores the address of that field in a numeric variable called X. The

Substring (SUBST) function is then used to move the nonblank characters of NAME into the left-most characters of the NAME field, and then pad the remaining positions of the NAME field with blanks.

For example, let's apply the code in Figure 5.1 to the following NAME field:

```
...+... 1 ...+... 2 ...+... 3
      SMITH
```

The results after the operation in Figure 5.1 look like this:

```
...+... 1 ...+... 2 ...+... 3
SMITH
```

TRANSLATE (XLATE) PERFORMS SINGLE-CHARACTER SUBSTITUTION WITHIN CHARACTER STRINGS

The XLATE op code is a handy tool when you need to perform character substitution within a character string. You can specify From and To characters to be translated, or entire strings of characters that need to be translated.

One of the more popular uses for this op code is to translate a lowercase character string to uppercase. This is a frequent requirement when you are importing data from an external source. Figure 5.2 is an example of how to address this issue.

Figure 5.2: Using XLATE to Translate Lowercase Character Strings to Uppercase

```
.....I...............Namedconstant+++++++++C.........Fldnme....................
     I              'abcdefghijklmnopqrst-C        LOW
     I              'uvwxyz'
     I              'ABCDEFGHIJKLMNOPQRST-C        UP
     I              'UVWXYZ'
.....CL0N01N02N03Factor1+++OpcdeFactor2+++ResultLenDHHiLoEqComments+++++++......
     C              LOW:UP    XLATEINNAME     NAME      P         TRANSLATE TO UPPER
      **                                                          CASE
```

USING *BITON/BITOF* OPERATION CODES

BITON and the converse op code BITOF allow you to change the status of the bits in a single-byte field. The BITON op code changes the specified bits from a 0 (off) to a 1 (on) (Figure 5.3). Conversely, the BITOF op code does just the opposite.

Figure 5.3: Example of the BITON RPG Op Code

Factor 1	Op Code	Factor 2	Result Field	Ext	HI	LO	EQ
—	**BITON**	'bit pattern'	1 byte field	—	N/A	N/A	N/A

In both of the operation codes, Factor 1 is left blank. Factor 2 can contain either a single-byte character field or a named constant containing a bit pattern. If a field is used in Factor 2, then the bits that are on in that field are set off in the results field. The bits that are off in the field in Factor 2 are ignored in the results field.

You should be aware of the horizontal method of addressing bits used in RPG. There are eight bits in a byte. The bits are numbered from left to right, beginning with 0.

One of our favorite uses of these operation codes is to change a display attribute of some portion of a text field. The DSPATR keyword is easy to use, but works on the complete field. You can not use it to highlight a single word inside a text field. But you can use the BITON/BITOF operation codes to accomplish this. Let's take at look a the code in Figure 5.4.

Figure 5.4: Using BITON/BITOF to Change Display Attributes

```
.....CL0N01N02N03Factor1+++OpcdeFactor2+++ResultLenDHHiLoEqComments+++++++......
     C                    BITOF'01234567'HI         1
     C                    BITON'26'      HI
     C                    BITOF'01234567'NM         1
     C                    BITON'2'       NM
     C                    BITOF'01234567'RV         1
     C                    BITON'27'      RV
     C                    MOVELHI        FIELD  20
     C                    MOVE NM        FIELD
```

We first use the BITOF op code to set off all of the bits in our field named HI (short for High Intensity). This is similar in function to initializing a field. We then use the BITON op code to set on bits 2 and 6. This combination of bits, when sent to a display device, translates into a command character that tells the system to turn on highlighting.

Again we use the BITON/BITOF op codes to set on bit 2 in a field called NM (short for Normal Intensity). (You might notice that we have included the bit pattern for the field named RV, which is short for Reverse Image. We are not using it in this example, but we thought you might find it useful.) We use the NM field to turn off the highlighting function. Next we move the field HI to the beginning of the field we want highlighted and move the field NM to the end of the field we want highlighted. When this field, named (cleverly enough) FIELD, is displayed on a device, it is highlighted. This field can then be embedded in an array or "substringed" (you will not find this word in your Webster's Dictionary, but consider it to be a derivative of the Substring op code) together with other text that would be displayed normally.

When using this technique, be sure to use the normal pattern to shut off the display attribute that you set. If you do not, the attribute remains in effect until the end of the displayed line.

USING RTNDTA IN FILE MAINTENANCE

A file maintenance program is like a sewer; it performs a very necessary function, but nobody likes to work there. Let's face it, file maintenance programs are boring and tedious. Every one of them performs pretty much the same routines—read a record, move the fields from the record to the screen, display the screen, edit the fields, move the fields back to the record, update the record. This a standard, low-tech, boring job that must be done (usually by junior programmers).

There is a DDS keyword, RTNDTA, that can eliminate a lot of code. While it can't actually make you *like* doing file maintenance programs, it simplifies the task by eliminating a lot of tedious move statements.

Figure 5.5 shows a typical file maintenance task. It reads a record, moves the fields in the record to the screen, and waits for the user to enter some data. The record is not locked at this point because we don't know how long this user will be at lunch while this record is on the screen. When the user comes back from their break and presses the Enter key, we get the database record (this time locking the record for update), move the fields from the screen to the record, and update the database record.

Figure 5.5: Routine File Maintenance Task

```
...CLON01N02N03Factor1+++OpcdeFactor2+++ResultLenDHHiLoEqComments++++++......
   C           CHKEY     CHAINCUSTOMER              N68
   C                     MOVE CUNAME    DSNAME
   C                     MOVE CUADR1    DSADR1
   C                     MOVE CUADR2    DSADR2
   C                     MOVE CUCITY    DSCITY
   C                     MOVE CUSTAT    DSSTAT
   C                     MOVE CUZIP     DSZIP
   C                     EXFMTFMT2
   C           CHKEY     CHAINCUSTOMER               68
   C                     MOVE DSNAME    CUNAME
   C                     MOVE DSADR1    CUADR1
   C                     MOVE DSADR2    CUADR2
   C                     MOVE DSCITY    CUCITY
   C                     MOVE DSSTAT    CUSTAT
   C                     MOVE DSZIP     CUZIP
   C                     UPDATCUSREC
```

Figure 5.6 shows the same function as Figure 5.5, but uses the RTNDTA keyword in the display file. All of the fields in the display file are named the same as the fields in the database file. This eliminates the need to code all of the move statements to get them from the database record to the display file record format.

Figure 5.6: Maintenance Function with RTNDTA Keyword

```
.....CLON01N02N03Factor1+++OpcdeFactor2+++ResultLenDHHiLoEqComments++++++......
    C           CHKEY     CHAINCUSTOMER              N68
    C                     EXFMTFMT2
    C           CHKEY     CHAINCUSTOMER               68
    C                     READ FMT2
    C                     UPDATCUSREC
```

But wait, you say, when it chains back out to the database record to get it for update, it will lose any of the data keyed into the fields in the display format. This is true, and so we have coded another read to the display file record format (FMT2). The RTNDTA keyword is coded on this record format and this was the last record format written to the screen, so the system gets the fields from the screen again, as the user keys them. But wait another minute, you say, the READ FMT2 statement will cause the program to wait for input from the user. Normally true, but the RTNDTA keyword also prevents this from happening.

This is a very powerful technique that potentially can eliminate tons of code and reduce the amount of maintenance that must be performed later. In this very simple example, we eliminated a lot of extraneous code. And, remember our motto—Less code, fewer errors.

PROCESSING MULTIPLE VIEWS OF THE SAME DATABASE FILE

Options, options, and more options. We are really in the business of providing people with options. The more the merrier. One of the options that every user seems to demand is the ability to display the records from a database file in a sequence other than the database designer intended. With DB/400's support of logical files, this does not present much of a problem. Remember the performance considerations when utilizing this technique (see Chapter 1, "Performance Starts with Program Design").

In Figure 5.7, we present our usual method of handling multiple views of the same file in a single program. The first step is to define the files in the File Description Specifications. The compiler frowns upon using two file definitions with the same record format, so we must rename one of the record formats. This is accomplished using the RENAME function of the File Description Specification Continuation line. We name the actual record format and then give it an alias with which to refer to it inside the RPG program.

Figure 5.7: Multiple Views of the Same File in a Single Program

```
.....FFilenameIPEAF........L..I........Device+......KExit++Entry+A....U1........
      FFILE1    IF   E         K          DISK
      FFILE1LOGIF    E         K          DISK
      F          FILREC                               KRENAMELOGREC
.....CL0N01N02N03Factor1+++OpcdeFactor2+++ResultLenDHHiLoEqComments++++++......
      C                     SELEC
      C          *IN71      WHEQ *ON
      C                     READ FILREC                    81
      C          *IN72      WHEQ *ON
      C                     READ LOGREC                    81
      C                     ENDSL
```

Now that the compiler is happy, we can continue on our merry way and read whichever view of the database file the user is happy with. The system keeps two independent file pointers for each "view" of your data. You do, however, need to be careful in handling the contents of individual fields.

One of our complaints with RPG is that the file access operation codes (e.g., READ and CHAIN) do not allow a field name in Factor 2. When dealing with multiple views of the same database file, this would greatly simplify the amount of code necessary to accomplish the task. So, the next time someone at a users' conference asks you to fill out a REQUIREMENTS form, you know what to ask for, right?

PASS THE PARAMETER, IF YOU PLEASE

As with everything else on the AS/400, there are numerous ways to handle passing information between programs. You can use files, data queues, message queues, data areas, parameters, and so on.

Parameters are defined in a program using a Parameter List (PLIST) statement, with *ENTRY defined in Factor 1. A PLIST statement must be followed by at least one Parameter (PARM) statement. This PARM statement defines the data being received by the program.

We see an example of this in Figure 5.8. Two parameters are being passed to this program: A two-character, alphanumeric return code and a two-digit, numeric location code.

Figure 5.8: Passing a Variable Number of Parameters between Programs

```
....I.................................PFromTo++DFieldL1M1FrP1MnZr..........
I          SDS
I                                      *PARMS     PARMS
I                                      254 263 USER
....CL0N01N02N03Factor1+++OpcdeFactor2+++ResultLenDHHiLoEqComments+++++++......
C          *ENTRY    PLIST
C                    PARM            RTNCOD  2
C                    PARM            PASLOC  20
C          PARMS     IFGE 1
C                    MOVE *BLANKS    RTNCOD
C                    ENDIF
C          PARMS     IFGE 2
C                    MOVE PASLOC     WKLOC   20
C                    ENDIF
```

The thing to remember about parameter passing is that the program neither checks, nor cares, about any of the parameters until it actually tries to use them. This means that, if a program calls another program and does not pass all of the parameters that the called program is expecting, nothing happens until—and if—the called program tries to access one of the passed parameters. If the called program does try to use a parameter and the program that initiated the call did not pass the field, you get introduced to one of the nifty little error handling routines of the operating system.

There is a simple method of avoiding this error. Code the Program Status Data Structure and use the keyword *PARMS as we did in Figure 5.9. The field PARMS contains the number of parameters that the calling program passed to the called program.

Figure 5.9: Using a RTNCOD Parameter between Programs

```
....CL0N01N02N03Factor1+++OpcdeFactor2+++ResultLenDHHiLoEqComments++++++......
     C           *ENTRY    PLIST
     C                     PARM            RTNCOD  2
     C                     EXFMTFORMAT1
     C           *INKC     IFEQ *ON
     C                     MOVE '03'       RTNCOD
     C                     SETON                      LR
     C                     ENDIF
     C           *INKL     IFEQ *ON
     C                     MOVE '12'       RTNCOD
     C                     ENDIF
```

If the field PARMS tells us that a parameter was passed to this program, we move it to a work field. Thereafter, the program only works with the work fields, unless it is passing data back to the calling program, in which case it must check the PARMS field again. At no time does the program attempt to access a parameter without first checking the PARMS field to see if the field was passed to it.

USING A *RTNCOD* PARAMETER BETWEEN PROGRAMS

We all know the problems associated with using one big program to do many different functions. The program is slow to load into memory, difficult to follow, and hard for others to maintain. In large and complex applications, it is far better to design many small programs controlled by one *driver* program. These smaller programs are generally referred to as *subprograms*. The subprograms only get loaded into memory when they are needed. Maintenance can usually be isolated to one small, easy-to-follow subprogram.

This technique can present something of a problem in that the calling program often needs to know what happened in the called program. If the driver program calls a subprogram that presents the user with a screen and the user presses F3 to Exit, the driver program must know this in order to end the job step. As usual, there are many ways to accomplish this—one of which is to use a parameter to pass the function key that was pressed. Figure 5.9 illustrates this technique.

USING THE INDICATOR ARRAY

One technique that we often take for granted is one that new programmers might not yet be aware of. You can use the array handling operation code Move Array (MOVEA) to set on and off many indicators at once. We use this technique quite often at the beginning of edit routines to set off all of the error indicators. Figure 5.10 demonstrates this technique.

Figure 5.10: Using the Indicator Array

```
.....I..............Namedconstant+++++++++C.........Fldnme....................
     I              '001100111110000111100-C          CONIND
     I              '000000'
.....CL0N01N02N03Factor1+++OpcdeFactor2+++ResultLenDHHiLoEqComments++++++......
     C                        EXFMTFORMAT1
     C                        MOVEA*ALL(0)     *IN,40
     C                        EXSR EDIT1
     C                        EXFMTFORMAT2
     C                        MOVEA'000000'    *IN,32
     C                        EXFMTFORMAT3
     C                        MOVEACONIND      *IN,50
```

In our example, after displaying FORMAT1, the MOVEA operation code is used to set off indicators 40 through 99. The reserved word *ALL is used to indicate the settings of the indicators. We could just as easily specify *ALL(1) to set all of the indicators on.

In the second example in Figure 5.10, after displaying FORMAT2, the MOVEA operation code is used to set off indicators 32 through 37. The length of Factor 2 is only eight characters, so this version of the technique is limited in the number of indicators affected by the operation code.

The third example in Figure 5.10 uses a named constant to set the status of 26 indicators, namely 50 through 75. This version of the technique can handle as many indicators as you want, and set them to any status required.

When you use this technique, be aware that the indicators that are affected by the MOVEA statement do not show up in the RPG compile listing as having been used. This is because they are individual elements in an array.

USING INDICATORS AS FIELD NAMES

You can also refer to an indicator as a named field. Every indicator has its own name using the format *INXX, where XX is the indicator number. The first two statements shown in Figure 5.11 basically are equal. And, you can, and should, test the status of indicators by using the indicator name in Factor 1.

Figure 5.11: Indicators as Named Fields

```
.....CLON01N02N03Factor1+++OpcdeFactor2+++ResultLenDHHiLoEqComments++++++......
     C                   SETON                          01
     C                   MOVE *ON      *IN01
     C         *IN01     IFEQ *ON
     C                   MOVE *ON      *INLR
     C                   ENDIF
```

We have a strong aversion to using indicators in positions 9 through 17 of the Calculation Specifications. This is because, while it's easier to code, it's harder to read, follow, and maintain.

RETRIEVING THE PROGRAM NAME

One very useful bit of information that you can extract from the Program Status Data Structure is the name of the program that is running. Why is this useful, you ask? After all, you wrote the program so you know its name. Why do you need the Program Status Data Structure to tell you this?

The obvious answer is maintenance. After you have been programming for some time, you should find that you almost never write programs from scratch anymore. You find something from your toolbox that is similar to the task at hand and you start there. So, the less hard coding you have in any program, the easier it is to clone and use for the basis of something else.

But there is another, less obvious, answer. The system sometimes changes the name of the program! If a program is executing and some inattentive programmer compiles that same program, the system moves the program that is executing into the QRPLLIB library. As it does this, it renames the object. The net result is that the program that is running still runs the old code, while any new instances of the program run the newly compiled version.

While that program is running in QRPLLIB, it has a different name. If you have hard coded the name of the program into any fields, (such as message queue name), you might experience the system handling error routine. This is kind of like meeting the Master Control Program (for all you TRON fans)—a very nasty experience.

So, the best way to code the name of the program is to retrieve it from the Program Status Data Structure. An example of this is shown in Figure 5.12. The program name is retrieved by using the keyword *PROGRAM and assigns it a field name of PGM.

Figure 5.12: Extracting the Program Name

```
.....I..............................PFromTo++DField+L1M1FrP1MnZr..........
     I          SDS
     I                              254 263 USER
     I                              *PROGRAM PGM
```

USING MULTIPLE FORMAT FILES

The AS/400 uses a very strong relational database file manager. File definitions are external to the programs processing the data, thus ensuring consistency and relieving the programmer of the necessity of defining the data.

But some people believe that this file management system can not handle multiple format files. While it is true that a single file can only contain one format, it is also true that a logical file can be built over multiple files (each file having a different format). The net result appears to be a multiple format file. This is especially useful in a header/detail type file relationship.

If you perform a read on the logical file, you get a record from either database file, (either the header record or the detail record), depending upon which was next in sequence. From a programming perspective, the problem becomes how to determine which record format was just read. This information can be obtained from the File Information Data Structure. Figure 5.13 shows the RPG code that demonstrates this technique.

Figure 5.13: Processing a Multiple-format Logical File

```
.....FFilenameIPEAF........L..I........Device+......KExit++Entry+A....U1........
     FLOGICAL IF  E          K        DISK
     F                                              KINFDSINFO
.....I..............................PFromTo++DField+L1M1FrP1MnZr..........
     IINFO        DS
     I                              *RECORD  FORMAT
.....CL0N01N02N03Factor1+++OpcdeFactor2+++ResultLenDHHiLoEqComments++++++......
     C                   READ LOGICAL            68
     C                   SELEC
     C          FORMAT   WHEQ 'HEDREC'
     C                   EXSR HEADER
     C          FORMAT   WHEQ 'DETREC'
     C                   EXSR DETAIL
     C                   ENDSL
```

You must be sure to read the file and not the record format. If you specify the file name on the read statement, then you read either the header record or the detail record. On the other hand, if you specify a record format name on the read statement, then you only read records that are in that format. Once we have read the file, the field we named FORMAT, which has been named with the special keyword *RECORD, contains the name of the record format that we just read. We use this field to determine if we have read a header record or a detail record.

LOCALIZED INDICATORS

It's unfortunate, but true—indicators are still a fact of life in RPG. We still need them to communicate to I/O devices. Complex programs can still use quite a few indicators. One way to hold down the number of indicators used in a program is to use the concept of localized indicators.

Simply put, when we enter a subroutine, we save the contents of the indicator array. We then clear the array. This allows the subroutine to use any indicator it needs without disturbing the normal flow of the program. At the end of the subroutine, we restore the indicator array to its original state.

The net effect of this technique is to make the entire subroutine "indicatorless." This can prove very useful if this subroutine will be used in many places. Figure 5.14 shows an example of this technique.

Figure 5.14: Code Sample for Localized Indicators

```
.....CL0N01N02N03Factor1+++OpcdeFactor2+++ResultLenDHHiLoEqComments++++++......
     C                        EXSR EXAMPL
     C           EXAMPL        BEGSR
     C                         MOVEA*IN,1      SAVIND 99
     C                         MOVEA*OFF       *IN,1
     C** PROCESSING STUFF HERE
     C                         MOVEASAVIND     *IN,1
     C                         ENDSR
```

DEFINING FIELDS

RPG makes defining a field simple. Just put the size of the field in columns 49 to 51, and the number of decimal positions in column 52, and you have a new field. Or, you can name a field in a data structure and define it that way.

A lot of times you need to define a new field to hold or save the values of another field. We typically call these fields *work* fields. Whenever you need to define a work field, take advantage of yet another way to define a field—the Definition (DEFN) op code. This op code allows you to define a field and to base that definition on another field! This is perfect for work fields because, if the size of the originating field ever needs to be changed, the size of the work field changes as well.

To define a field and base it on another field, use the keyword *LIKE in Factor 1 of the DEFN op code. In Factor 2, put the name of the field to be used as the base. In the result field, put the name of the new field you are defining. Now, if sometime in the future someone comes along and changes the size of the base field, the size of the work field also changes when this program is recompiled.

In addition to defining the new field exactly the same as the base field, you can use the base field as a base and increase the size of the new field. In other words, you can say, "Make this new field the same size as the base field and then increase it by X number of digits." This is particularly useful when you are accumulating numeric values.

To define a field larger than the field on which you are basing the new field, you again use *LIKE in Factor 1 of the DEFN keyword, the base field in Factor 2 and the new field in the result columns. Then, in the size column, you put the number of digits by which to increase the base size.

In the example in Figure 5.15, the new field being defined (NEWFLD) is two digits longer than the base field. If the base field is defined as a seven-digit field with two decimals, the new field is a nine-digit field with two decimals.

*Figure 5.15: Extending the Size of New Fields Using *LIKE*

Factor 1	Op Code	Factor 2	Result Field	Size
*LIKE	**DEFN**	BASFLD	NEWFLD	+02

USING THE CLEAR OP CODE

We have already seen how the use of the RTNDTA keyword can eliminate a bunch of tedious move statements to update fields. The CLEAR op code can do the same thing when you want to blank out all of the fields on a screen.

Normally, before you present an input screen, you blank out the input fields so that, whatever the user entered into those fields the last time the screen was displayed, it will not show up this time around. If there are 10 fields on the screen, 10 move statements are required to clear them. You can clear all 10 fields with one CLEAR statement. And best of all, if someone comes along later and adds a new field to the screen, it too is cleared with the same CLEAR statement without any additional coding changes.

Figure 5.16 shows the Clear op code. If you specify a format name in Factor 2, all fields in the format are cleared. You can also use the Clear op code to clear a field or all fields in a database file record format. Fields that are numeric are set to all zeros; alphanumeric fields are set to all blanks. While this, in itself, does nothing to help future maintenance (after all, it's not likely that the field will change from alphanumeric to numeric), it does relieve you from having to know what type of field you are clearing.

Figure 5.16: Clear Op Code

Factor 1	Op Code	Factor 2	Result Field
—	CLEAR	Format Name	—

DIVERSITY IN YOUR ARSENAL IS YOUR BEST DEFENSE

Regardless of how long you remain in this business, you can never have too many tools in your toolbox. Knowing where to get the tool to get the job done is usually the most important step in programming. It is not necessarily how much you know that is important, but rather, do you know what tools are available to you and where to get them.

Chapter 6

The Power of QCMDEXC

The QCMDEXC program is used to call AS/400 commands from within your RPG or CL programs. It is a powerful tool and should certainly be in every RPG programmer's arsenal. Almost anything you would ever want to do with a single command can be done right from within your program!

THE WHAT, THE WHY, AND THE HOW

Think about the possibilities. You can submit jobs, manipulate library lists, override printer parameters, sort database files, plus a veritable plethora of other tasks, all from within your RPG program.

In this chapter, we give you three examples of ways to use the QCMDEXC program to give you more flexibility with your RPG programs:

- Running the OPNQRYF command from within a print program to sequence a file into the order you want before listing it.

- Overriding printer parameters within the RPG program to allow you to send the printed output to a specific printer and change the number of copies.

- Submitting a job from within an RPG program.

The QCMDEXC program is not only versatile, it is also very easy to use. All you need to do is call the program and pass it two parameters: The command you want to run, and the length of the command (you can even fudge a little on this one because the system does not seem to mind if you pad the back end of your command with blanks). The length of the second parameter, which specifies the command length, must be a 15-digit field with 5 decimal positions. It is that easy!

The example in Figure 6.1 shows how to embed the Work with Spool Files (WRKSPLF) command into an RPG program. Let's get into some more practical examples of the QCMDEXC program.

Figure 6.1: Using QCMDEXC to Run WRKSPLF from within an RPG Program

```
C                   CALL  'QCMDEXC'                QCMDEXC COMMAND TO
C                   PARM 'WRKSPLF' CMD      7      RUN WRKSPLF
C                   PARM 7         LEN      155
```

RUNNING OPNQRYF TO SORT A DATABASE FILE FROM WITHIN AN RPG PROGRAM

If your system has multiple report programs that produce the same output, the odds are pretty good that the reason they are different programs is because they have different sequence or selection criteria. When output change requests are made, you may be asked to make the same changes to all of them. By sequencing and selecting your data dynamically, you could add a great deal of flexibility to your programs and reduce the amount of maintenance performed.

The first sample program in this chapter gives you the ability to accomplish just that. The RPG program is a simple file listing program that prints our Customer File in customer name or customer number order. When the program is called, a parameter is passed that determines the sequence in which the records are printed. If a 1 is passed to the program, the list is printed in customer name sequence. Otherwise, the list prints in customer number order.

Note that UC is in positions 71 and 72 of the File Description Specification for the CUST file. This tells the system that the file open and close to our CUST file is user-controlled within the program (see Chapter 1 for more information on user-controlled file opens). Before we can open the file, we must perform the file overrides on the file. The override we use tells the system that we want our RPG program and the OPNQRYF command to share the same data path of our CUST file. We do this by using the Override Data Base File (OVRDBF) command.

Also note that the program uses QCMDEXC to call the commands specifying that the program use a shared access path for the CUST file and then again to perform the Open Query File (OPNQRYF) operation to sequence the data. The option ALLWCPYDTA(*OPTIMIZE) is specified to enhance the performance of the OPNQRYF function (this option allows OPNQRYF to make the decision as to whether or not the file should be sorted). A Concatenate (CAT) operation is used to concatenate the primary element of the OPNQRYF command to the appropriate KEYFLD parameter. The KEYFLD parameter chosen is dependent upon the value within the parameter passed to the program. Once the OPNQRYF command has been performed, the CUST file can be opened for use within our RPG program.

The QCMDEXC program is called upon three different times in the example in Figure 6.2. First it is used to run the Override Data Base File (OVRDBF) command so the system knows to share the open data path between the OPNQRYF command and the RPG program. Second, QCMDEXC is used to perform the OPNQRYF command where the data is then sequenced. And third, the QCMDEXC command is used to close the CUST file once we are finished with the list. Failure to close the file could cause some interesting and unintended results in subsequent programs that use the CUST file.

Figure 6.2: Using QCMDEXC to Run OPNQRYF from within an RPG Program

```
FCUSTOMERIF   E                    DISK                              UC
FQSYSPRT  O   F   132     OF       PRINTER
E                 ACMD     1    5 80
C             *ENTRY   PLIST
C                      PARM              SEQ     1
C                      MOVELACMD,1       CMD     80       OVER-RIDE
C                      Z-ADD80           LEN              FILE TO SHARE
C                      CALL 'QCMDEXC'                     THE OPEN DATA PATH
C                      PARM              CMD
C                      PARM              LEN     155
C             SEQ      IFEQ '1'
C             ACMD,2   CAT  ACMD,3:1     CMD        P
C                      ELSE
C             ACMD,2   CAT  ACMD,4:1     CMD        P
C                      ENDIF
C                      Z-ADD80           LEN
C                      CALL 'QCMDEXC'                     PERFORM OPNQRYF
C                      PARM              CMD              TO SEQUENCE DATA
C                      PARM              LEN
C                      OPEN CUSTOMER
C                      EXCPTHEDING
C             *IN50    DOUEQ'1'
C                      READ CUSREC                     50
C             *IN50    IFEQ *OFF
C                      EXCPTDETAIL
C                      ENDIF
C                      ENDDO
C                      MOVELACMD,5       CMD     80       CLOSE FILE
C                      CALL 'QCMDEXC'
C                      PARM              CMD
C                      PARM              LEN     155
C                      SETON                           LR
OQSYSPRT E  202        HEDING
O         OR       OF
O                                       72 'CUSTOMER LIST'
O         E  1        HEDING
O         OR       OF
O                                       15 'CUSTOMER NUMBER'
O                                       45 'CUSTOMER NAME'
O         EF 1        DETAIL
O                     CUST#    15
O                     NAME     65
**
OVRDBF FILE(CUSTOMER) SHARE(*YES)
OPNQRYF FILE((CUSTOMER)) ALWCPYDTA(*OPTIMIZE)
KEYFLD((NAME))
KEYFLD((CUST#))
CLOF CUSTOMER
```

Employing this methodology, we create a listing program to sequence the data dynamically. This may eliminate the need to code and maintain additional programs with similar output. It also allows us to process the data in the CUST file in arrival sequence, rather than the less-efficient method of reading the file by key (see Chapter 1).

OVERRIDING PRINTER PARAMETERS FROM WITHIN AN RPG PROGRAM

Allowing users to decide where they want a report printed is pretty standard stuff. The odds are good that you already have found a way to handle this request. But, if you are not familiar with the QCMDEXC program, you may want to check out this next example.

In Figure 6.3, we use the QCMDEXC program to change printers and the number of copies printed, from within our RPG print program. Parameter one of our program is the number of copies to print, and parameter two is the printer device to which to direct the output.

Figure 6.3: Using QCMDEXC to Override Printer Attributes

```
      FCUSTOMERIF E           DISK
      FQSYSPRT O   F    132     OF    PRINTER                        UC
       *
      E                ACMD      1   1 70           PRINT JOB CMD
       *
      I         DS
      I                               1  70 CMDDS
      I                              30  31 COPIES
      I                              38  47 PRINTR
       *
      I         SDS
      I                          *PARMS    PARMS
       **
      C         *ENTRY    PLIST
      C                   PARM         PASCPY  2
      C                   PARM         PASPRT 10
       *
B1    C         PARMS     IFGT *ZEROS           ONLY PERFORM THE
      C                   MOVEAACMD,1  CMDDS    PRINTER OVER-RIDES
      C                   MOVE PASCPY  COPIES   IF THE PARAMETERS
      C                   MOVE PASPRT  PRINTR   ARE PASSED TO THE
      C                   CALL 'QCMDEXC'        PROGRAM...
      C                   PARM         CMDDS
      C                   PARM 70      LEN    155
E1    C                   ENDIF
       *
      C                   OPEN QSYSPRT
      C                   EXCPTHEDING
B1    C         *IN50     DOUEQ*ON
      C                   READ CUSREC                  50
B2    C         *IN50     IFEQ *OFF
      C                   ADD  1       COUNT   50      PRINT DETAIL RECORDS
      C                   EXCPTDETAIL
E2    C                   ENDIF
E1    C                   ENDDO
      C                   EXCPTTOTALS
      C                   CLOSEQSYSPRT
      C                   SETON                  LR
       **
      OQSYSPRT E 302        HEDING
      O        OR       OF
      O                               5 'DATE:'
      O                   UDATE Y    14
      O                              70 'CUSTOMER LIST'
```

```
     O                                121 'PAGE:'
     O                      PAGE  Z    127
     O        E   1         HEDING
     O       OR        OF
     O                                 20 'CUSTOMER NUMBER'
     O                                 46 'CUSTOMER NAME'
     O        EF  1         DETAIL
     O                      CUST#       20
     O                      NAME        66
     O        E  21         TOTALS
     O                      COUNT 1     14
     O                                 35 'TOTAL RECORDS LISTED'
**
OVRPRTF FILE(QSYSPRT) COPIES(  ) DEV(           ) OUTQ(*DEV)
```

As in our previous example, the file we are overriding must remain closed while we perform the file overrides. Notice the UC in positions 71 and 72 of the printer file (QSYSPRT), which tells the system this file is a user-controlled file. We code the open and close of QSYSPRT ourselves, once we have performed our desired file overrides.

We choose to use the PARMS field in the Program Status Data Structure to indicate to the program whether or not parameters are passed to the program (the Program Status Data Structure is discussed in Chapter 4). If the customer file listing program is called with parameters 1 and 2 specified (the PARMS field is greater than zero), we perform printer file overrides to specify our desired printer and number of copies. If no parameters are passed to the program, the override is not performed.

The only element of the ACMD table (which is defined in the Extension Specification in Figure 6.3) holds the shell of the Override Printer File (OVRPRTF) command. We choose to use a data structure as a tool to load the parameters of the OVRPRTF command because it is generally easier to follow than using the CAT command to concatenate the various components. We begin by loading the ACMD table element into our data structure and then overlaying it with the values passed into the program as parameters 1 and 2. The net result is a complete OVRPRTF command that is ready to be executed. This is done by calling the QCMDEXC program. Once the override to the printer file is performed, the printer file is opened and the rest of the simple list program is completed.

SUBMITTING A JOB TO THE JOB QUEUE FROM WITHIN AN RPG PROGRAM

As an RPG programmer on the AS/400, you may have wondered why there is no SMBJOB op code that allows you to submit jobs from within your RPG program. The good news is that, by using the QCMDEXC program, you can do just that.

For our next example, we use a little RPG prompt program, which prompts for a printer ID and the number of copies, validates the values entered, and then submits a program to the job queue. The program we are submitting is the customer list program, which we wrote in our previous example (Figure 6.3). The display file coded in Figure 6.4 is used to present the prompt screen as it is seen in Figure 6.5.

Figure 6.4: Customer List Prompt Screen Display File

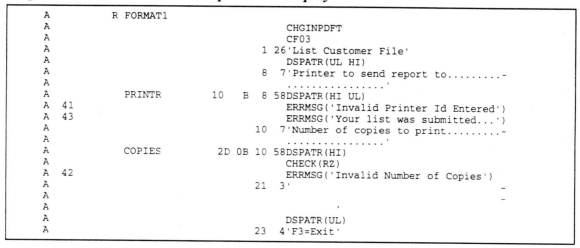

```
A              R FORMAT1
A                                    CHGINPDFT
A                                    CF03
A                                  1 26'List Customer File'
A                                    DSPATR(UL HI)
A                                  8  7'Printer to send report to.........-
A                                    ................'
A              PRINTR      10   B  8 58DSPATR(HI UL)
A  41                                ERRMSG('Invalid Printer Id Entered')
A  43                                ERRMSG('Your list was submitted...')
A                                 10  7'Number of copies to print.........-
A                                    ................'
A              COPIES     2D  0B 10 58DSPATR(HI)
A                                    CHECK(RZ)
A  42                                ERRMSG('Invalid Number of Copies')
A                                 21  3'                                  -
A                                    '                                    -
A                                    DSPATR(UL)
A                                 23  4'F3=Exit'
```

Figure 6.5: Customer List Prompt Screen

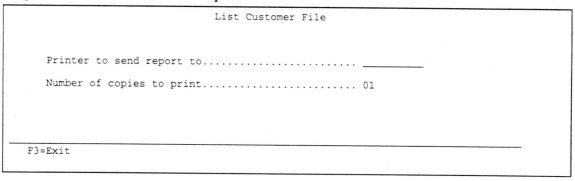

```
                         List Customer File



    Printer to send report to....................... _____

    Number of copies to print....................... 01




  _____
   F3=Exit
```

In the RPG program in Figure 6.6, we first establish the default values for the number-of-copies field and then present our prompt screen. The program has been coded to continue presenting the prompt screen until F3 is pressed. If the entries keyed pass the edits, the print job is submitted to the job queue and a confirmation message is sent to the screen.

Figure 6.6: *Using QCMDEXC to Submit Jobs from within an RPG Program*

```
      FLCUSTDSPCF   E                   WORKSTN
        *
      E                     ACMD    1   1 80              SUBMIT JOB CMD
        *
      I           IDS
      I                                       1   80 CMDDS
      I                                      35   36 PASCPY
      I                                      40   49 PASPRT
        *
      C                     MOVEAACMD,1     CMDDS          SETUP DEFAULTS
      C                     Z-ADD1          COPIES
   B1 C           *INKC     DOUEQ*ON                       DO UNTIL EOJ REQUEST
      C                     EXFMTFORMAT1
      C                     MOVEA'000'      *IN,41
   B2 C           *INKC     IFEQ *OFF
      C                     CALL 'EXIST'                   VALIDATE PRINTER
      C                     PARM            PRINTR
      C                     PARM '*LIBL'    LIBR    10
      C                     PARM '*DEVD'    OBJTYP  10
      C                     PARM            VALID    1
   B3 C           VALID     IFNE 'Y'                       SEND ERR MESSAGE IF
      C                     MOVE *ON        *IN41          NOT VALID
      C                     ITER
   E3 C                     ENDIF
   B3 C           COPIES    IFEQ *ZEROS                    MUST SPECIFY NUMBER
      C                     MOVE *ON        *IN42          OF COPIES
      C                     ITER
   E3 C                     ENDIF
      C                     MOVE *ON        *IN43          SUBMIT JOB IF NO
      C                     MOVE COPIES     PASCPY         ERRORS FOUND
      C                     MOVE PRINTR     PASPRT
      C                     CALL 'QCMDEXC'
      C                     PARM            CMDDS
      C                     PARM 80         LEN     155
   E2 C                     ENDIF
   E1 C                     ENDDO
        **
      C                     SETON                       LR
    **
   SBMJOB CMD(CALL PGM(LSTCUS) PARM('99' 'Printer ID')) JOB(LISTCUST)
```

The next step is to edit the printer ID that is keyed by the program operator. We use the EXIST API program (shown in Figure 6.7), which is explained in further detail when we cover system APIs in Chapter 9. The purpose of the API program is to make sure the device description of the printer ID keyed does, in fact, exist on the system.

Figure 6.7: RPG API Program to Validate Printer Existence

```
     IERROR     IDS
     I                                 B   1    40BYTPRV
     I                                 B   5    80BYTAVA
     I                                     9  15 MSGID
     I                                    16  16 ERR###
     I                                    17 116 MSGDTA
     I          DS
     I                                 B   1    40RCVLEN
     C          *ENTRY   PLIST
     C                   PARM          OBJECT 10
     C                   PARM          LIB    10
     C                   PARM          OBJTYP  8
     C                   PARM          YESNO   1
     C                   Z-ADD116      BYTPRV
B1   C          LIB     IFEQ *BLANKS
     C                   MOVEL'*LIBL'  LIB
E1   C                   ENDIF
     C                   MOVELOBJECT   FILLIB 20
     C                   MOVE LIB      FILLIB
     C                   CALL 'QUSROBJD'              ATTEMPT TO RETRIEVE
     C                   PARM          RCVVAR100        OBJECT DESC
     C                   PARM 100      RCVLEN
     C                   PARM 'OBJD0100'FILFMT  8
     C                   PARM          FILLIB
     C                   PARM          OBJTYP
     C                   PARM          ERROR
     C                   MOVE 'Y'      YESNO
B1   C          MSGID   IFNE *BLANKS
     C                   MOVE 'N'      YESNO
E1   C                   ENDIF
     C                   SETON                      LR
```

If either the printer ID or the number-of-copies fields are deemed invalid, the prompt screen is redisplayed with the appropriate error message indicator on. The operator may then press Error Reset, correct the value in error, and press Enter; or press F3 to terminate the program.

If the field entries keyed pass the edits, the QCMDEXC program is called and the program is submitted to the job queue passing along the printer ID and number of copies keyed as parameters. The confirmation indicator (*IN43) is then turned on and the screen is redisplayed. A message is displayed indicating that the requested job was submitted to the job queue.

All in all, the QCMDEXC program is a very powerful and easy-to-use tool. Once you have the hang of it, you may be surprised at how many different uses you can find for it.

Chapter 7

Array and String Handling

Webster's Dictionary defines an array as "an orderly grouping." While that definition does describe an array in RPG, perhaps a better description for our purposes is found in the IBM *RPG/400 Reference Guide*. The guide refers to an array as "a systematic program-internal arrangement of data fields (array elements) with the same field length, data type (character or numeric), and number of decimal positions (if numeric)."

WHAT IS AN ARRAY?

As the description indicates, an array consists of a consecutive set of like data elements that are stored in main memory while your RPG program is running. Unlike data queues and user spaces, arrays require a fixed amount of main storage that is defined to the system when your program is compiled. Arrays also have a fixed number of elements, and each element must be the same size and data type.

Do not let the apparent inflexibility deter you. As you will see, arrays definitely have their place on the AS/400. We begin by defining the different types of arrays and giving you a couple of examples so you will see that they are quite useful.

WHAT WOULD I USE AN ARRAY FOR?

Up until the introduction of the string handling op codes a few years ago, arrays were a major component of every RPG programmer's toolbox. Whether you needed to pack a name into "Last name, First" or pack "city, state, and zip code" together, arrays were the best tool available for the job.

Introduction of the string handling op codes in RPG/400 changed all that. Arrays were instantly outdated for this purpose because they required too much code compared to their successors. What used to take 10 or more lines of code could now be done in 2. Less code meant fewer opportunities for error.

But arrays are still a valuable tool. They are great for accumulating totals when printing a report. They are useful for validating data in your interactive programs. They can be used to pull like data elements together so they can be processed from within a loop. And, as you will see, they are often without peer when it comes to formatting data that is to appear on reports and screens.

ARRAY BASICS

Within your RPG program, you define the field size, the data type, and the maximum number of data elements that will exist within the array. Also within your program, you manage the sequence and content of the data elements with techniques that we demonstrate within this chapter.

Prior to ILE RPG and V3R1, the only way to define an array was with an Extension Specification. The Extension Specification tells the system the name of your array and how many elements it has, as well as the size and type of the elements. If your array happens to be numeric, this specification also tells the system the number of decimal positions that belong to each element.

RPG allows you to address arrays wholly or as individual array elements. When you use the array name followed by a comma and a numeric field or value (commonly referred to as an array index), you are addressing an individual array element.

Array indices must contain valid array address values when used. If a statement is encountered where an array index is zero or it is greater than the maximum number of array elements allowed, the result is an *array index error*, which causes the program to be interrupted. You need to use care when coding arrays to make sure these conditions can not possibly exist.

RPG allows you to specify both compile-time and run-time arrays. As the name implies, the data for a compile-time array is loaded when the program is compiled (we explain this array type in further detail later in this chapter). The run-time array is loaded and managed from within the RPG program while it is running. It is the run-time array that we focus most of our attention on within this chapter.

Before we get too carried away with run-time arrays, however, we need to mention that there is a third type of two-dimensional array that is not really an array. It is a Multiple-occurrence Data Structure. It differs from arrays in that each element is itself a data structure with fields of varying size and data type. Refer to the chapter on data structures (Chapter 8) for a more detailed description of this special type of array.

THE RUN-TIME ARRAY

In Figure 7.1, we define two run-time arrays. The first array is called STAT, which has 50 array elements and each element is two characters long. This array is used to hold the two-character abbreviation for each of the 50 United States. Because there are only 50 states, we are able to set the size of the array at a maximum size of 50. We also know that the size of the field we use as an index only needs to be two digits because it will never be over 50.

Figure 7.1: Defining Run-time Arrays with an Extension Specification

```
FMT E    .....E....FromfileTofile++Name++N/rN/tbLenPDSArrnamLenPDSComments+++++++++......
0005.00      E                      STAT      50  2          STATE CODE
0006.00      E                      TOT       50  5 0        COUNT PER STATE
```

Setting the size of your array can be something of a science. It can not be increased from within your program. The idea is to set a size that is at least as large as the maximum number of elements you could possibly encounter, but at the same time keep the number of elements to a minimum because main storage (memory) is being allocated every time your program is run. The number of elements multiplied by the size of each element translates into how much main storage is being allocated each time your program is run.

The second array in Figure 7.1 is called TOT and is used to store the total number of customers that reside in each state. Each TOT array element is five digits with zero decimal positions.

In Figure 7.2, we use the arrays defined in the previous example to accumulate and store the total number of customers we have in each state. This method to accumulate totals is especially valuable if you can not control the sequence of the records being read.

Figure 7.2: Accumulating Totals in Run-time Arrays

```
FMT C
.....CLON01N02N03Factor1+++OpcdeFactor2+++ResultLenDHHiLoEqComments+++++++.....
B1   C           *IN50    DOUEQ*ON
     C                    READ CUSREC                      50 READ ALL CUSTOMER
B2   C           *IN50    IFEQ *OFF                           RECORDS AND ADD UP
     C                    Z-ADD1        X         30        68 TOTALS BY STATE
     C           STATE    LOKUPSTAT,X                       68
B3   C           *IN68    IFEQ *OFF
     C           '    '   LOKUPSTAT,X                       68
E3   C                    ENDIF
     C                    MOVE STATE    STAT,X
     C                    ADD  1        TOT,X
E2   C                    ENDIF
     C                    EXCPTDETAIL
E1   C                    ENDDO
```

For example, let's say you need to write a Customer List RPG program that is to be printed alphabetically by customer name, but you need to print summary totals at the bottom of the report showing how many customers are in each state. The totals are to be printed in the sequence of the two-character abbreviation for each state.

This poses a potential problem. Reading the customer records in a sequence that presents the records alphabetically by customer name will, in all likelihood, result in totals that are recorded in a sequence that does not match our desired output for the summary by state.

Do you resequence the file into state order and read all of the records a second time just to print the totals in the desired sequence? Probably not. As we talked about in Chapter 1, reducing I/O can have a big impact on overall system performance.

Do you create a totals-output field for each of the 50 states? This would be very tedious and the repetition creates a situation that leaves room for error. Would this solution even be viable if we were talking about 500 totals-output fields? Probably not.

Figure 7.2 demonstrates a technique that allows us to accumulate totals into array elements that may be processed for output later. By accumulating the totals as you read the records, you are prepared to output a summary later without making another pass through the data. In Figure 7.2, we read and print the customer file records as we process them in alphabetical order, and at the same time store our totals in the TOT array. We use the STAT array to keep track of which state the corresponding TOT array element represents.

After the totals have been accumulated, the final result looks something like this:

STAT Array:

CA	NV	AZ	OR	ID	NY

TOT Array:

451	103	55	28	12	1033

A quick glance at the arrays tell us that we have 451 customers in California, 55 in Arizona, 12 in Idaho, and so on. Each data element in the TOT array directly corresponds to the element in the STAT array.

Using Run-time Arrays to Store and Accumulate Totals

Let's analyze the code in Figure 7.2 to see how our totals are accumulated. If the first customer record read is from California, the program uses the LOKUP op code to perform a *lookup* in the STAT array to see if we have already processed a customer record from California.

The LOKUP op code is unique to tables and arrays. Its name aptly describes its function. The LOKUP op code performs a lookup operation to see if the search argument specified in Factor 1 already exists somewhere within the array. If the search argument does, in fact, exist, the indicator specified in position 58 (=) is turned on and the number of the element where the search argument was found is returned to the field specified in the Result Field (position 43). Note that, prior to the lookup operation, the index was reset to 1 and the result indicator was preset to OFF. This must be done because the search begins from where the index happens to be set.

Back to our example. Let's assume that this was the first record read. The lookup failed to find an array element of CA and needs to add it. We have coded the program to look for the first available array element in the STAT array by performing another lookup using the LOKUP op code to find the first array element filled with blanks.

Once the first available blank element is found, the CA state code is moved into the STAT array and a count of 1 is added to the corresponding array element in the TOT array. After reading our first customer record and processing the record, our arrays look like this:

STAT Array:

CA					

TOT Array:

1					

If the next customer record read is from Nevada, the STAT array lookup is performed with the NV state code, and, as before, the NV code is added when NV is not found initially. After reading and processing our second customer record from Nevada, our arrays look like this:

STAT Array:

CA	NV				

TOT Array:

	1	1			

Let's assume that the third customer record read is again from California. In this case, the lookup in the STAT array for CA is successful (as indicated when indicator 68 comes on) and the appropriate array index is returned and stored in the field X.

This time, we simply add 1 to the TOT array element that directly corresponds to the STAT array element that was found in the lookup operation. After reading and processing the third customer record, our arrays look like this:

STAT Array:

CA	NV				

TOT Array:

	2	1			

When all of the customer records have been read and processed, we end up with a STAT array that contains state codes for each and every customer record in our file. The TOT array contains a count representing the number of customers we have in each state.

Sequencing Run-time Arrays for Output Operations

We now have the data we need to print our totals by state summary at the bottom of our report. But there is a problem. How are we going to get the totals to print out in state order? Our arrays have been built based upon the customer name arrival sequence of the records because that is what our report specifications called for. The solution to this problem lies in a technique that is demonstrated in Figure 7.3.

Figure 7.3: Using Sort Array (SORTA) to Resequence Array Elements

```
     FCUSTOMERIF  E                     DISK
     FSTATES  IF  E         K           DISK
     FQSYSPRT O   F    132     OF        PRINTER
        *
     E                     STAT     50  2              STATE CODE
     E                     TOT      50  5 0            COUNT PER STATE
     E                     SWRK     50  2              STATE WORK ARRAY
        *
     C                     EXCPTHEDING
B1   C         *IN50       DOUEQ*ON
     C                     READ CUSREC                 50 READ ALL CUSTOMER
B2   C         *IN50       IFEQ *OFF                      RECORDS AND ADD UP
     C                     Z-ADD1        X       30    68 TOTALS BY STATE
     C         STATE       LOKUPSTAT,X                 68
B3   C         *IN68       IFEQ *OFF
     C         ' '         LOKUPSTAT,X                 68
E3   C                     ENDIF
     C                     MOVE STATE    STAT,X
     C                     ADD  1        TOT,X
E2   C                     ENDIF
E1   C                     ENDDO
        *
     C                     MOVE STAT     SWRK             MOVE STATES TO WORK
     C                     SORTASWRK                      ARRAY AND SORT BY
        *                                                 STATE
B1   C                     DO   50       Y       30
B2   C         SWRK,Y      IFNE *BLANKS
     C                     Z-ADD1        X       30    68 READ SORTED ARRAY
     C         SWRK,Y      LOKUPSTAT,X                 68 AND FIND THE STATE
     C         STAT,X      CHAINSTATES               68   CODE IN THE ORIGINAL
     C                     ADD  TOT,X    TOTAL   70       ARRAY TO FIND THE
     C                     EXCPTDETAIL                    APPROPRIATE TOTAL
E2   C                     ENDIF
E1   C                     ENDDO
     C                     EXCPTTOTALS
     C                     SETON                    LR
     OQSYSPRT E   302        HEDING
     O        OR        OF
     O                              70 'SUMMARY BY STATE'
     O        E  1         HEDING
     O        OR        OF
     O                              16 'STATE'
     O                              42 'TOTAL'
     O        EF 1         DETAIL
     O                     STAT,X    4
     O                     STDESC   31
     O                     TOT,X 1  40
     O        E 21         TOTALS
     O                     TOTAL 1  14
     O                              30 'TOTAL CUSTOMERS'
```

In Figure 7.3, we code a print program that simply prints the customer-summary-by-state report, similar to the summary we have been talking about. We employ a loop to load the arrays, much as we did in the previous example. The program is a little different, though, in that we added an additional array called SWRK. It is important to note that the SWRK array has the exact same definition as the STAT array.

In order to print our totals in state code order, we need to sort the STAT array. The Sort Array (SORTA) op code is perfect for this purpose, except that the array sequence is what binds the STAT and TOT arrays together. If we sort the STAT array and leave the TOT array alone, our totals no longer correspond to the state code and the results are a mess. We solve this problem with a third array that matches the attributes of the array we want to sequence.

In Figure 7.3, the SWRK array matches the attributes of the STAT array. Once we have used our loop to compile our totals, we copy the entire contents of the STAT array into the SWRK array and then sort the SWRK array so it is in state code order. The net result is that the SWRK array has all of the state codes we want to print and they have been sorted into our desired sequence.

Next, we code a print loop that "walks" through the SWRK array, which then does a lookup on the original STAT array to retrieve the appropriate array index (of the STAT array) and store it in field X. We know the correct element will be found because the contents of the SWRK array were initially identical to those of the STAT array.

The results after the SWRK array is sorted look something like this:

SWRK Array:

AZ	CA	ID	NV	NY	OR

STAT Array:

CA	NV	AZ	OR	ID	NY

TOT Array:

451	103	55	28	12	1033

The totals in the TOT array still correspond to the state codes in the STAT array, so the index stored in field X happens to represent the correct total in the TOT array as well. When we perform our print operation, we are able to print our array in state code order by using the array index stored in field X.

USING RUN-TIME ARRAYS TO FORMAT DATA FOR OUTPUT

In our next example, we are going to use arrays to solve a common output problem. We want to print a customer phone list, but it needs to be a three-column alphabetical list, much like a phone book. This output is desirable on multicolumn alphabetic reports because the format makes it easier to look up entries.

Our customer phone list program in Figure 7.4 uses two arrays to store the data that is printed. The program reads the customer file and stores the fields we are going to print in the ONAM and ONUM arrays. The ONAM array holds the customer name, and the ONUM array holds the phone number. Storing the data in the arrays gives us the flexibility to produce the list in the desired format.

Figure 7.4: Multicolumn Customer Phone List Using Arrays to Format Output

```
     FCUSTOMERIF  E                      DISK                    UC
     FQSYSPRT O   F     132      OF      PRINTER
         *
     E                      ACMD    1   3 80
     E                      ONAM       120 29              CUSTOMER NAMES
     E                      ONUM       120 10 0            CUSTOMER PHONE NUMBERS
         *
     C                      CALL  'QCMDEXC'               OVERRIDE FILE TO
     C                      PARM ACMD,1    CMD      80     SHARE OPEN DATA PATH
     C                      PARM 80        LEN     155
     C                      CALL  'QCMDEXC'               PERFORM OPNQRYF
     C                      PARM ACMD,2    CMD            TO SEQUENCE DATA
     C                      PARM 80        LEN
     C                      OPEN CUSTOMER
B1   C           *IN50      DOUEQ'1'
     C                      READ CUSREC                50
B2   C           *IN50      IFEQ *ON                      END OF FILE?
B3   C           X          CASGT*ZEROS    OUTPUT         DUMP OUTPUT ARRAYS
E3   C                      ENDCS                         IF ANY DATA IS LEFT
     C                      LEAVE                         AND GET OUT OF LOOP
E2   C                      ENDIF
```

```
      C                    ADD  1          X        30
      C                    MOVELNAME       ONAM,X              LOAD OUTPUT ARRAYS
      C                    MOVE PHONE       ONUM,X
B2    C          X         CASEQ120        OUTPUT              PERFORM OUTPUT IF
E2    C                    ENDCS                               ARRAYS ARE FULL
E1    C                    ENDDO
      C                    CALL 'QCMDEXC'                       CLOSE THE FILE
      C                    PARM ACMD,3     CMD
      C                    PARM 80         LEN      155
      C                    SETON                             LR
      CSR        OUTPUT    BEGSR
      C                    EXCPTHEDING                         PRINT HEADING
B1    C          1         DO   40         X                   CREATE INDICES FOR
      C          X         ADD  40         Y        30         EACH OUTPUT COLUMN
      C          X         ADD  80         Z        30         AND OUTPUT DATA
      C                    EXCPTDETAIL
E1    C                    ENDDO
      C                    MOVE *ZEROS     X                   CLEAR OUTPUT
      C                    CLEARONAM                           FIELDS
      C                    CLEARONUM
      CSR                  ENDSR
      OQSYSPRT E  202          HEDING
      O       OR       OF
      O                            78 'CUSTOMER PHONE LIST'
      O       E  1          HEDING
      O       OR       OF
      O                            15 'CUSTOMER'
      O                            40 'PHONE#'
      O                            59 'CUSTOMER'
      O                            84 'PHONE#'
      O                           103 'CUSTOMER'
      O                           128 'PHONE#'
      O       EF 1          DETAIL
      O                ONAM,X  29
      O                ONUM,X  42 '  /  -   0'
      O                ONAM,Y  73
      O                ONUM,Y  86 '  /  -   0'
      O                ONAM,Z 117
      O                ONUM,Z 130 '  /  -   0'
**
OVRDBF FILE(CUSTOMER) SHARE(*YES)
OPNQRYF FILE((CUSTOMER)) ALWCPYDTA(*OPTIMIZE) KEYFLD((NAME))
CLOF CUSTOMER
```

The program first runs OPNQRYF from within the RPG program to sequence the customer file into customer name order. We use the QCMDEXC API program to perform the OPNQRYF operation (we first examined this technique in Chapter 6).

Once our file is in the desired sequence, we load our output arrays accordingly. The ONAM array is loaded alphabetically by customer name because that is the sequence in which we are reading the file. The customer phone numbers are loaded into the corresponding ONUM array elements.

Our program specifications call for a phone list that prints 3 columns across and 40 records deep. To be able to output the data in our desired sequence, we fill all 120 array elements (3 columns multiplied by 40 records deep) and then use a print loop to dump the array contents. Because we also need to print the partially filled arrays when our end-of-file is reached, we have separated the output operation into a subroutine called OUTPUT (seems appropriate enough, does it not?).

In the output subroutine, we use three separate array indices to stagger the output to meet our desired format. In other words, we want the 1st array element to print on the same line as the 41st and the 81st array elements. The end result is a list designed so that you can look for a customer name alphabetically down the first column and, if not found, look down the second column, and so on.

The X index is used to print array elements 1 through 40, which are listed in the first column. The Y index is used to print elements 41 through 80 (the second column), and Z is used to print elements 81 through 120 (column three).

By using this technique, our list prints alphabetically top to bottom and then left to right. This phone-book style of output is made easy thanks to the use of arrays.

RUN-TIME ARRAY HANDLING RPG OP CODES

Now that we have defined and discussed the value of run-time arrays, we need to look at how the various RPG op codes affect arrays. Some of these op codes only apply to arrays and others work differently than you might expect.

Most of the arithmetic op codes work with numeric arrays. You specify that you are performing the operations on the entire array or just on a specific array element through the use of an array index. If you specify the index (by following the array reference with a comma and number or numeric field), the operation is performed on the specified array element. If you do not specify an index, the operation is performed on the entire array.

Using the MOVE and MOVEL op codes on single-array elements (by specifying the array index) works in the same fashion as if you had specified individual fields. Using these operations on whole arrays may not produce the kind of results you expect. Performing a MOVE or MOVEL from a field, constant, or data structure into an entire array performs the move as if it is being performed with a single field, but the same results are recorded into all elements of the array.

For example, let's say we wanted to move the literal SMITH into an array of single, one-character elements. We call our array NAM. If we simply perform a MOVEL:

```
.....CLON01N02N03Factor1+++OpcdeFactor2+++ResultLenDHHiLoEqComments++++++......
     C                   MOVEL'SMITH'     NAM
```

the results in the NAM array look like this:

S	S	S	S	S

While this may, in fact, be our intended result, it is more likely that we wanted to put each character of our constant into an element of the array.

That is where the MOVEA op code comes in. MOVEA was introduced to allow you to perform moves that cross the boundaries of the array when the move is performed. Let's see what the results are when we perform the same operation using MOVEA in place of MOVEL.

```
.....CLON01N02N03Factor1+++OpcdeFactor2+++ResultLenDHHiLoEqComments++++++......
     C                   MOVEA'SMITH'     NAM
```

the results in the NAM array look like this:

S	M	I	T	H

Table 7.1 outlines the op codes that are used specifically with arrays (with the exception of the LOKUP op code that may be used for tables as well).

Table 7.1: Op Codes That are Used Specifically with Arrays

Op Code	Description
LOKUP	The Lookup (LOKUP) op code can actually be used for tables or arrays. It is used to perform a "seek and find" operation to determine if the search argument specified in Factor 1 exists in the table or array. If the search argument is found, the EQ indicator (in position 58) is turned on and the address of the array element found is returned to the index field of Factor 2 (position 33) if the index field was specified. When an index is specified, the lookup begins at the array element initially specified in the index. If you want the search to begin at the start of the array, you must make sure the index is set to 1. You may also use the LOKUP operation to perform high or low lookups that seek out the array elements that are closest to the search argument specified, but still satisfy the search conditions. The high or low lookups are done by utilizing the indicators in positions 54 and 55 (HI) or 56 and 57 (LO), depending upon the desired search criteria.
MOVEA	Move Array (MOVEA) is used to move values to and from arrays. This op code may be used to move an array to a field, a field to an array, or an array to another array. In this case, a data structure or any constant qualifies as a field too. MOVEA may be used for alphanumeric or numeric arrays and fields, but the Factor 2 and Result field types must match. An index may be specified in Factor 2 or the Result field and the move operation begins at the point of the index. The move that is performed is similar to a Move Left (MOVEL) in that the move begins with the left-most point of Factor 2 and begins loading the value into the left-most portion of the Result field. If Factor 2 and the Result fields are not equal in length, the move is performed for the length that matches the shorter of the two.
SORTA	Sort Array (SORTA) performs the function that the name of the op code implies. The name of the array you want to sort goes into Factor 2. The array elements are automatically resequenced into an order that coincides with the value of the array elements. If array elements include blanks or zeros, these

Op Code	Description
	entries appear first after SORTA is executed.
XFOOT	Cross Foot (XFOOT) sums all of the values of a numeric array in a single command. The Result field must contain a valid numeric field or array element where the total is placed when the operation is performed.

THE COMPILE-TIME ARRAY

Another type of array is the compile-time array. Like the name implies, data is loaded into this type of array when a program is compiled. The data used to load the array is coded right into the source of your RPG program.

This type of array can be useful when you need to work with a small number of data elements that always remain constant and are not subject to change. An example of this type of data is days of the week. There are a limited number of days in a week and they are not likely to change. Rather than store them in a file or data area, it is easier to simply store them in a compile-time array at the end of a program.

Compile-time array data is actually stored *after* the source to your program. Directly following the last source statement (generally an Output or Calculation Specification), an asterisk (*) is keyed into positions 1 and 2 of the next source statement. The two asterisks act as a trigger record to tell the compiler that table or compile-time-array data follows.

The source records that follow the trigger record represent the data for the compile-time array. Figure 7.5 is an example of what compile-time array data looks like. In this example, the first array element is AL (for Alabama).

Figure 7.5: Example of Compile-time Array Data

```
   ...+... 1 ...+... 2 ...+... 3 ...+... 4 ...+... 5 ...+... 6 ...+... 7
**
AL
AK
AZ
```

In Figure 7.6, we have defined a compile-time array with an Extension Specification. Our array is named STAT, has 50 total elements that are each two characters in length (representing each of the 50 United States), and there is one entry per source record. Figure 7.5 shows the trigger record and the first few array entry source records.

Figure 7.6: Defining Compile-time Arrays with an Extension Specification

```
.....E....FromfileTofile++Name++N/rN/tbLenPDSArrnamLenPDSComments+++++++++
      E                 STAT    1  50 2              STATE CODES
```

This array can be used to validate the state entered on a data entry screen. You can use the Lookup (LOKUP) op code with the value entered on the screen against the STAT array to see if the value keyed exists in the array. If the value keyed is not found, you can issue an error message so the program operator can correct the field before the data keyed is accepted.

ALTERNATIVE DEFINITION OF ARRAYS

The most common way to load an array is with some form of logic loop as in our previous examples. But, there are some other very useful ways to load data into arrays that will help you at input, output, and calculation time.

You can use File Input Specifications to redefine data fields into array elements. The specifications can be used to take entire fields from a file and split them up into array elements. They can also be used to take individual fields and redefine them so the system considers them to be part of an array.

In Figure 7.7, we define an array called AGE. The array is used to store and process aged accounts receivable amounts that are stored in our customer file. We could load each aging field stored in the customer file into our array, perform the necessary processing, and then move the fields back prior to output. But this would be time-consuming and tedious.

Figure 7.7: Redefining Run-time Arrays Using Input Specifications

```
.....E....FromfileTofile++Name++N/rN/tbLenPDSArrnamLenPDSComments+++++++++
      E                  AGE           6  9 2
.....I.............Ext-field+.....................Field+L1M1..PlMnZr.....
      ICUSREC
      I               CUS000                       AGE,1
      I               CUS030                       AGE,2
      I               CUS060                       AGE,3
      I               CUS090                       AGE,4
      I               CUS120                       AGE,5
      I               CUS150                       AGE,6
```

A better way is to tell the system at file-definition time that each of the aging fields in our customer file represents a specific array element. The example in Figure 7.7 does exactly that. Even though our customer file is externally described, we use an internal definition of the CUSREC record format to tell the system that field CUS000 is the first array element in the AGE array, CUS030 is the second element, and so on.

Another example of redefining input file data fields into array elements is shown in Figure 7.8. While our first example uses field names from our externally described customer file, this second example uses the field positions within the file to tell the system which fields in our customer file to use as array elements. In lieu of the field names that exist in the external description of the file, we place the array name along with the index that is used to describe which element within the array represents the specified field positions. This method is less desirable than the method demonstrated in Figure 7.7 because changes in the size and type of data can cause a lot of extra, tedious work that would not be necessary otherwise.

Figure 7.8: Redefining Run-time Arrays with Multiple Input Specifications

```
.....E....FromfileTofile++Name++N/rN/tbLenPDSArrnamLenPDSComments+++++++++
      E                  AGE           6  9 2
.....I...............................PFromTo++DField+L1M1FrPlMnZr
      ICUSREC
      I                              P 101 105 AGE,1
      I                              P 106 110 AGE,2
      I                              P 111 115 AGE,3
      I                              P 116 120 AGE,4
      I                              P 121 125 AGE,5
      I                              P 126 130 AGE,6
```

Notice that there are no decimal positions specified on the Input Specifications, even though the array definition reflects the array elements as being nine digits with two decimal places. The compiler will not allow you to specify decimal positions at the input level when you are redefining array elements. Instead, it takes the definition from the Extension Specification describing the array.

Interestingly enough, the compiler insists that you handle the data type in the opposite manner. Our example in Figure 7.8 shows that the data in our customer file is in a packed format, as specified in column 43 of the Input Specifications, but the compiler will not let you specify in position 39 of the Extension Specification that the array is packed. The compiler takes the data type definition from the Input Specification describing the input file.

The aging fields from the customer file shown in the example in Figure 7.8 are contiguous fields (stored consecutively in the file). It is easier to redefine the array elements with a single Input Specification, as shown in Figure 7.9.

Figure 7.9: Redefining Multiple Run-time Array Elements with a Single Input Specification

```
.....E....FromfileTofile++Name++N/rN/tbLenPDSArrnamLenPDSComments++++++++++
     E                         AGE          6  9 2
.....I.................................................PFromTo++DField+L1M1FrPlMnZr
     ICUSREC
     I                                     P 101 130 AGE
```

You can also use data structures to redefine arrays just like you do with file input specifications. If you choose to use this method, however, you must be careful to initialize your numeric data structures before your program tries to use them. As we will discuss in the next chapter, numeric data structures are considered to have blanks in them until you initialize or load data into them. Failure to perform one of these options will likely result in a Data Decimal Error, which occurs when the system encounters non-numeric data in a numeric field.

STRING HANDLING IS NOT JUST FOR PEOPLE WITH YO-YOS ANYMORE

String handling op codes were a significant (and long-awaited) announcement as part of the Version 2 operating system. These tools allow us to concatenate, scan, and parse results from data fields without having to load them into arrays first. The op codes listed in Table 7.2 make the process of string manipulation a far more palatable task.

Table 7.2: String Handling Op Codes

Op Code	Description
CAT	Concatenates (joins) two character or constant fields into a single result field. You can specify how many (if any) blanks you want to exist between the two fields once they have been concatenated.
CHECK	Used primarily to validate data in one string of data and checking to see if all of the characters from the string being checked happen to exist in another string. If invalid characters exist in the string being searched, the address position(s) of illegal characters can be returned to a field or array.
CHECKR	Functions similarly to the CHECK op code, except the check for character validity is performed from the right-most character to the left. Just like the CHECK Op code, the check is discontinued once an illegal character is found unless the Result field specified happens to be a numeric array.
SCAN	Scans (searches) a data field or array for a specific search argument and returns the positional address(es) of where within the searched field or array the search argument is found. No positional address is returned if the search argument is not found. If the result field of this op code is a numeric array, multiple positional addresses may be returned if there are multiple occurrences of the search argument within the field or array being searched.
SUBST	Substrings (extracts) a portion of a character field, array element, or data structure element and places it into another. You specify the start position of the extract and the size of the result field is used to determine how many characters are moved. This op code generally is used in conjunction with the SCAN or CHECK op codes.
XLATE	Translates characters of a field, array element, or data structure from one value (or set of values) to another. An example of how to use this op code is the translation of fields from lowercase to uppercase.

EVERYBODY WANTS TO BE A CAT

For many years, arrays were the only tool RPG programmers could use for string handling and manipulation. As you can see from the example in Figure 7.10, array handling was not always terribly efficient.

Figure 7.10: Using Arrays to Pack City, State, and Zip Code

```
.....E....FromfileTofile++Name++N/rN/tbLenPDSArrnamLenPDSComments+++++++++......
     E                    WRK       40 1                      WORKING ARRAY
     C*
.....CL0N01N02N03Factor1+++OpcdeFactor2+++ResultLenDHHiLoEqComments++++++++......
     C                    MOVE *BLANKS   WRK
     C                    MOVEACITY      WRK
     C          WRK,X     DOWEQ*BLANKS                         FIND LAST NON-BLANK
     C                    SUB  1         X          68         CHARACTER
     C    68              END
     C                    ADD  1         X
     C                    MOVEA',' WRK,X                       ADD A COMMA
     C                    ADD  2         X
     C                    MOVEASTATE     WRK,X                 ADD THE STATE
     C                    ADD  3         X
     C                    MOVEAZIPCOD    WRK,X                 ADD THE ZIP
     C                    ADD  5         X
     C                    MOVE '-' WRK,X
     C                    ADD  1         X
     C                    MOVEAZIP4      WRK,X                 ADD ZIP + 4
     C                    MOVEAWRK       CSZ   40              MOVE RESULT TO FIELD
     C*
```

The objective of this routine is to take the contents of the following fields and pack them together into one field:

Field	Size and Attributes	Contents
CITY	15A	San Diego
STATE	2A	CA
ZIPCOD	5A	92126
ZIP4	4A	4440

The result after the routine is run looks something like this:

```
San Diego, CA 92126-4440
```

As you can see from the example in Figure 7.11, it requires significantly less code to use the CAT op code to perform the same operation shown in Figure 7.10. As you already know, less code means less maintenance and fewer chances for error

Figure 7.11: Using the CAT Op Code to Pack City, State, and Zip Code

```
.....CLON01N02N03Factor1+++OpcdeFactor2+++ResultLenDHHiLoEqComments++++++......
     C           CITY      CAT  ',':0        CSZ    40 P      PACK CITY, STATE, &
     C                     CAT  STATE:1      CSZ              ZIP CODE
     C                     CAT  ZIPCOD:1     CSZ
     C                     CAT  '-':0        CSZ
     C                     CAT  ZIP4:0       CSZ
```

The first statement of the example in Figure 7.11 uses the CAT op code to concatenate the contents of the field CITY in Factor 1 to a constant comma (,) found in Factor 2. Because the P extender is specified in position 53, our Result field (CSZ) is *padded,* or filled with blanks, prior to placing the results of our CAT operation there. After filling the CSZ field with blanks, the results of the concatenation are placed into the Result field:

Factor 1	Op Code	Factor 2	Result Field	Ext	HI	LO	EQ
[1st character string]	**CAT**	2nd string[:# of blanks]	concatenation result	[P]	----	----	----

Placing a colon (:) and a numeric value or field after the constant or field specified in Factor 2 tells the system how many blanks to have between the Factor 1 and Factor 2 values once the concatenation is complete. On the first line of the example in Figure 7.11, we tell the system that we want a comma (represented by the constant specified in Factor 2) to directly follow the field value of Factor 1 with no spaces between them. The results recorded in the CSZ field after the first line of the example in Figure 7.11 looks like this:

```
San Diego,
```

The second line of our example is used to concatenate the STATE field to the current value of the CSZ field, leaving a single space between the two values. Factor 1 is left blank here because the system automatically assumes that Factor 1 is the same as the Result field unless you specify otherwise.

The remaining statements concatenate the ZIPCOD, a dash (-), and the ZIP4 field to the end of the CSZ field to attain the desired results. We are able to accomplish our goal with approximately one quarter the number of statements. Another advantage is that we did not need to worry about array index errors because arrays are no longer part of the equation.

Note that this operation was made more simple because the zip code is stored as an alphanumeric field. If it were stored as numeric, we would have had to move the code to an alphanumeric field before performing the CAT operation.

In Figure 7.12, you can see how much code is required if we want to use arrays to "pack" a first name, middle initial, and last name into a single field. This operation was made much simpler when the CAT op code was announced, as you can see in Figure 7.13.

Figure 7.12: Using Arrays to Pack First Name, Middle Initial, and Last Name

```
.....E....FromfileTofile++Name++N/rN/tbLenPDSArrnamLenPDSComments+++++++++......
     E                    WRK       30 1             WORKING ARRAY
     E*
.....CL0N01N02N03Factor1+++OpcdeFactor2+++ResultLenDHHiLoEqComments++++++......
     C                    MOVE *BLANKS   WRK
     C                    MOVE *BLANKS   NAME
     C                    MOVEAFIRST     WRK
     C                    Z-ADD10        X         20    FIND LAST NON-BLANK
 B1  C          WRK,X     DOWEQ*BLANKS   '               CHARACTER
     C                    SUB  1         X            68
 E1  C     68             ENDDO
     C                    ADD  2         X
 B1  C          INIT      IFNE *BLANKS                    ADD MIDDLE INITIAL
     C                    MOVE INIT      WRK,X
     C                    ADD  2         X
 E1  C                    ENDIF
     C                    MOVEALAST      WRK,X       '   ADD LAST NAME
     C                    MOVEAWRK       NAME
```

Figure 7.13: Using CAT to Pack First Name, Middle Initial, and Last Name

```
.....CL0N01N02N03Factor1+++OpcdeFactor2+++ResultLenDHHiLoEqComments++++++......
     C          FIRST     CAT  INIT:1    NAME      P
     C                    CAT  LAST:1    NAME
```

CHECK, PLEASE

The CHECK op code is a useful tool for validating data in a string or to remove leading blanks from a field (also referred to as left justify). Figure 7.14 uses the CHECK op code to validate data in the alphanumeric field called TSTAMT to make sure the data is entirely numeric. If the test determines that all characters in the field are numeric, it moves the value in TSTAMT to the field called AMOUNT. Otherwise, the AMOUNT field is filled with zeros.

Figure 7.14: Using CHECK to Validate a Numeric Field

```
.....I.............Namedconstant++++++++C.........Fldnme...................
     I          '0123456789'           C          NUMBER
.....CL0N01N02N03Factor1+++OpcdeFactor2+++ResultLenDHHiLoEqComments++++++......
     C          NUMBER    CHECKTSTAMT                   68
B1   C          *IN68     IFEQ *OFF                         FIELD IS ALL NUMERIC
     C                    MOVE TSTAMT    AMOUNT   92
     C                    ELSE
     C                    MOVE *ZEROS    AMOUNT
E1   C                    ENDIF
```

You may have occasion to perform this test to avoid Data Decimal Errors. As you are aware, the AS/400 is very particular about data types. If a field is defined as being numeric, the AS/400 tends to get a little upset if it finds data other than numbers. Unfortunately, data imported into the AS/400 often comes from other systems (including some of the AS/400's predecessors) that are not nearly as vigilant in checking the validity of their data.

You can also specify a result field with the CHECK op code that will be used to store the address(es) of the digits that were found to be invalid. The result field can be a numeric field or array.

Factor 1	Op Code	Factor 2	Result Field	HI	LO	EQ
validation string	**CHECK**	string to check[:start position]	[position(s)]	----	[Err]	[Found]

If the Result field specified happens to be a numeric array, the CHECK operation checks the entire contents of the string specified in Factor 2, and returns the address of the fields found to be invalid to the Result field array.

USING THE CHECK OP CODE TO REMOVE LEADING BLANKS

The CHECK op code is very useful for removing leading blanks. When used in conjunction with the Substring (SUBST) op code, leading blanks can be removed from a field with two simple statements. The example in Figure 7.15 shows how to use the CHECK op code to find the first nonblank character in the NAME field and store the address of that field in a numeric variable called X.

Figure 7.15: Using CHECK to Remove Leading Blanks

```
.....CL0N01N02N03Factor1+++OpcdeFactor2+++ResultLenDHHiLoEqComments++++++
     C              ' '       CHECKNAME     X         20
     C                        SUBSTNAME:X   NAME        P
```

The Substring (SUBST) function is then used to move the nonblank characters of NAME into the left-most characters of the NAME field, and then pad the remaining positions of the NAME field with blanks.

For example, let's apply the code in Figure 7.15 to the following NAME field:

```
...+... 1 ...+... 2 ...+... 3
     SMITH
```

The results after the operation look like this:

```
...+... 1 ...+... 2 ...+... 3
SMITH
```

CHECKR VALIDATES CHARACTER STRINGS FROM RIGHT TO LEFT

The CHECKR op code serves basically the same function as the CHECK op code, except that the string is validated from the right-most characters of the string being validated back to the left-most character.

Factor 1	Op Code	Factor 2	Result Field	HI	LO	EQ
validation string	**CHECKR**	string to check[:start position]	[position(s)]	----	[Err]	[Found]

If you choose to use indexing on Factor 2 (the string being searched), the CHECKR operation begins at the character address specified by the index field and searches from right to left, back to the beginning character of the string.

SEEK AND FIND WITH SCAN

SCAN allows you to search a character string for a specific search argument, and then return a character address if the search argument happens to be found. Figure 7.16 is an example of how to use the SCAN op code to find the address of the comma that is embedded into a name field that was keyed as Last, First. The objective of the routine is to look for the comma and then extract the first and last names if the comma is found. If no comma is found, blank out the first name field and put the rest of the characters in the last name field.

Figure 7.16: Using SCAN to Extract First and Last Names from a Field That was Keyed as Last, First

```
.....CL0N01N02N03Factor1+++OpcdeFactor2+++ResultLenDHHiLoEqComments++++++......
      C              ','       SCAN NAME:1     POS      20      68 FIND COMMA
B1    C              *IN68     IFEQ *ON
      C              POS       ANDGT1                              IF COMMA WAS FOUND,
      C                        SUB  1          POS
      C              POS       SUBSTNAME:1     LAST       P        EXTRACT LAST NAME
B2    C              POS       IFLT 26
      C                        ADD  3          POS
      C              28        SUB  POS        LFT      20
      C              LFT       SUBSTNAME:POS   FIRST      P        EXTRACT FIRST NAME
E2    C                        ENDIF
X1    C                        ELSE
      C                        MOVE *BLANKS    FIRST               COMMA NOT FOUND...
      C                        MOVELNAME       LAST       P
E1    C                        ENDIF
```

In our example in Figure 7.16, the length of the search argument happened to be a single character (we could have used the CHECK op code to perform this same function). But the SCAN op code can look for entire strings of data too.

For example, let's say we want to know how many of the customers in our customer file are corporations. We could search the customer names for the characters INC and get a pretty good idea. The code looks something like Figure 7.17.

Power RPG III

Figure 7.17: Using SCAN to Find Customers with INC in the Customer Name Field

```
.....CL0N01N02N03Factor1+++OpcdeFactor2+++ResultLenDHHiLoEqComments+++++++......
        C           'INC':3    SCAN CUSNAM                 68 FIND CORPORATIONS
B1      C           *IN68      CASEQ*ON       PRINT           AND PRINT THEM
E2      C                      ENDCS
```

The search argument of the SCAN op code is always specified in Factor 1. The argument can be a constant, all or part of a field, an array element, or a table name. You can specify that you only want to use the first portion of a field by indicating the field length in Factor 1. The field length is specified by following the value in Factor 1 with a colon (:) and a numeric field or constant.

Factor 1	Op Code	Factor 2	Result Field	HI	LO	EQ
search argument[:length]	**SCAN**	string to scan[:start position]	[position(s)]	----	[Err]	[Found]

Factor 2 contains the string that you want searched. The string must be a character, but it can be a field, constant, array element, or table.

If you choose to specify the optional result field, it is loaded with the positional address of the search argument if it happens to be found. If you choose to omit the Result field, you must specify an indicator in position 58. The indicator is turned on if the search argument is found and turned off if it is not.

Note that the SCAN op code is case sensitive. Using SCAN to detect an uppercase character string does not detect the same string in lowercase, and vice versa. If you want to perform a search that crosses the case boundaries, you can do so if you utilize the SCAN op code in conjunction with the Translate (XLATE) op code we discuss later in this chapter.

176

Substring (SUBST) Ties the Whole String-handling Thing Together

You can use Substring (SUBST) to extract a value or values from a character string and move the results to the desired target character string, all from within a single operation. The character strings involved must be alphanumeric data. These elements may be arrays, array elements, data structures, etc.

Factor 1	Op Code	Factor 2	Result Field	Ext	HI	LO	EQ
[Length to be extracted]	**SUBST**	Base string[:start]	Target string	[P]	----	[Err]	--

The Substring (SUBST) function really performs two or three functions at the same time. It extracts the data you desire and then performs a "move left" function into the result field. If you specify a P in the extender field (formerly known as the half adjust column), the remainder of the Result field is padded with blanks.

The character string from which you want to extract data is specified in Factor 2. Optionally, you may indicate the position within the string where you want the extraction to begin by following the string specified in Factor 2 with a colon (:) and a number or numeric field that contains the character address where the search should begin.

You tell the system how many characters to extract by the numeric value or numeric field that you specify in Factor 1. If Factor 1 is omitted, the system calculates the length of the extraction based upon the start position and the length of the string that was specified in Factor 2.

The example in Figure 7.18 shows how to take an alphabetical date field that is stored as YYMMDD (year, month, day) and parse it out (split it up) into three distinct fields.

Figure 7.18: Using SUBST to Parse Out an Alpha DATE Field into Month, Day, and Year

```
C           2        SUBSTDATE:1     YEAR    2
C           2        SUBSTDATE:3     MONTH   2
C           2        SUBSTDATE:5     DAY     2
```

Factor 1 is specified to indicate the number of characters we want to extract. Factor 2 contains the name of the original field (DATE) followed by a colon (:) and a number that represents the position within the string where the extraction should begin.

In this simple example of the use of SUBST, numeric values are specified for the length to extract and the beginning positions. More advanced examples of this tool are shown in Figure 7.19, where both the starting position and the length to extract are specified as variables.

Figure 7.19: Using SUBST to Separate a Name Field That is "Last, First" into Separate First and Last Name Fields

```
.....CL0N01N02N03Factor1+++OpcdeFactor2+++ResultLenDHHiLoEqComments+++++++......
     C              ',':1    SCAN NAME      X       20      68 LOOK FOR COMMA
B1   C              *IN68    IFEQ *ON
     C                       SUB  1         X                  EXTRACT LAST NAME
     C              X        SUBSTNAME:1    LAST    P
     C                       ADD  2         X                  EXTRACT FIRST NAME
     C                       SUBSTNAME:X    FIRST   P
     C              ' '       CHECKFIRST     X                  REMOVE ANY
     C                       SUBSTFIRST:X   FIRST              LEADING BLANKS
X1   C                       ELSE
     C                       MOVELNAME      LAST    P          COMMA NOT FOUND
     C                       MOVE *BLANKS   FIRST
E1   C                       ENDIF
```

In Figure 7.19, we have a name field that is stored as LAST NAME, FIRST NAME, and we want to separate the data into two separate fields. We first use the SCAN op code to determine if the names are stored as LAST, FIRST. If a comma is found, we use SUBST to parse the data into distinctly different fields.

The SCAN operation returns the character address of the comma within the NAME character string, so we are able to ascertain that all characters prior to the comma belong in the last name field (LAST). We subtract 1 from X (so the comma is not included in the data we extract) and perform the SUBST operation on the NAME field beginning in position 1 for a length of X (which now stores the length of the last name field). We use the P extender to pad the rest of the LAST name field with blanks in case there are characters in the field from a prior operation.

The next step is to add 2 to X to move the character address past the comma in the NAME string. We assume that all characters beyond the comma belong in the first name field, so we perform the SUBST operation beginning at the character address, which places us a single character beyond the comma. We do not indicate the number of characters to extract in the SUBST operation because we want all characters through the end of the string to be moved into our target field. Again, we use the P extender to clear undesired characters from the FIRST field.

At this point, we have performed our desired function of separating the first and last names. We put an additional step into the code to ensure that leading blanks are stripped from the first name field. If the initial NAME character string came from a data entry process somewhere, you are likely to have inconsistencies in the way the field is keyed. Some operators may be inclined to key the name with a blank after the comma where others would not. By using the CHECK and SUBST operations we are able to suppress the leading blanks in this field.

Translate (XLATE) Performs Single-character Substitution within Character Strings

The XLATE op code is a handy tool when you need to perform character substitution within a character string. You can specify From and To characters to translate, or entire strings of characters that need to be translated.

Factor 1	Op Code	Factor 2	Result Field	Ext	HI	LO	EQ
From value:To value	**XLATE**	Base string[:start]	Target string	[P]	----	[Err]	--

One of the more popular uses for this op code is to translate a lowercase character string to uppercase. This is a frequent requirement when you are importing data from an external source. Figure 7.20 is an example of how to address this issue.

Figure 7.20: Using XLATE to Translate Lowercase-character Strings to Uppercase

```
.....I..............Namedconstant+++++++++C.........Fldnme....................
     I              'abcdefghijklmnopqrst-C        LOW
     I              'uvwxyz'
     I              'ABCDEFGHIJKLMNOPQRST-C        UP
     I              'UVWXYZ'
.....CL0N01N02N03Factor1+++OpcdeFactor2+++ResultLenDHHiLoEqComments+++++++......
     C              LOW:UP    XLATEINNAME    NAME       P    TRANSLATE TO UPPER
       **                                                    CASE
```

In Figure 7.20, we take an input field named INNAME that may or may not contain lowercase characters, and translate them to uppercase characters, placing the end results in a field called NAME. To do this, we use a named constant field (LOW) that contains all the lowercase characters that we want to translate. We use another named constant (UP) that holds the corresponding uppercase characters.

The XLATE operation looks for characters in the INNAME field that happen to exist in the LOW named constant and replaces them with the corresponding character found within the UP named constant.

In Figure 7.21, we use the XLATE op code to translate brackets in the field called INFLD to parentheses.

Figure 7.21: Using XLATE to Translate Brackets to Parentheses

```
.....CL0N01N02N03Factor1+++OpcdeFactor2+++ResultLenDHHiLoEqComments++++++++......
     C              '{':'('   XLATEINFLD     INFLD
     C              '}':')'   XLATEINFLD     INFLD
```

FINAL WORDS ABOUT ARRAYS AND STRING HANDLING

As you have seen in reading this chapter, arrays and string handling are a vital part of RPG programming. Array handling is invaluable for performing data validation, formatting output, and storing totals that will be output later in a program. The string handling op codes make difficult character manipulation chores much easier for us to perform.

Take the time to become familiar with the tools discussed in this chapter. You will find that it is time well spent.

Chapter 8

Data Structures, Data Areas, and the Local Data Area

In this chapter, we discuss three valuable components that are used for definition, composition, and transportation of data elements both to and from your RPG programs. As the AS/400 has continued its logical evolution, these three components have become a bigger part of the overall scheme of things. We have seen a myriad of APIs announced, which use data structures to pass system data back and forth to our programs. Multiple-occurrence Data Structures have been added to reduce the number of fields and arrays required as well as to give us a method for creating two-dimensional arrays. And the local data area (LDA) is still one of the best ways to pass localized data from one program to the next.

You will find that a thorough knowledge of these tools can give you a distinct competitive advantage over your programming counterparts. Once you have mastered these techniques, you will find that you are able to write more efficient code that also performs better. Let us continue on our path of education by example to discuss the merit and functions of each of these methods.

THE DATA STRUCTURE

Data structures are used primarily to define and redefine data elements. In its simplest form, you can consider a data structure to be a sum of all of its parts. It is used to subdivide larger fields into smaller subfields, or compose smaller fields into larger ones.

By allowing you to create subdivisions in the data, a unique condition is created where data in the lesser subfields is directly bound to the larger fields that are being divided. If data in the subfield is changed, the value of the larger field is changed as well. Consequently, if values in the larger field are changed, the subdivided data is changed at the same time. This can eliminate an awful lot of code that would otherwise be needed to move data back and forth.

Let's begin by looking at a hypothetical point-of-sale transaction. In the following example, we look at a stock keeping unit (SKU) number that might be used in a retail application. SKU numbers are used to identify a particular product or service.

The SKU number usually can be parsed out into codes that represent the department, manufacturer, vendor, model number, and stock number. As a general rule, the SKU number is used to record and track sales as well as to help manage the inventory.

When we read an SKU number from our hypothetical point-of-sale transaction, we could perform a series of MOVE and MOVEL operations to parse, or separate out, our department, manufacturer, vendor, model, and stock numbers. But it is time-consuming to code and involves setting up a series of work fields. Another option is to use the new string handling op codes that we covered in Chapter 7.

A much simpler way to perform this same task is to use a data structure to subdivide the number for you. Every time the SKU number changes, the subfields that make up the data structure defining the SKU number change as well.

In the following example, our sample SKU number is 22502807224089123491A405. While this number appears to be large and unwieldy, it is not nearly as overwhelming if you break it down as follows:

Sample SKU number:

Department	Manufacturer	Vendor	Model	Stock Number
22	502	80722	4089123491A	405

Figure 8.1 shows a data structure that breaks down the SKU number for us. Note that the subfields (DEPT, MANUF, VENDOR, MODEL, and STOCK#) are all subsets of the field positions that make up the SKU# field.

Figure 8.1: Using Data Structure Input Specifications to Break Down an SKU Number

```
.....IDsname....NODsExt-file++.............OccrLen+..........................
     I          DS
.....I.............................PFromTo++DField+L1M1FrPlMnZr..........
     I                               1   24 SKU#
     I                               1   20DEPT
     I                               3    50MANUF
     I                               6   100VENDOR
     I                              11   21 MODEL
     I                              22   24 STOCK#
```

This data structure, in effect, redefines the SKU number field into the various subfields we desire. Notice that we have told the system that the first three fields (DEPT, MANUF, and VENDOR) are all numeric fields, even though they are subelements of a larger alphanumeric field (SKU#).

If our retail point-of-sale application reads a database or display file record that contains the field called SKU#, our program could address and use the various subfields without having to worry about any additional overhead or work to extract the subfields. In this particular case, the SKU# field in the database or display file needs to be 24 alphanumeric characters, just like it is defined in the data structure. The compiler gives you a hard time if you try to define it otherwise.

In the next example, we do not define the length of the SKU# field in our data structure. We define just the subfields instead.

Figure 8.2 serves essentially the same function as the data structure in Figure 8.1. The difference is that instead of defining the field SKU# down in the Input Specifications with the subfields, SKU# has been used as the name of the data structure.

Figure 8.2: An Alternate Data Structure Definition to Break Down an SKU Number

```
.....IDsname....NODsExt-file++.............OccrLen+...........................
     ISKU#          DS
.....I.........................................PFromTo++DField+L1M1FrP1MnZr..........
     I                                          1    20DEPT
     I                                          3     50MANUF
     I                                          6    100VENDOR
     I                                         11   21 MODEL
     I                                         22   24 STOCK#
```

In this example, we do not need to specify the size of the SKU# field. We define the buffer positions within the SKU# data structure that represent the various subfields. The length of the SKU# data structure does not require that we specify the length (in positions 48 through 51) because the SKU# field is already defined by our database or display file.

As a general rule, if you do not specify the size of a data structure, the compiler defines the length of it by computing the length of all of the subfields within the structure. However, if the name of the data structure also happens to be an input field from a file, the definition comes from the file instead.

RULES REGARDING DATA STRUCTURES

Data structures can be externally or program described (as you saw in Figure 8.1) and are defined in the Input Specifications of your RPG program. They support character, zoned-decimal, packed, and binary data types. Data types are defined in the same manner, and follow the same rules, as you adhere to when coding program-described files.

The definition of a data structure begins with the characters DS in positions 19 and 20 of an Input Specification. If your data structure is internally described, you may optionally name your data structure in columns 7 through 12 of the same Input Specification. This field is required if the data structure is externally described, (we discuss more on that later in the chapter when we cover "Externally Defined Data Structures"). Optionally, you also define the length of the data structure in positions 48 through 51 of this same line.

The fields for a data structure and its subfields must all appear together within the Input Specifications (they may not be mixed in with file definitions or other data structures). The compiler does not allow field names within a data structure to exist in any other data structures within the program. As shown in the previous example, however, they may exist in database or display file definitions.

Where the field length of an alphanumeric field in RPG can only be 256 characters, a data structure can go all the way up to 9,999 characters in size. If you need a field larger than 256 characters, you can simply make your field name the name of a data structure to eliminate the field size restriction.

SPECIAL DATA STRUCTURES

There are four very unique data structures on the AS/400 that are used for special purposes:

- **File Information Data Structure.** A special data structure that serves as a feedback area used to retrieve additional information about a file from the system. This data structure is initiated by the use of a special continuation line that is specified in the File Description Specifications. This data structure is used primarily for error detection and prevention (i.e., record lock conditions or errors trying to open a database file). Chapter 4 offers a detailed explanation of the File Information Data Structure and its potential uses.

- **Program Status Data Structure.** Used to retrieve information about the program that is running. This information includes program name, job number, user ID, library name where the program resides, and a variety of other job information that may be pertinent to the task at run time. Chapter 4 illustrates examples of what information can be retrieved and where you may want to use it within your programs.

- **Data Area Data Structure.** Used to describe the information inside a data area. A data area is kind of like a single-record data file that happens to come in two flavors: Local and global. The local data area (LDA) is unique to each program session and is used primarily to pass information from one job stream component to the next. On the other hand, global data areas can reside in any library and can be accessed by programs and CL alike. Data Area Data Structures may be used to describe and define both types of data areas. Examples of this type of data structure are covered later in this chapter.

- **Multiple-occurrence Data Structure.** Offers a way to define multiple data structures at once or establish two-dimensional arrays from within your RPG program. The Multiple-occurrence Data Structure introduces flexibility into your RPG programs that may be used to eliminate arrays, fields, and work files from your RPG programs. If you eliminate work files, you are also eliminating unnecessary I/O processing. We visit the topic of Multiple-occurrence Data Structures a little later in the chapter.

There are also other special data structures like the Program Initialization (PIP) Data Structure and those involving system APIs (Application Program Interfaces, which are covered in detail in Chapter 9).

DYNAMICS OF DATA STRUCTURES

As stated, one of the advantages of using data structures is that, when you change data in one of the components, it can dynamically change the data fields or subfields being used to redefine the component. In Figure 8.1, we saw how reading a database or display file record with the SKU# field in it dynamically changed the values of the data structure subfields to redefine the SKU# field.

What happens when the situation is reversed? Let's calculate a follow-up date that might be used in an Accounts Receivable application. The objective of this routine is to create a follow-up date that is exactly one month from the current date (Figures 8.3 and 8.4).

Figure 8.3: Using Data Structure Input Specifications to Breakdown a Date Field

```
.....IDsname....NODsExt-file++.............OccrLen+.............................
     I            DS
.....I.........................................PFromTo++DField+L1M1FrPlMnZr..........
     I                                         1   60YMD
     I                                         1   20YY
     I                                         3   40MM
     I                                         5   60DD
```

Although there are many ways to perform this type of operation, we are going to use a data structure to help us perform this simple calculation. The first step is to load today's date into our data structure field.

The task of retrieving the current date could easily be performed in a variety of ways. Our options include using the TIME op code; loading UYEAR, UMONTH, and UDAY into the appropriate subfields (YY, MM, and DD); or moving UDATE into the YMD data structure field (if your system date format is Year/Month/Day). The method chosen to load our date field is unimportant for our example.

Let's say that our current date is December 31, 1995.

After loading our YMD data structure field, the value of the YMD field is 951231. The values of the various subfields are:

YY	MM	DD
95	12	31

Applying the code shown in Figure 8.4 results in a date field in the YMD data structure that is one month from the original date.

Figure 8.4: RPG Code Using the Data Structure in Figure 8.3 to Add a Month to a Date Field

```
B1   C                        ADD  1       MM
     C              MM         IFGT 12
     C                         SUB  12      MM
     C                         ADD  1       YY
E1   C                        ENDIF
```

After applying the code in Figure 8.4, the YMD data structure field contains a value of 960131, and the subfield values are:

YY	MM	DD
96	01	31

Although this code amply demonstrates the power of dynamically changing data within a data structure, you probably have noticed that this code is tragically flawed. If your current date is January 31, 1996, and you apply the code shown in Figure 8.4, you end up with the invalid date of February 31, 1996.

The proper way to perform this function is to convert the date to Julian, perform the math, and then convert it back to YYMMDD. See Chapters 5 and 9, "Tips and Techniques for RPG Programmers" and "System APIs," for more information on this subject.

THE DATA STRUCTURE AND THE DATA DECIMAL ERROR

As you are no doubt aware, your AS/400 is terribly picky about data types. If you define a field as signed numeric, then that is exactly what the AS/400 expects to see. If it encounters blanks or alphanumeric data where it expects to see numeric data, the system complains very loudly in the form of a Data Decimal Error.

Data structures are one area of RPG where it is very easy to create a condition where Data Decimal Errors occur. This is because data structures are initially assumed to be alphanumeric data, regardless of the data type of the subfields defined within.

This potential error condition exists because data structures are not automatically initialized at program initiation unless you instruct your program to do so. If the data defined in your data structure is defined as signed numeric, and your program tries to refer to the numeric field prior to initializing or loading numeric data into the field, your program experiences a Data Decimal Error condition.

For example, let's say your program contains the data structure shown in Figure 8.5. If your program refers to the AMOUNT, DOLARS, or CENTS numeric fields prior to loading data into them, or moving zeros to them, you have a Data Decimal Error on your hands when the program is run.

Figure 8.5: Example of a Data Decimal Error Waiting to Happen

```
.....IDsname....NODsExt-file++.............OccrLen+............................
     I              DS
.....I.....................................PFromTo++DField+L1M1FrPlMnZr..........
     I                                        1   92AMOUNT
     I                                        1   70DOLARS
     I                                        8   90CENTS
```

One way to address this potential problem is to always load data into the field(s) prior to using them. An even easier way to address this problem is to instruct the system to automatically initialize the data structure at program initiation time.

To initialize a data structure at program initiation time, simply put an I in position 18 of the Input Specification that defines the data structure. The I should appear just prior to the DS in positions 19 and 20.

Figure 8.6 shows an example of the same data structure shown in Figure 8.5, except that this one is initialized automatically at program run time just prior to running the optional Initialize (*INZSR) subroutine, which, when present in your RPG program, runs prior to the execution of all other Calculation Specifications.

Figure 8.6: Performing Data Structure Initialization

```
.....IDsname....NODsExt-file++.............OccrLen+............................
     I          IDS
.....I...............................PFromTo++DField+L1M1FrPlMnZr..........
     I                                  1    92AMOUNT
     I                                  1    70DOLARS
     I                                  8    90CENTS
```

The data structure in Figure 8.6 has an I in position 18 of the data structure definition line, so there are no Data Decimal Errors associated with the AMOUNT, DOLARS, or CENTS fields unless the same fields happen to be defined in a database file with invalid numeric data.

Because we did not specify otherwise, the three numeric fields in our example are initialized as zeros. Data structure initialization is performed based upon data type. In other words, alphanumeric fields are initialized to blanks and numeric fields are initialized to zeros, unless you specify otherwise. The next section deals with situations where we want fields initialized to values other than blanks or zeros.

DEFAULT VALUES AND DATA SUBFIELD INITIALIZATION

As we saw in the previous example, data structure initialization is a handy way to clear the fields in an entire data structure. But subfields within a data structure may be initialized as well, and not necessarily to blanks or zeros as dictated by the data type.

To initialize subfields in a data structure, simply put an I in position 8 of the Input Specification describing the data structure subfield. Figure 8.7 shows the same data structure as the previous two examples, except the initialization is performed on a subfield level instead of the entire data structure.

Figure 8.7: Data Structure Subfield Initialization

```
.....IDsname....NODsExt-file++.............OccrLen+............................
     I              DS
.....I..............................PFromTo++DField+L1M1FrPlMnZr..........
     I I                                    1    92AMOUNT
     I I                                    1    70DOLARS
     I I                                    8    90CENTS
```

This example serves essentially the same purpose as the example in Figure 8.6. The AMOUNT, DOLARS, and CENTS fields are initialized to zeros because their data type is signed numeric and an I has been specified in position 8 of the Input Specifications.

What sets subfield initialization apart from data structure initialization is that default values may be established for each subfield. The default values are placed in positions 21 to 42 of the Input Specifications describing the subfield. Just like Calculation Specifications, defaults for alphanumeric fields are placed in quotes, while numeric values are not.

In Figure 8.8, we choose to use both forms of data structure initialization at the same time. We specify an I in position 18 of the data structure Input Specification telling the system to initialize the entire data structure based upon data type. We then place an I in position 8 of the Input Specification describing the DOLARS subfield with a default value of 5 in positions 21 to 42.

Figure 8.8: Data Structure Subfield Initialization with Default Values

```
.....IDsname....NODsExt-file++.............OccrLen+............................
     I              IDS
.....I..............................PFromTo++DField+L1M1FrPlMnZr..........
     I                                      1    92AMOUNT
     I I          5                         1    70DOLARS
     I                                      8    90CENTS
```

In this example, the entire data structure is initialized according to data type (in this case zeros) and then the default value of 5 is placed in the DOLARS subfield. Consequently, the value of the AMOUNT field after initialization is 5.00.

This same technique can be applied to alphanumeric fields too. For instance, let us say that we could initialize a description field with the value of Not on File, with the assumption that we probably will replace the initial value with a valid description later.

The example in Figure 8.9 establishes the definition of the field called DESC and initializes the original value of the field as Not on File (by placing an I in position 8, and the literal default in positions 21 to 42).

Figure 8.9: Alphanumeric Subfield Initialization with Default Values

```
.....IDsname....NODsExt-file++.............OccrLen+...........................
    I            DS
.....I..................................PFromTo++DFie1d+L1M1FrP1MnZr..........
    I I           'Not on File'          1  35 DESC
```

In lieu of the literal default value in positions 21 to 42, we could have specified the name of a named constant. The value in the named constant would then serve as the default entry.

> **Note**: Default values may be re-established by using the RESET op code.

In Figure 8.9, we established the initial value of the field called DESC as Not on File with the idea that we would replace the value once a valid entry was made. If the RESET op code is specified later in the program, the default values are re-established at that time. The RESET op code may be specified for a single field, or for an entire data structure like that shown in Figure 8.10.

Figure 8.10: Data Structure Subfield Initialization with Default Values

```
.....IDsname....NODsExt-file++.............OccrLen+...........................
    IRESETDS     IDS
.....I..................................PFromTo++DFie1d+L1M1FrP1MnZr..........
    I                                    1  92AMOUNT
    I I          5                       1  70DOLARS
    I                                    8  90CENTS
    I I          'Not on File'          11  45 DESC
```

If RESET is applied to the RESETDS data structure, all of the subfields in the data structure are reinitialized to their original values. The DOLARS and DESC fields are reset to include the default values specified, and the CENTS field is reinitialized to zeros because of its numeric data type.

The AMOUNT field in this example is simply a redefinition of the DOLARS and CENTS fields, so the value of the AMOUNT field is reset to 5.00 and the DESC field is reset to Not on File.

Externally Described Data Structures

Many of the same attributes that make externally described data files such a powerful tool on the AS/400 also apply to Externally Described Data Structures. Because they are defined in a single place, there is consistency in definition. Programs using the data structure are easier to maintain because they do not necessarily need to be modified when the data structure changes, unless the program happens to use the fields within the data structure that were changed.

If an external data structure does change, programs using the data structure only need to be recompiled, with two notable exceptions. The first exception is if the program uses one of the fields in the data structure that was changed. The second exception is if new fields were added to the end of the data structure. In this case, only the programs using the new additional field(s) need to be modified or compiled.

Externally Described Data Structures can be used to define LDA, data areas, program-described files, and parameter lists. We discuss these topics more as this chapter progresses.

External data structure definitions are coded with DDS just like you would code any other data file. In fact, an external definition really is just a physical file, and you can use other physical file specifications as external data structures. This technique can come in handy when your program uses a work file that exactly matches another physical file.

Basically, it does not matter whether the external definition you refer to in your Input Specifications ever has data or not. The physical file specifications are simply being used as a data structure that is being used to describe and define your data.

Figure 8.11 shows the DDS for a simple externally defined data structure. Figure 8.12 shows the RPG Input Specifications defining the external definition called EXTDEF.

Figure 8.11: DDS for an Externally Described Data Structure

```
A..........T.Name++++++RLen++TDpB......Functions++++++++++++++++++++++++++++
A          R EXTDEF                    TEXT('EXTERNAL DATA STRUCTURE')
A            COMP#         3S 0         COLHDG('COMPANY NUMBER')
A            CONAME        40A          COLHDG('COMPANY NAME')
```

Figure 8.12:RPG Input Specifications for an Externally Described Data Structure

```
.....IDsname....NODsExt-file++.............OccrLen+............................
     IDEF        E DSEXTDEF
```

The name of the data structure defined by the RPG Input Specifications in Figure 8.12 is DEF. The data structure subfields called COMP# and CONAME are defined and ready for use from within the RPG program, just as if you had defined the data structure from within the program.

To get a full appreciation for the value of the Externally Described Data Structure, we really need to see how this methodology applies when used in conjunction with data areas, LDA, program-described files, and parameter lists.

DATA AREAS

As the name implies, data areas are areas on disk that are used to store data. Data areas are similar to data files in that they reside in a library, are used to store data, and may be externally or program-described. They are unlike files in that they may not have multiple record formats or multiple records.

As we mentioned earlier in this chapter, data areas come in two flavors: Local and global. Data kept in the LDA is temporary in nature and is pertinent only to the session with which it is associated. In other words, the LDA is unique to each program session and is used primarily to pass information from one job stream component to the next. Consequently, workstation sessions may not share the LDA, and the information is unique to each workstation session. The information in the LDA is only available until the session is terminated.

Data kept in a global data area is permanent in nature and is available to all. This type of data area can reside in any library and can be accessed by programs and CL alike. Data areas can be accessed by any job and may be shared throughout the system.

You may have your RPG program open, close, and lock global data areas automatically for you, or you may perform these functions yourself. Similar to record level locks for data files, you can lock a data area to prevent another program from updating it while you need it.

Global Data Areas

Global data areas are generally created on demand by keying the Create Data Area (CRTDTAARA) command, or from within a CL program. We discuss three ways your RPG programs can define data areas. These three ways consist of using a Data Area Data Structure, using an externally described data area, or simply using a program-described data area.

Data Area Data Structures

Data Area Data Structures are the easiest of the three to code, but are less flexible than the other two methods mentioned. Defining a Data Area Data Structure instructs your RPG program to read and lock the data area at program initialization and then perform an update to the data area and release the lock at last record time.

Unless you use the Unlock (UNLCK) or Write Data Out to a Data Area (OUT) operation codes within your RPG program, the initial lock on the data area remains in effect until your program ends. This is not always practical when your data area is shared by many programs throughout the system.

Data Area Data Structures are defined by placing a U in position 18 of the Input Specification that defines the data structure. We see an example of this in Figures 8.13 and 8.14. In Figure 8.13, we define a Data Area Data Structure named DTADEF. As you can see, the DDS resembles specifications that you would use for any physical file.

Figure 8.13: Data Definition Specifications for a Data Area Data Structure

```
.....A..........T.Name+++++RLen++TDpB......Functions++++++++++++++++++++++++++++++
     A          R DTADEF
     A            DEVICE        10A          COLHDG('TAPE DEVICE')
     A            PRINTR        10A          COLHDG('PRINTER NAME')
     A            OUTQ          10A          COLHDG('OUT QUEUE')
```

Figure 8.14: Input Specifications for a Data Area Data Structure

```
.....IDsname....NODsExt-file++.............OccrLen+..............................
     I            EUDSDTADEF
```

By specifying a U in position 18 of the Input Specification (as seen in Figure 8.14), we are telling the system to read in and lock the DTADEF data area when the program is initialized, and then write out and unlock the data area when the program ends. The data stored in the data area is available throughout the program, and the field values may be updated as needed. The results of the update are recorded when the program ends.

Externally Described Data Areas

Externally described data areas are very similar in nature to the Data Area Data Structure. The principle difference is that they offer a little more flexibility with regard to lock state conditions and when data is retrieved or written to the data area. You will find this to be true of the program-described data areas as well, but you lose the rigidity and standardization with regard to data area definition.

Externally described and program-described data areas offer more control of when the data area is read, locked, written to, and released. Unlike Data Area Data Structures, data areas are not automatically read and locked during program initiation and written to at Last Record time.

Instead, there are four specific operation codes that you use in your RPG program when working with data areas. These are Define (DEFN), Read IN Data from a Data Area (IN), Write Data OUT to a Data Area (OUT), and UNLOCK a Data Area or Other Object (UNLCK).

The DEFN op code is useful for a variety of definition functions, but we want to discuss how it relates to data areas.

Factor 1	Op Code	Factor 2	Result Field
*NAMVAR	**DEFN**	[Data Area Name]	Data Structure Name

Specifying *NAMVAR in Factor 1 of the DEFN statement tells the system that we are defining a variable (field or data structure) representing a data area. We may optionally put the name of the data area in Factor 2, but for the examples here, we use the Input Specifications to indicate the name of our data area. The Result field contains the field or data structure name that is used to represent the data area.

The IN operation code is used to perform a controlled read of a single data area or all data areas defined in the program. If you specify *LOCK as Factor 1 of the IN operation code, the data area(s) in Factor 2 are locked until the data area is unlocked using the UNLCK or OUT operation codes, or the job is terminated.

Factor 1	Op Code	Factor 2
[*LOCK]	**IN**	Data Area or *NAMVAR

Factor 2 of the IN operation code is either the name of the data area in question or the literal *NAMVAR. Choosing the *NAMVAR option causes all data areas defined in the program to be read. Also, the data areas are all locked if specified to do so in Factor 1.

The OUT operation code is used to perform a controlled update of a data area(s).

Factor 1	Op Code	Factor 2
[*LOCK]	**OUT**	Data Area or *NAMVAR

If you specify *LOCK as Factor 1 of the OUT op code, the locks on the data area(s) in Factor 2 remain in effect after data has been written to them. The locks remain in effect until the data area is unlocked using the UNLCK op code, using a subsequent OUT operation code that does not have *LOCK specified, or when the job is terminated.

Factor 2 of the OUT op code is either the name of a data area or the literal *NAMVAR. Just like the IN operation code, the *NAMVAR option specified in Factor 2 causes all data areas defined in the program to be written to and the locks either remain in effect or are released depending upon the contents of Factor 1.

The UNLCK operation code is used to release a data area or record of a file that has been opened for update.

Op Code	Factor 2
UNLCK	Data Area or File Name

Note: When used with data areas, the IN, OUT, and UNLCK op codes may only refer to data areas that have been defined with the DEFN statement.

In our next example (Figure 8.15), we look at the same data structure we looked at in Figures 8.13 and 8.14, but this time we use the definition for an Externally Described Data Structure.

Figure 8.15: Input Specifications for an Externally Described Data Area

```
.....IDsname....NODsExt-file++.............OccrLen+...........................
    IDTAARA     E DSDTADEF
```

In the following example, we define a data structure named DTAARA. By specifying an E in column 17 of our Input Specification, we tell the compiler that this data structure is externally defined and the name of the external definition can be found in columns 21 through 42 (DTADEF in this case) of the same line. The name identified in these columns must refer to a physical file found somewhere in the library list at the time the RPG program is compiled. Figure 8.16 shows the Calculation Specifications that define, lock, read, write, and unlock the DTADEF data area.

Figure 8.16: Calculation Specifications for Opening, Locking, and Updating an Externally Described Data Area

```
.....CL0N01N02N03Factor1+++OpcdeFactor2+++ResultLenDHHiLoEqComments++++++......
    C          *NAMVAR   DEFN           DTAARA 30         READ DATA AREA
    C          *LOCK     IN    DTAARA
    C                    MOVE  PRINT     PRINTR
    C                    MOVE  TAPE      DEVICE
    C                    OUT   DTAARA                      WRITE CHANGES
```

By using *NAMVAR in the DEFN statement, we tell the system that we are defining a data area. In this case, we did not put the name of the data area in Factor 2, but instead put the name of a data structure in the Result field (DTAARA). This definition (in conjunction with the Input Specifications) tells the system that we are using the DTAARA data structure to redefine the DTADEF data area. The process of redefining the data area is similar to when we redefined the SKU# earlier in this chapter.

In the next step, we read the data from the DTADEF data area using the IN op code, placing a lock on the data area at that time. Remember that the IN operation is a destructive read, and whatever was in the fields defined by the DTADEF data structure is replaced with the data from the data area. Consequently, as long as the IN operation is performed prior to any reference to the fields specified in the data structure, we do not need to worry about data structure initialization.

After performing our IN operation, we move data into the externally described fields that we want to change, and write the data back out to the data area. We did not specify otherwise on the OUT statement, so the lock we previously placed on the data area when performing the IN operation is released.

Program-described Data Areas

The last category of global data areas to cover is program-described data areas. In the following example, we use a data area that has no external definition. We have decided, instead, to define the data area and then move it to an internal Program-described Data Structure for processing. Once we are done manipulating the data, we move data defined by our Program-described Data Structure back into the data area.

In Figure 8.17, we define a data area variable named DTAARA using the DEFN statement. The fact that we used *NAMVAR in Factor 1 of this statement tells the system that we are defining a variable that is to be supported by a data area.

Figure 8.17: RPG Calculation Specifications to Lock and Read a Data Area

```
.....CL0N01N02N03Factor1+++OpcdeFactor2+++ResultLenDHHiLoEqComments++++++......
     C           *NAMVAR   DEFN          DTAARA 30         READ DATA AREA
     C           *LOCK     IN    DTAARA                    AND PUT DATA IN
     C                     MOVE DTAARA   DATADS            DATA STRUCTURE
```

We then read and lock our data area and move the data area contents to a data structure named DATADS, as seen in Figure 8.18. It should be noted here that a lock remains in effect on our DTAARA data area until we perform an OUT or an UNLCK operation (on the data area), or until our job terminates. Just like file record locks, no other job is able to obtain a lock on the data area until we have released our lock.

Figure 8.18: Program-described Data Structure Used to Define a Data Area

```
.....IDsname....NODsExt-file++.............OccrLen+............................
     IDATADS      DS
     I                                     1  10 DEVICE
     I                                    11  20 PRINTR
     I                                    21  30 OUTQ
```

In Figure 8.19, we move the contents of our DATADS data structure back into our variable (DTAARA) and then write the contents back out to the data area. The lock is released automatically at this time, because we did not specify *LOCK in Factor 1 of our OUT statement. If we had used *LOCK as Factor 1 of our OUT statement, the data area would have been updated and the lock would have remained in effect.

Figure 8.19: RPG Calculation Specifications to Write to and Unlock a Data Area

```
.....CL0N01N02N03Factor1+++OpcdeFactor2+++ResultLenDHHiLoEqComments+++++++......
     C                   MOVE DATADS    DTAARA         PUT DATA STRUCTURE
     C                   OUT  DTAARA                    BACK INTO DATA AREA
```

THE LOCAL DATA AREA

For those of you who were around for the IBM System/34 and System/36, you will recognize the local data area as one of the most powerful tools that could be used for passing limited amounts of data from one program to the next. The data in the LDA is special in that the data residing there is "local" and only available for the current job. Submitted jobs, jobs in other workstation sessions, and jobs running on other workstations each have their own unique local data areas.

In the case of the AS/400, the size of the LDA has been expanded to 1K—or 1024 bytes. You can use any or all of the LDA from any of your programs.

LDA on the AS/400 is still a powerful tool for program-to-program communications. It can be externally described with a data structure and is useful in reducing the number of parameters that must be passed from one program to the next. This is especially true if the data only needs to be accessible to a few links within a chain of programs. Instead of using the same parameters from one program to the next, you can place the data in LDA and only access or update it in the programs that need it.

In the case of submitted jobs, the LDA originally consists of the same contents as the LDA of the workstation that submitted the job. Once the submitted job is running, however, the LDA takes on a life of its own. Changes occurring to the data in the LDA are isolated within the submitted job only, and the data is only held in the system as long as the submitted job is still running.

Program-described Local Data Area

The designation of LDA is very similar to the data area definitions we just studied. In Figure 8.20, we show the simplest form of LDA. In this case, we used a Data Area Data Structure to describe LDA.

Figure 8.20: Program-described Input Specifications Defining the Local Data Area

```
.....IDsname....NODsExt-file++.............OccrLen+............................
     I           UDS
     I                                    1  10 DEVICE
     I                                   11  20 PRINTR
     I                                   21  30 OUTQ
```

The U in position 18 of the data structure Definition Specification tells the system we are defining a Data Area Data Structure. The system knows we are defining the LDA (as opposed to a global data area) because positions 7 through 12 of that same statement are blank.

In Figure 8.20, we define the first 30 bytes of LDA. The total size of LDA is 1024 bytes of character data, but your program only needs to define the portion of the local data area that it will use.

Using a Program-described Data Structure to Define the LDA

In Figures 8.21, 8.22, and 8.23, we read the LDA in our Calculation Specifications and then move the data into our LDADS data structure. We write that data back out to the LDA using our Program-described Data Structure (LDADS).

Figure 8.21: Program-described Data Structure Used to Redefine the LDA

```
.....IDsname....NODsExt-file++.............OccrLen+............................
     ILDADS      DS
     I                                    1  10 DEVICE
     I                                   11  20 PRINTR
     I                                   21  30 OUTQ
```

Figure 8.22: RPG Calculation Specifications Used to Read the LDA and Move It to a Program-described Data Structure

```
.....CL0N01N02N03Factor1+++OpcdeFactor2+++ResultLenDHHiLoEqComments++++++......
     C           *NAMVAR DEFN *LDA     LDADS         READ DATA FROM LDA AND
     C                   IN   LDADS                  MOVE INTO DATA STRUCTURE
```

Figure 8.23: RPG Calculation Specifications Used to Write Data to the LDA via a Program-described Data Structure

```
.....CLON01N02N03Factor1+++OpcdeFactor2+++ResultLenDHHiLoEqComments++++++......
   C                  OUT  LDADS                      LOCAL DATA AREA
```

In Figure 8.22, we define LDA to our program using the special keyword *LDA in Factor 2 of the DEFN statement. At the same time, we tell the system that we are using the LDADS data structure to redefine LDA within our program. Note that we did not use the *LOCK parameter of the IN op code in our example because the local data area is unique to the current session and may not be accessed by any other job. On the subsequent statement, we read in LDA and consequently move the data into our data structure.

Later in our program we write the contents of our data structure back out to LDA by performing the code in Figure 8.23. The changed data in LDA is then available to any subsequent programs in the job stream.

Using Externally Described Data Structures to Define the Local Data Area

External Data Structures can be useful to define your LDA too. By using an external definition, you assure consistent definitions from program to program, and also reduce the amount of maintenance required when the definition of LDA must change. This is especially true when you have many programs that use the same definitions of LDA (Figures 8.24 through 8.27).

Figure 8.24: Data Description Specifications for an External Data Structure Used to Define the Local Data Area

```
A..........T.Name++++++RLen++TDpB......Functions+++++++++++++++++++++++++++++
A          R LDADEF
A            CUST#        10A          COLHDG('CUSTOMER#')
A            NAME         40A          COLHDG('NAME')
A            ADDRES       30A          COLHDG('ADDRESS')
A            CITY         30A          COLHDG('CITY')
A            STATE         2A          COLHDG('STATE')
A            ZIP           9A          COLHDG('ZIP CODE')
A            SLSMAN        5A          COLHDG('SALESMAN')
A            PHONE        10S 0        COLHDG('PHONE NUMBER')
```

Figure 8.25: Input Specifications Designating an External Data Structure Used to Define the LDA

```
.....IDsname....NODsExt-file++.............OccrLen+.............................
     ILDA       EUDSLDADEF
```

Figure 8.26: Calculation Specifications Defining and Reading the LDA via an External Data Structure

```
.....CL0N01N02N03Factor1+++OpcdeFactor2+++ResultLenDHHiLoEqComments+++++++......
     C          *NAMVAR    DEFN *LDA     LDA               INITIALIZE AND CLEAR
     C                     IN   LDA                         LOCAL DATA AREA
     C                     CLEARLDA                         BEFORE LOADING DATA
```

Figure 8.27: Calculation Specifications Writing Data to the LDA via an External Data Structure

```
.....CL0N01N02N03Factor1+++OpcdeFactor2+++ResultLenDHHiLoEqComments+++++++......
     C                     OUT  LDA                         LOCAL DATA AREA
```

USING EXTERNALLY DESCRIBED DATA STRUCTURES TO DEFINE PROGRAM-DESCRIBED DATA FILES

Externally Described Data Structures also offer a viable alternative to program-described files. This is of particular interest to those programmers working on legacy systems that happen to be running under the System/36 environment.

Instead of internally describing all of the fields in a file within the RPG program, you can use an external data structure to define the data fields within the file. This allows you to define the file in a single place and simply call on that definition each time you use the file. Changes in the file definition are made once, and programs requiring that change only need to be recompiled.

This method is particularly useful when you wish to store multiple formats of data in the same file. You can use a record-type code to determine which data structure to move the data to, and create your own multiple-format data file.

The biggest benefit to this method must be field name consistency. You do not have to worry about a field being named something different in every program. Consistency helps eliminate errors.

This method is certainly not a substitute for externally described files, but it is definitely a step up from leaving all of the file definitions as program-described. You still are unable to use any of the database tools like query or Display File Field Description (DSPFFD) because the system file definition still does not have that level of detail.

In Figure 8.28, we see a conventional program-described file. Figures 8.29 and 8.30 represent the same file, but with an external data structure used for file definition.

Figure 8.28: Program-described Customer File

```
.....IDsname....NODsExt-file++.............OccrLen+...........................
     ICUSTOMER    NS
I                                             1  10 CUST#
I                                            11  50 NAME
I                                            51  80 ADDRES
I                                            81 110 CITY
I                                           111 112 STATE
I                                           113 121 ZIP
I                                           122 126 SLSMAN
I                                           127 1360PHONE
```

Figure 8.29: Data Description Specifications for an External Data Structure Describing the Customer File

```
A..........T.Name++++++RLen++TDpB......Functions++++++++++++++++++++++++++++
A          R CUSREC
A            CUST#        10A          COLHDG('CUSTOMER#')
A            NAME         40A          COLHDG('NAME')
A            ADDRES       30A          COLHDG('ADDRESS')
A            CITY         30A          COLHDG('CITY')
A            STATE         2A          COLHDG('STATE')
A            ZIP           9A          COLHDG('ZIP CODE')
A            SLSMAN        5A          COLHDG('SALESMAN')
A            PHONE        10S 0        COLHDG('PHONE NUMBER')
```

Figure 8.30: Input Specifications Designating an External Data Structure Used to Describe the Customer File

```
.....IDsname....NODsExt-file++.............OccrLen+...........................
     ICUSDTA     EUDSCUSREC
```

Power RPG III

By using the data structure in Figure 8.29 to redefine the data in the customer file, all of the fields defined by the externally described data structure become available.

USING DATA STRUCTURES TO REDUCE PROGRAM PARAMETERS

Programs that pass too many parameters are a common problem in many AS/400 systems. Programs that are initially written with 2 or 3 parameters end up with 10, 12, or even more.

When you have that many parameters being passed back and forth between programs, you have plenty of room for error. The programs being called, and those doing the calling, must be in constant synchronization. When a subprogram is called by multiple calling programs, the room for error gets multiplied. Program maintenance can become a nightmare.

A simple solution to this problem that is just waiting to happen is to use an external data structure as a parameter in lieu of a parameter list. The data structure can hold many fields and, because the definition is external, you have consistency between the various programs.

In the example in Figure 8.31, we define a data structure for use as a parameter in Figure 8.32. The data description specifications in Figure 8.31 are compiled as a physical file, even though the "file" will not contain data.

Figure 8.31: Data Definition Specifications for a Parameter Data Structure

```
.....A..........T.Name++++++RLen++TDpB......Functions++++++++++++++++++++++++++
     A          R DTADEF
     A            DEVICE      10A          COLHDG('TAPE DEVICE')
     A            PRINTR      10A          COLHDG('PRINTER NAME')
     A            OUTQ        10A          COLHDG('OUT QUEUE')
```

Figure 8.32: Calculation Specifications Defining a Parameter Data Structure

```
.....CL0N01N02N03Factor1+++OpcdeFactor2+++ResultLenDHHiLoEqComments+++++++......
     C           *ENTRY    PLIST
     C                      PARM           PARMDS
```

204

Figure 8.33 shows the Input Specifications necessary to define the external data structure to our program. The PLIST in Figure 8.32 refers the program to the PARMDS data structure for a list of the parameters that are passed between the programs.

Figure 8.33: Input Specifications for a Parameter Data Structure

```
.....IDsname....NODsExt-file++............OccrLen+...........................
     IPARMDS     E DSDTADEF
```

In the example here, we only have a few fields in our DTADEF external data structure, but you can use your imagination. Instead of using extensive parameter lists, your programs could simply reference the PARMDS Externally Defined Data Structure. The length of the parameter does not need to be specified because the Externally Defined Data Structure length is used instead.

Maintenance could be made considerably easier. No matter how many fields in the Externally Defined Data Structure get changed, the program does not require additional maintenance (unless the program in question uses the fields that have changed).

If the external data structure changes, programs using the data structure only need to be recompiled. There are two exceptions to this rule. One is if the program uses one of the fields in the data structure that was changed. The other exception is if fields are simply added to the end of the data structure. In this case, only the programs using the new additional field(s) need to be modified or compiled.

MULTIPLE-OCCURRENCE DATA STRUCTURES AND THE TWO-DIMENSIONAL ARRAY

A Multiple-occurrence Data Structure is a data structure like any other, except it has multiple copies (referred to as occurrences), each containing different data. Each occurrence or copy is actually treated as a separate, self-contained data structure, except that you do not have to define each occurrence separately. The occurrences are accessed with an index, much as you would access an array.

Figure 8.34 shows an example of the code necessary to define a multiple-occurring data structure. The name of the data structure (DSNAME) is specified in positions 7 through 14, and columns 44 through 47 are used to indicate how many occurrences of the data structure exist. Columns 48 through 51 are used for the length of the data structure, but as with all data structures, this field is optional. If you do not specify the length, the system automatically assigns the data structure the length of the accumulated subfields within it.

Figure 8.34: Input Specifications Defining a Multiple-occurrence Data Structure

```
.....IDsname....NODsExt-file++.............OccrLen+............................
     IDSNAME      DS                      5
I                                         1    72TOTAMT
I                                         8   130TOTCNT
I                                        14   150LOCCOD
I                                        16   45 LOCNAM
```

In our example, we have indicated that our data structure has five occurrences. Because we did not specify the length of the data structure in columns 48 through 51, the length assigned to this data structure is 45 characters (that is where the last subfield ends).

Table 8.1 represents the DSNAM Multiple-occurrence Data Structure defined in Figure 8.34 after data has been loaded into it. As you can see in the example, it is almost as if we had defined five separate data structures with the same four fields defined for each.

Table 8.1: Example of Data Stored in a Multiple-occurrence Data Structure

Occurrence	TOTAMT	TOTCNT	LOCCOD	LOCNAM
1	50.00	1	01	Store number 1
2	150.00	3	05	Store number 5
3	250.00	5	19	Store number 19
4	150.00	3	14	Store number 14
5	50.00	1	12	Store number 12

The data structure index is either set or retrieved using the OCUR op code. When setting the data structure index, the OCUR statement tells the system which copy of the structure to use. The OCUR statement can also be used to retrieve the current index and return it to a variable as well.

Factor 1	Op Code	Factor 2	Result Field
[index pointer]	**OCUR**	Data Structure Name	[Occurrence Value]

If you want to set the occurrence (i.e., index) of a Multiple-occurrence Data Structure named DSNAME to 1, do so by employing the following code:

```
.....CLON01N02N03Factor1+++OpcdeFactor2+++ResultLenDHHiLoEqComments++++++......
     C            1           OCUR DSNAME
```

In effect, you are telling the system that you want to work with the first of multiple data structures. Using the previous example, all references to subfields within the data structure refer to the first occurrence of the data structure. This remains the case until the OCUR operation is performed again with a different index specified.

The index you use for the OCUR operation could be a numeric literal as specified in the previous example, or it could be any other numeric field. You need to make sure, however, that the index specified falls within the range of the number of elements (occurrences) that are defined for the Multiple-occurrence Data Structure.

The OCUR operation allows you to retrieve the index value of where the index pointer is set currently. If your goal is to find the occurrence to which the data structure is currently pointing, use code somewhat like the following:

```
.....CLON01N02N03Factor1+++OpcdeFactor2+++ResultLenDHHiLoEqComments++++++......
     C                        OCUR DSNAME    X
```

In this example, the current occurrence pointer value is retrieved from the system and written to the variable X.

Initializing the Multiple-occurrence Data Structure

As we have previously stated, data structures are considered to be alphanumeric, regardless of the data type specified in the subfields within. If you attempt to access a numeric subfield within a data structure prior to initializing it or loading it with numeric data, you find yourself with a Data Decimal Error. Multiple-occurrence Data Structures are no exception to this rule.

Placing an I in position 18 of the Input Specification defining the Multiple-occurrence Data Structure causes all occurrences within the data structure to be initialized for you when the program is initialized. If you specify default subfield values (by placing an I in position 8 of the subfield Input Specification), the default is copied automatically to all occurrences.

 If you need to reinitialize the Multiple-occurrence Data Structure (to be reused, for example), you find that the system does not automatically initialize each copy of the structure for you. Using the CLEAR or RESET operations simply clears or resets the occurrence where the index happens to be set.

If you want to clear the entire data structure, you need to establish a loop to do so. In Figure 8.35, we have coded a loop to step through the occurrences of the data structure and reset the subfields within all of the occurrences of the Multiple-occurrence Data Structure.

Figure 8.35: Resetting a Multiple-occurrence Data Structure to Its Original Values

```
IDSNAME         DS                          5
I                                           1    72TOTAMT
I                                           8   130TOTCNT
,I                                          14  150LOCCOD
I I                   'Not on File'         16   45 LOCNAM
  *
C                         DO   5       X        10
C               X         OCUR DSNAME
C                         RESETDSNAME
C                         ENDDO
```

The numeric fields are cleared and reset to zero because there are no default values coded for them. The LOCNAM field, however, is initialized to Not on File in each occurrence of the data structure. The I in position 8 of the Input Specification for the LOCNAM subfield tells the system to initialize the field with the constant specified in positions 21 through 42. We could have used a named constant for this purpose instead of the literal.

The Two-dimensional Array

Reproducing the function of the Multiple-occurrence Data Structure coded in Figure 8.35 could be accomplished easily by replacing each field in the structure with its own array. But this would require four arrays, each of five elements, instead of the Multiple-occurrence Data Structure. Both methods work, but the data structure is probably easier to manage. The power of multiple-occurring data structures, however, is unmatched when you combine the power of arrays and Multiple-occurrence Data Structures together to create the two-dimensional array. By defining an array within the Multiple-occurrence Data Structure, you are, in effect, creating a two-dimensional array.

For an example of the two-dimensional array in action, let's establish a scenario that we might encounter when asked to write a sales analysis report. Say we want to create a 31-element array, called AR$, that holds the total dollar amount of goods sold for each day of the month. Further, let's create another 31-element array called AR#, to hold the number of sales transactions performed for each day of the month. On top of that, we want to keep each month's totals separate within the fiscal year.

To code this without multiple-occurring data structures requires 24 arrays! You need one array to represent total dollar amount sold for each month of the year as well as an array to represent the number of sales for each month. That is quite a bit of code to write and maintain.

By using a simple multiple-occurring data structure with 12 occurrences (1 for each month), we are able to trim down the amount of code required for this operation considerably. In the following example, we code two arrays called AR$ ($ amount sold per month) and AR# (number of sales per month). These arrays exist as separate copies within each occurrence of the Multiple-occurrence Data Structure. As you can see from the code in Figure 8.36, it is not difficult to code this two-dimensional structure.

Power RPG III

Figure 8.36: Creating Two-dimensional Arrays Using Multiple-occurrence Data Structures

```
.....E....FromfileTofile++Name++N/rN/tbLenPDSArrnamLenPDSComments+++++++++......
     E                    AR$         31  7 2
     E                    AR#         31  5 0
       **
.....IDsname....NODsExt-file++.............OccrLen+...........................
     IDSNAME     IDS                       12
     I                                      1 2172AR$
     I                                    218 3720AR#
       **
.....CL0N01N02N03Factor1+++OpcdeFactor2+++ResultLenDHHiLoEqComments+++++++......
     C           MONTH     OCUR DSNAME
     C                     Z-ADDDAY     D        20
     C                     ADD  AMOUNT  AR$,D              Amount sold
     C                     ADD  1       AR#,D              Count sold
```

The first dimension of our structure is indexed using the month of the sales transaction and is used to set the occurrence of the structure. The second dimension is indexed by the day of the sale, and is used as the index for each of the arrays.

In Figure 8.36, the MONTH field represents the month of the sale. In our example, we use this field to set the occurrence of the data structure prior to adding any data to the arrays. This, in effect, tells the system which copy of the arrays to use. The DAY field is moved to the index field called D because the Calculation Specification Result field is not big enough to use DAY as the index.

If the code specified in the Calculation Specifications of our example is run against all sales transactions that met our report criteria, the net result is that we effectively have 24 arrays potentially filled with data. We can then establish a loop to step through the data structure occurrences and print the data from each.

YOUR RPG TREASURE CHEST

By now, you realize all of the power that can be at your disposal by simply being well-versed on the components covered in this chapter. Scenarios in which you can exhibit this new-found power are only limited by your imagination.

Using these tools properly results in far more efficient code (and far less of it). Ultimately, this results in less program maintenance and more time to work on those projects that you like.

Chapter 9

System APIs

You are about to embark upon a brave new world. It is the wonderful world of APIs. You will find that it is a world of speed, efficiency, and information—lots of information.

If you do not know how to use APIs, if they are not part of your toolbox, a whole world of information remains behind closed doors. The good news is that opening those doors is not very difficult once you have the key. We are confident that you will have found that key after you finish reading this chapter.

WHAT IS AN API?

Let us begin by defining an API. API stands for application program interface. The interface referred to here is the missing link between your programs and the IBM operating system.

An API is an IBM program that you can call from within your RPG programs to perform work. This work includes, but is not limited to, retrieving system information. Your program passes parameters to indicate the work you want performed, and the API returns the data you requested in the form of a parameter or data structures placed into a user space (which we discuss in detail later in this chapter). Understanding these parameters and data structures serves as your master key and opens many doors inside your system.

The information provided for and returned from APIs usually is defined in a data structure, or series of data structures. One of the principle advantages of using APIs is that IBM will not change the data structure in future releases. If they decide to alter an API in order to show more information, they will add another data structure and leave the existing data structures intact. We define these data structures in detail as we go along.

You can find a complete listing of all APIs in the *System Programmer's Interface Reference Manual* (QBKA8402, SC41-8223). IBM insiders refer to this manual as the SPI (pronounced SPY) manual. The SPI manual defines each parameter for every API, and is extremely helpful when getting started with most of the APIs. Another great place for information on APIs is QUSRTOOL (which came free with your operating system prior to V3R1).

Many APIs return information into a variable data structure(s), which can be quite complex and tedious to code. However, many of these structures are defined in various members in the QUSRTOOL library. If you happen to have QUSRTOOL, you can copy the code that defines these data structures right into your programs.

Many APIs are not all that complex. In fact, some APIs are very simple. The Command Execute (QCMDEXC) program, covered in Chapter 6, is probably the most powerful, but at the same time it's one of the most basic. It allows you to run any command from within your program. The QCMDEXC program is simple in that it has only two parameters. The first parameter consists of the command to be executed and the second parameter defines the length of the command within the first parameter.

Even easier to use than QCMDEXC is the Command Line API (QUSCMDLN). This API has no parameters, you simply call it and a command entry window appears on your screen.

In this chapter, we unravel some of the mystery and confusion surrounding APIs. We cover Retrieve, Message, Spool Files, Document Handling, Conversion, Edit, and List APIs. We explain the whys and hows of user spaces. And last, but not least, we show you how APIs are used in one of our favorite programming utilities.

After reading this chapter, you should feel comfortable navigating through any of the APIs that you will need to perform your job. Although Table 9.1 lists the many APIs that we cover, there are hundreds more.

Table 9.1: Application Program Interfaces Covered in Chapter 9

API Name	Description
QCMDEXC	Command execute
QDBLDBR	List data base relations
QDBRTVFD	Retrieve file description
QECCVTEC	Convert edit code
QECEDT	Edit field
QHFCLSDR	Close directory
QHFOPNDR	Open directory
QHFRDDR	Read directory
QMHRMVPM	Remove program message
QMHSNDPM	Send program message
QOCCTLOF	Control Office Services
QSPMOVSP	Move spooled file
QUSCMDLN	Command entry line
QUSCRTUS	Create user space

API Name	Description
QUSLSPL	List spooled file
QUSROBJD	Retrieve object description
QUSRTVUS	Retrieve user space
QWCCVTDT	Convert date

RETRIEVE APIs

As the name implies, Retrieve APIs are used to extract information from the system. These APIs have both input and output parameters. You pass information to tell the APIs what kind of information you are trying to retrieve, and the APIs retrieves the requested information into a variable for you.

Before the advent of APIs, this type of programming was performed with a CLP command that directed its output to an OUTFILE (usually with all the speed of a fast turtle). You then had to process the OUTFILE to get the information you wanted.

With APIs, you can execute one quick call within an RPG program and the information you seek is loaded into a data structure for you. Another advantage to APIs is that you have some measure of control over the speed of the API. As you would expect, the more information you ask for, the longer it takes to retrieve. Asking for just the information you need speeds up the process.

When using the Retrieve APIs, the format name parameter is where you indicate the type of information you want returned. In general, APIs where the lower-numbered format names are specified run faster than those where the higher-numbered formats are specified. The variation in speed is due primarily to the amount of information involved. The Retrieve Job Information (QUSRJOBI) API is one notable exception to this rule—its formats have nothing to do with performance.

One of the more complex Retrieve APIs is the Retrieve File Description (QDBRTVFD) API. It has 10 parameters and, like many APIs, directs its output to a user space. Prior to using the QDBRTVFD API, the user space must be created. We can perform this function using the Create User Space (QUSCRTUS) API.

PUTTING THE POWER OF RETRIEVE APIs TO USE

Suppose we want to issue a warning error message to the system operator reminding them to back up their files. If we simply send the message every day, it becomes familiar and tends to get ignored. The warning message is more effective if it is sent only when the files have not been backed up within a prescribed time frame. In order to do this effectively, we need to know the last time the files were saved.

To find the date a file was last saved, use the Retrieve Object Description (QUSROBJD) API. The chart in Table 9.2 shows the parameters for this specific API. You can find a similar chart for every API in the aforementioned *System Programmer's Interface Reference Manual* (QBKA8402, SC41-8223).

Table 9.2: Required Parameter Group for the Retrieve Object Description (QUSROBJD) API

Parameter	Parameter Description	Type	Size
1	Receiver variable	Output	Char(*)
2	Length of receiver variable	Input	Binary(4)
3	Format name	Input	Char(8)
4	Object and library name	Input	Char(20)
5	Object type	Input	Char(10)

Optional Error Data Structure Parameter:

Parameter	Parameter Description	Type	Size
6	Error	Output	Char(*)

Parameter Definitions:

Receiver variable: This parameter represents the variable, or data structure, into which the system returns the requested information. Notice that the field is output in nature and the size column has CHAR(*), indicating that the field is a variable-length field.

Length of receiver variable: The second parameter of the API is the receiver variable length, which defines the length of the preceding parameter. This field is an input type and it is here that we tell the system the length of the receiver variable parameter that we want returned.

Format name: The third parameter of this API is the format name. The format parameter is where we indicate to the system exactly what information we are looking for. The format name we enter here tells the system how to format the data returned in the receiver variable parameter.

Object and library name: Here is where we specify the name and library of the object about which we are requesting information.

Object type: Defines the object type.

Error structure: The sixth parameter of this API is the optional error data structure we are about to discuss.

THE OPTIONAL API ERROR CODE PARAMETER

Most APIs include an optional error code parameter. It is a variable-length data structure, but do not let that deter you. The fact that it is variable in length simply means that, the larger you define the data structure, the more information there is to return to you. The required components of the Optional API Error Code Parameter are shown in Table 9.3.

Table 9.3: Required Parameter Group for the Optional API
Error Code Data Structure

Parameter	Description	Type	Size
1	Bytes provided	Input	Binary(4)
2	Bytes available	Output	Binary(4)
3	Message identification code	Output	Char(7)
4	Error number	Output	Char(1)
5	Message data	Output	Char(*)

Parameter Definitions:

Bytes provided: A field whereby we tell the API the length of the message data we want returned in the Message Data field.

Bytes available: The actual length of the data returned if an error occurs. If this field is 0, you can safely assume the API executed properly. If its value is greater than 0, an error occurred and the parameter returns the number of bytes returned to your program.

Message ID: If an error was detected, and the Bytes Available field is greater than zero, the Message Identification field contains the message identifier of the error that was detected.

Error number: The fourth parameter, Error Number, is reserved by the system and should be ignored.

Message data: If an error occurs, this parameter contains the substitution variables for the system message ID.

If the error code parameter is available to the API and you do *not* include it in the call, the API returns both diagnostic and escape messages. This means you get the normally cryptic system error message screen.

On the other hand, if you do code the program to use the error code parameter, only escape messages are returned to the program and the system does not present an error message screen. In general, if the error code parameter is available, use it. Once you have performed the error routine's initial deployment, the structure is easily cloned from program to program.

USING APIS TO RETRIEVE OBJECT DESCRIPTIONS

Output from the OBJD0300 format of the Retrieve Object Description (QUSROBJD) API is depicted in Table 9.4. Data is returned in this format if the format name in parameter 3 of the input parameters is specified as OBJD0300.

Table 9.4: Retrieve Object Description (USROBJD) API
Output Descriptions for Format OBJD0300

Dec	Hex	Type	Description
—	—	—	Everything from OBJD0100/OBJD0200 formats
180	B4	Char(13)	Source file updated date and time
193	C1	Char(13)	Object saved date and time
206	CE	Char(13)	Object restored date and time
219	DB	Char(10)	Creator's user profile
229	E5	Char(8)	System where object was created
237	ED	Char(7)	Reset date
244	F4	Binary(4)	Save size
248	F8	Binary(4)	Save sequence number
252	FC	Char(10)	Storage
262	106	Char(10)	Save command

Dec	Hex	Type	Description
272	110	Char(71)	Save volume ID
343	157	Char(10)	Save device
353	161	Char(10)	Save file name
363	16B	Char(10)	Save file library name
373	175	Char(17)	Save label
390	186	Char(9)	System level
399	18F	Char(16)	Compiler
415	19F	Char(8)	Object level
423	1A7	Char(1)	User changed
424	1A8	Char(16)	Licensed program
440	1B8	Char(10)	Program temporary fix (PTF)
450	1C2	Char(10)	Authorized program analysis report (APAR)

The QUSROBJD API returns data in one of the four possible formats seen in Table 9.5. We choose the OBJD0300 format for the following example because it contains the date and time an object was last saved.

Table 9.5: Formats for Retrieve Object Description (QUSROBJD) API

QUSROBJD API Format	Description
OBJD0100	Basic information
OBJD0200	Information similar to PDM
OBJD0300	Service information
OBJD0400	Full information

As is the case for the input parameters, the output parameters are also defined in the SPI manual. Note that the offsets in the table begin at 0, so you must add 1 to the given decimal position when you define it in an RPG Input Specification.

For instance, suppose we want to know the volume ID of the tape that holds the last copy of this file. The chart in Table 9.4 shows the save volume ID resides in position 272 for a length of 71 bytes. The RPG input specifications to access that field are shown in Figure 9.1 and begin in 273.

Figure 9.1: Sample Input Specifications Representing an API Data Structure Offset

```
IOFFSET         DS
I                                273 343 VOLID
```

Figure 9.2 shows the GETDAT RPG program, which has all the necessary code to use the Retrieve Object Description (QUSROBJD) API. The GETDAT program has the file and library names as input parameters, and date/time last saved as an output parameter.

Figure 9.2: Sample of the Retrieve Object Description API

```
**   Program name - GETDAT

IERROR      IDS
I                                    B   1    40BYTPRV
I                                    B   5    80BYTAVA
I                                        9   15 MSGID
I                                       16   16 ERR###
I                                       17  116 MSGDTA
IRCVVAR     DS                              206
I                                      194  206 DATESV
I           DS
I                                    B   1    40RCVLEN
I                                        5   24 FILLIB
I                                        5   14 FILNAM
I                                       15   24 LIBNAM
C           *ENTRY    PLIST
C                     PARM            INFILE 10
C                     PARM            INLIB  10
C                     PARM            DATSAV 12
C                     Z-ADD116        BYTPRV
C                     MOVELINFILE     FILNAM
C                     MOVE INLIB      LIBNAM
C                     CALL 'QUSROBJD'
C                     PARM            RCVVAR
C                     PARM 206        RCVLEN
C                     PARM 'OBJD0300'FILFMT  8
C                     PARM            FILLIB
C                     PARM '*FILE'    OBJTYP 10
C                     PARM            ERROR
C           MSGID     IFEQ *BLANKS
C                     MOVE DATESV     DATSAV
C                     ENDIF
C                     SETON                      LR
```

When reviewing the GETDAT program, you see that, if the Error Message ID field is blanks after the call to QUSROBJD, the DATESV field contains the date and time the file was last saved. The GETDAT program, in turn, returns the date last saved to the calling program in the DATSAV parameter. The calling program can then use the returned parameter information to determine how many days have elapsed since the file was last saved. If the number of days that have elapsed are considered to be too many, the warning message is sent to the program operator.

CHECKING FOR OBJECTS USING THE RETRIEVE OBJECT DESCRIPTION API

With slight variations to the previous program used in Figure 9.2, we could use the same API to create a program that checks for the existence of any object. And that's exactly what we've done in the EXIST RPG program shown in Figure 9.3.

Figure 9.3: Sample RPG Program to Validate Object Existence

```
        ** Program name - EXIST

        IERROR    IDS
        I                                 B   1    40BYTPRV
        I                                 B   5    80BYTAVA
        I                                     9   15 MSGID
        I                                    16  16 ERR###
        I                                    17 116 MSGDTA
        I         DS
        I                                 B   1    40RCVLEN
        C         *ENTRY    PLIST
        C                   PARM          OBJECT 10
        C                   PARM          LIB    10
        C                   PARM          OBJTYP  8
        C                   PARM          YESNO   1
        C                   Z-ADD116      BYTPRV
        C         LIB       IFEQ *BLANKS
        C                   MOVEL'*LIBL'  LIB
        C                   ENDIF
        C                   MOVELOBJECT   FILLIB 20
        C                   MOVE LIB      FILLIB
        C                   CALL 'QUSROBJD'               ATTEMPT TO RETRIEVE
        C                   PARM          RCVVAR100        OBJECT DESC
        C                   PARM 100      RCVLEN
        C                   PARM 'OBJD0100'FILFMT  8
        C                   PARM          FILLIB
        C                   PARM          OBJTYP
        C                   PARM          ERROR
        C                   MOVE 'Y'      YESNO
        C         MSGID     IFNE *BLANKS
        C                   MOVE 'N'      YESNO
        C                   ENDIF
        C                   SETON                    LR
```

An example of where you might want to use the EXIST program would be when prompting for a report or list. If you ask the operator which printer to direct the output to, you should check the device to see if it exists as well as if it is the correct device type. Checking the response at time of entry prevents potential errors down the line.

When running the program in Figure 9.3, you pass it the object name, library, and object type. The program, in turn, passes back a Yes/No parameter indicating whether or not an object with the specified name, type, and library exists. If you choose not to specify a library name for the object being validated, the program uses the library list.

In the example, we modify the FILFMT parameter so the QUSROBJD API returns the data defined by format OBJD0100. The objective in this case is simply to know if the object exists, so we don't really care what information is returned. Therefore, we choose to use the format with the smallest number of fields for maximum API performance.

The EXIST RPG program in Figure 9.3 may be called from other application programs to verify the existence, type, and library of an object.

MESSAGE APIs

Let's continue our lessons by example and demonstrate how to send a message to a program message queue using the Send Program Message (QMHSNDPM) API. Message APIs provide a method for you to design your programs to work with AS/400 messages.

Examine the RPG program shown in Figure 9.4 to see how to use the QMHSNDPM API. The DDS for the program in Figure 9.5 is shown so you can compile and run this utility.

Figure 9.4: Sample RPG Program Using the Send Program Message (QMHSNDPM) API

```
     ** Program name - MSGEX

    FMSGEXDSPCF   E                    WORKSTN
    IERROR        IDS
    I                               B    1    40BYTPRV
    I                               B    5    80BYTAVA
    I                                    9   15 MSGID
    I                                   16   16 ERR###
    I                                   17  116 MSGDTA
    I             DS
    I                               B    1    40MSGDLN
    I                               B    5    80MSGQNB
    I                               B    9   120MSKLEN
    I                               B   13   160LENRTN
    I                               B   17   200PRECSN
    I                               B   21   240DECMAL
    I             DS
    I                                    1    60MDY
    I                                    1    40MMDD
    I                                    5    60YY
    ISAVEDS       DS
    I                                    1    10CENTRY
    I                                    2   7 SAVED
    I                                    8   130DSTIME
    I                                   14   160MILSEC
    I             'WARNING - Customer f-C            DATERR
    I             'ile last backed up o-
    I             'n '
    C                     MOVEL'*'      PGMQ    10
    C                     SETON                        90
    C                     CALL  'GETDAT'
    C                     PARM  'CUSTOMER'FILE    10
    C                     PARM  'TESTLIB' LIB     10
    C                     PARM          DATSAV  12
    C                     MOVELDATSAV   SAVED
    C                     MOVE  UDATE   MDY
    C                     MOVELYY       TODAY    6
    C                     MOVE  MMDD    TODAY
```

```
C                TODAY       IFGT SAVED
C                            EXSR FMTMSG
C                            EXSR SNDMSG
C                            WRITEMSGCTL
C                            ENDIF
C                            EXFMTFMTC
C                            EXSR CLRMSG
C                            SETON                      LR
CSR              CLRMSG      BEGSR
C                            Z-ADD116     BYTPRV
C                            CALL 'QMHRMVPM'                       REMOVE MESSAGES
C                            PARM '*'     MSGQ    10
C                            PARM         MSGQNB
C                            PARM         MSGKY    4
C                            PARM '*ALL'  MSGRMV  10
C                            PARM         ERROR
C                            ENDSR
C                SNDMSG      BEGSR
C                            Z-ADD116     BYTPRV
C                'QCPFMSG' CAT  'QSYS':3  MSGF
C                            MOVE 'CPF9898' MSGID
C                DATERR      CAT  DATE8:1  MSGDTA      P
C                            Z-ADD60      MSGDLN
C                            Z-ADD0       MSGQNB
C                            CALL 'QMHSNDPM'                       SEND ERROR MESSAGE
C                            PARM         MSGID
C                            PARM         MSGF    20
C                            PARM         MSGDTA
C                            PARM         MSGDLN
C                            PARM '*DIAG' MSGTYP  10
C                            PARM '*'     MSGQ    10
C                            PARM         MSGQNB
C                            PARM         MSGKY
C                            PARM         ERROR            ERROR CODE
C                            ENDSR
C                FMTMSG      BEGSR
C                            CALL 'QWCCVTDT'
C                            PARM '*YMD'  INPFMT  10
C                            PARM         SAVEDS
C                            PARM '*MDY'  OUTFMT  10
C                            PARM         SAVOUT  16
C                            PARM         ERROR
C                            MOVE SAVOUT  SAVEDS
C                            Z-ADD6       PRECSN
C                            Z-ADD1       DECMAL
C                            CALL 'QECCVTEC'
C                            PARM         EDTMSK256
C                            PARM         MSKLEN
C                            PARM         LENRTN
C                            PARM         ZEROHD   1
C                            PARM 'Y'     EDITCD   1
C                            PARM         FILLCD   1
C                            PARM         PRECSN
C                            PARM         DECMAL
C                            PARM         ERROR
C                            MOVE SAVED   PASDAT
C                            CALL 'QECEDT'
C                            PARM         DATE8    8
C                            PARM         LENRTN
C                            PARM         PASDAT  60
C                            PARM '*PACKED' PASCLS 10
```

```
C                    PARM          PRECSN
C                    PARM          EDTMSK
C                    PARM          MSKLEN
C                    PARM          ZEROHD
C                    PARM          ERROR
C                    ENDSR
```

Figure 9.5: DDS for the MSGEX RPG Program Using the Send Program Message (QMHSNDPM) API

```
A                                       DSPSIZ(24 80 *DS3)
A          R FMTC
A                                       CF03(03 'End of job')
A                                       CF12(12 'Return to Previous')
A                                       OVERLAY
A                                  21  3'                                    -
A                                                 '                          -
A                                       DSPATR(UL)
A                                  22  5'F3=Exit'
A                                  22 19'F12=Previous'
A                                   9 21'Customer Number:'
A          FLD001      10A  B       9 38
A                                   1 27'Customer Inquiry'
A                                       DSPATR(HI)
A                                       DSPATR(UL)
A          R MSGSFL                     SFL
A                                       SFLMSGRCD(24)
A          MSGKEY                       SFLMSGKEY
A          PGMQ                         SFLPGMQ
A          R MSGCTL                     SFLCTL(MSGSFL)
A                                       OVERLAY
A                                       SFLSIZ(3) SFLPAG(1)
A                                       SFLDSP SFLINZ
A 90                                    SFLEND
A          PGMQ                         SFLPGMQ
```

In the example in Figure 9.4, the GETDAT program is called to find the date the customer file was last saved. This function is performed prior to bringing up a screen format. (See Figure 9.2 for the code to the GETDAT program.)

If the current date happens to be greater than the date last saved, it can be safely assumed that the customer file has not been saved today. When this happens to be the case, our warning is sent to the program operator via the MSGEX program we just examined. It is in the MSGEX program where the FMTMSG subroutine is then executed.

The FMTMSG subroutine formats the date field (see "Date Conversion" later in this chapter) and executes the SNDMSG subroutine. The SNDMSG subroutine uses the Send Program Message (QMHSNDPM) API to send the message. The required parameter group for the QMHSNDPM API is shown in Table 9.6.

Table 9.6: Required Parameter Group for the
Send Program Message (QMHSNDPM) API

Parameter	Description	Type	Size
1	Message ID	Input	Char(7)
2	Message file name and library	Input	Char(20)
3	Message data	Input	Char(*)
4	Message data length	Input	Binary(4)
5	Message type	Input	Char(10)
6	Message queue name	Input	Char(10)
7	Job invocation number	Input	Binary(4)
8	Message key	Input	Char(4)
9	Error data structure	Both	Char(*)

Parameter Definitions:

Message ID: The message identification code of the message to be sent or blanks for an immediate message. If you specify a message ID code, you must also specify the message file name and library in parameter 2.

Message file name and library: The name of the file and library that contain the message ID specified in parameter 1. The first 10 characters of the parameter are file name, and the last 10 characters are the library name. You may also specify the following special values: *CURLIB (Current Library) or *LIBL (Library List).

Message data: If using a predefined Message ID in parameter 1, this parameter is used to pass the data to insert into the message substitution variables. If sending an immediate message (indicated by sending blanks in parameter 1), this parameter field is the complete text of the immediate message.

Message data length: The number of bytes occupied by the message data field in the preceding parameter.

Message type: One of the following values: Completion (*COMP), Diagnostic (*DIAG), Escape (*ESCAPE), Informational (*INFO), Inquiry (*INQ), Notify (*NOTIFY), Request (*RQS), or Status (*STATUS). The Inquiry (*INQ) message type is only valid if the message is sent to the external message queue.

Message queue name: The name of the external message queue, the call stack entry to which to send the message, or the name of the entry to start counting from if job invocation number is 0.

Job invocation number: The location in the call stack that identifies the target entry to which message queue the message is sent. The number is relative to the message queue name parameter, indicating how many calls up the stack the target entry is from the message queue name entry.

Message key: The key to the message being sent. This parameter is ignored if the message type is specified as *STATUS.

Error data structure: The standard Optional Error Code Data Structure.

For the program in Figure 9.4, we choose to use the system-provided Message ID CPF9898 in message file QCPFMSG in library QSYS. This is a useful general purpose message and can be used to format any message on the fly, including any variable you want displayed with the message.

The CPF9898 message has no incoming text associated with it, and only one data field. We create our message using the CAT op code to embed the date the file was last saved into our message and put it in the message data field for the system to display.

We have loaded an asterisk (*) in the message queue parameter indicating that the message is to be sent to the current job's message queue. The job invocation stack is 0, so the message is sent to the current program's message queue. Any other number put in this field causes the message to be sent back up the invocation stack. The number placed in the job invocation number parameter determines how far back in the stack the message is sent.

Our MSGEX program issues a warning message to the program operator. It displayed via the write to the MSGCTL format, and then followed by a general input screen (FMTC in this case).

To prevent the error from reappearing after entering data on the screen (this is only an informational warning message), the program executes the clear message subroutine. This subroutine uses another useful API—the Remove Program Messages (QMHRMVPM) API.

In this particular example, it is really not necessary to remove the messages from the program message queue because the program is going to set on the last record indicator and terminate. But in a working application, you would probably edit the data entered on the screen and loop back up to issue any error messages. You want to clear the message queue before issuing new messages so the old ones do not redisplay.

The Remove Program Messages API accepts five input parameters and two sets of optional parameters. For our purposes, we only cover the required entries and they are shown in Table 9.7.

Table 9.7: Required Parameter Group for the Remove Program Messages (QMHRMVPM) API

Parameter	Description	Type	Size
1	Message queue	Input	Char(10)
2	Call stack counter relative to parameter 1. Indicates how many entries up the stack to go to find the message queue to remove.	Input	Binary(4)
3	Message key	Input	Binary(4)
4	Messages to remove	Input	Char(10)

Parameter	Description	Type	Size
5	Error	Both	Char(*)

Parameter Definitions:

<u>Message queue</u>: The name of the call stack entry to which to send the message, or the name of the entry to start counting from if job invocation number is 0. You can also specify the external message queue, or *, for the current job's message queue.

<u>Call stack counter</u>: The location in the call stack identifying the entry to whose message queue the message is to be sent. The number is relative to the message queue name parameter, indicating how many calls up the stack the target entry is from the message queue name entry. Special values are:

*	The message queue of the current call stack.
* ALLINACT	All message queues for inactive call stack entries.
* EXT	The external message queue.

<u>Message key</u>: The message file key to the message being removed.

<u>Messages to remove</u>: The message or group of messages being removed. Valid values are:

*ALL	All messages in the message queue.
*BYKEY	Only the message specified by the key parameter.
*KEEPRQS	All messages except request messages.
*NEW	All new messages in the queue.
*OLD	All old messages in the queue.

<u>Error</u>: The standard Optional Error Code Data Structure.

We code an asterisk (*) in the Message Queue field (MSGQ) indicating that we want to clear this job's message queue. We also place a 0 in the call stack counter indicating that we want to clear the message queue of the program in which this command is coded. The Message Key (MSGKY) field is left blank. The Message Type to Remove (MSGRMV) is coded with *ALL to indicate that all messages are to be removed from the message queue.

DATE CONVERSION

The warning message issued with our program in Figure 9.4 contains the date the file was last saved. To format the date in a readable format, we use the FMTMSG subroutine. This routine converts the date format from YYMMDD to MM/DD/YY.

The first thing the FMTMSG subroutine in Figure 9.4 does is call the Convert Date API. The input parameters for the convert date API are shown in Table 9.8.

Table 9.8: Required Parameter Group for the QWCCVTDT Convert Date API

Parameter	Description	Type	Size
1	Input format	Input	Char(10)
2	Date to be changed	Input	Char(*)
3	Output format	Input	Char(10)
4	Output date in new format	Output	Char(*)
5	Error	Both	Char(*)

Parameter Definitions:

Input format: Parameter 1 describes the format of the input date you want to convert. The valid values for this format are described in Table 9.9.

Date to be changed: Parameter 2 is the date format to be converted. The required format of this parameter is described in Table 9.10.

<u>Output format</u>: Parameter 3 tells the API which format to convert the date into. Valid values for this parameter are the same as for the input format with the exception of the *CURRENT format. The *CURRENT format tells the API to use the current system date format.

<u>Output date</u>: Parameter 4 is the converted date in the new format. It also follows the same data structure format as the input field.

<u>Error</u>: The optional parameter 5 is the standard Optional Error Code Data Structure (see "The Optional API Error Code Parameters" earlier in this chapter).

After executing the Convert Date API, we have the date in MMDDYY format, but the field is not in an edited format. So we need to edit the date to get it in the desired MM/DD/YY format. To perform that function, we needed to use the editing APIs.

Table 9.9: Valid Values for the First Parameter of the Convert Date (QWCCVTDT) API

Format	Description
*YMD	Year, month, day (YYMMDD).
*MDY	Month, day, year (MMDDYY).
*DMY	Day, month, year (DDMMYY).
*JUL	Julian date (YYDDD).
*SYSVAL	The format given in QDATFMT system value.
*JOB	The format given in QDATFMT job attribute.
*DTS	System time stamp format.
*CURRENT	Current machine clock time.

Table 9.10: Valid Values for the Second Parameter of the Convert Date (QWCCVTDT) API

Position	Description
1	Century digit, 0/20th, 1/21st.
2-7	Date to be converted, left justified.
8-13	Time in hours, minutes, seconds (HHMMSS).
14-16	Milliseconds (can not be blanks).

EDITING APIs

The edit function APIs allow you to take an *edit code* or an *edit word*, to create an *edit mask* and apply it to a numeric input field. Edit masks are byte strings that tell the system how to format a numeric value into an edited character field. An edit code is a standard predefined description of how a numeric value should be formatted. Edit words serve essentially the same function as edit codes, except that they are user-defined.

Edit functions are always performed in pairs. You first select your desired edit format, and then apply the selected format to an input field. The first step is to call either the Convert Edit Code (QECCVTEC) API or the Convert Edit Word (QECCVTEW) API. Either one of these APIs returns an edit mask. You then pass the edit mask along with the numeric input field to be edited to the Edit (QECEDT) API, which returns the formatted output character field.

In our case, in order to display the date as if a Y (the standard RPG date edit code) edit code has been applied (MM/DD/YY), we call the Convert Edit Code (QECCVTEC) API. The input parameters for this API are shown in Table 9.11.

Table 9.11: Required Parameter Group for the Convert Edit Code (QECCVTEC) API

Parameter	Description	Type	Size
1	Edit mask	Output	*Char(256)
2	Edit mask length	Output	Binary(4)
3	Receiver variable length	Output	Binary(4)
4	Zero-balance fill character	Output	Char(1)
5	Edit code	Input	Char(1)
6	Fill or floating currency indication	Input	Char(1)
7	Source variable precision	Input	Binary(4)
8	Source variable decimal positions	Input	Binary(4)
9	Error data structure	Both	Char(*)

Parameter Definitions:

Edit mask: Parameter 1 is the edit mask that can be applied against the numeric field we want to edit. The mask that is output in this API parameter is subsequently applied to our numeric input field when we call the Edit (QECEDT) API.

Edit mask length: The second parameter returned is the length of the edit mask returned in parameter 1. This value is also passed to the Edit (QECEDT) API.

Receiver variable length: The third parameter returned in this API is used to describe the length of the output that is produced once the edit mask is used. This value, obviously, is also passed to the Edit (QECEDT) API.

Zero-balance fill character: This parameter indicates how to handle zero-balance suppression (for those edit codes that have zero-balance suppression). This value is passed to the Edit (QECEDT) API.

Edit code: The fifth parameter is the edit code for which a mask is to be created.

Fill or floating currency indication: The sixth parameter indicates how the output should be padded; put in the character between x'41' and x'FE'.

Source variable precision: Parameter 7 is the number of positions of the field preceding the decimal point.

Source variable decimal positions: Parameter 8 is the number of digits after the decimal point.

Error data structure: Parameter 9 is the standard Optional Error Code Data Structure.

The next step is to call the Edit (QECEDT) API to apply the mask to the numeric date field. Table 9.12 shows the input requirements for the QECEDT API. After performing these two API jobs the date is in the desired format of MM/DD/YY.

Table 9.12: Required Parameter Group for the Convert Edit Code (QECEDT) API

Parameter	Description	Type	Size
1	Receiver variable	Output	Char(*)
2	Length of receiver variable	Input	Binary(4)
3	Field to be edited	Input	Char(256)
4	Class	Input	Char(*)
5	Precision	Input	Binary(4)
6	Edit mask	Input	Char(256)
7	Edit mask length	Input	Binary(4)
8	Zero-balance handling	Input	Char(1)
9	Error data structure	Both	Char(*)

Parameter Definitions:

<u>Receiver variable</u>: The edited field returned that we want as output from calling this API.

<u>Length of receiver variable</u>: The length of the preceding receiver variable. We retrieve this value when we run the Convert Edit Code (QECCVTEC) API.

<u>Field to be edited</u>: The raw data to which the edit mask is to be applied. In our example, this is the input date.

<u>Class</u>: The class parameter describes the type of raw input data. Valid entries are: *PACKED, *ZONED, *BINARY(2), or *BINARY(4).

<u>Precision</u>: Parameter 5 is the number of positions of the field preceding the decimal point.

<u>Edit mask</u>: The edit mask that can be applied against the field we want to edit. Remember that this value is retrieved by the APIs that convert the edit code or the edit word to the edit mask.

<u>Edit mask length</u>: The length of the edit mask (also retrieved from the previously run API).

<u>Zero-balance handling</u>: This parameter indicates how to handle zero-balance suppression (for those edit codes that have zero-balance suppression).

<u>Error data structure</u>: Parameter 9 is the standard Optional Error Code Data Structure.

As you can see, the amount of code necessary to apply an edit mask to a field is minimal. In this particular example, you could have used even less code by simply concatenating the month, day, and year fields with the slash to form the edited field (you have to move the numeric data to alphanumeric fields before using the CAT code). But, if you need to edit an amount field, there is no better way than with APIs. Once you have put this code into a program, it is very simple to clone and requires only minor modifications from field to field.

USER SPACES

A user space is an area created and defined by the user, and used for storing any kind of information that you want to put in it. All of the list APIs direct their output to a user space that must exist at the time the API runs. Consequently, you must be able to use the Create User Space (QUSCRTUS) API if you intend to use any of the list APIs.

The maximum size of a user space is 16 megabytes (as opposed to 2000 bytes for a data area). If you create a space that is too small to hold the complete list from the API, it is extended to the nearest memory page boundary. If the space is still too small to hold the list, the API puts as much data as possible in the space and returns an error message in the Optional Error Code parameter.

Creating User Spaces

An example of how to create a user space is shown in Figure 9.6. After this code is executed, library QTEMP contains an object called SPACENAM (of type *USRSPC) that is 1024 bytes long. The user space is initialized to value X'00', which allows the creation of the user space to execute faster than the default of *BLANKS.

Figure 9.6: Sample RPG Code to Create a User Space

```
IINPUT          DS
I                                       1  20 USRSPC
I                                       1  10 SPCNAM
I                                      11  20 SPCLIB
I                                    B  21  240LENSPC
C                     MOVEL'SPACENAM'SPCNAM
C                     MOVEL'QTEMP'  SPCLIB
C                     CALL 'QUSCRTUS'                  CREATE USER SPACE
C                     PARM          USRSPC
C                     PARM *BLANKS  ATRSPC 10
C                     PARM 1024     LENSPC
C                     PARM X'00'    VALSPC  1
C                     PARM '*CHANGE' AUTSPC 10
C                     PARM *BLANKS  TXTSPC 50
C                     PARM '*YES'   RPLSPC 10
C                     PARM          ERROR
```

Retrieving Data from a User Space

You extract data from a user space by using the Retrieve User Space (QUSRTVUS) API. This API gets information from the user space and puts it in a data area. It is relatively easy to use.

The Retrieve User Space API accepts four parameters: the name and the library that contain the user space, the starting position, the length of the data to extract, and the name of the data structure for the retrieved data.

Figure 9.7 shows an example of the code necessary to use this API. After the call to the Retrieve User Space (QUSRTVUS) API, the data structure GENDS contains whatever was in the user space beginning at location 1 for 140 bytes.

Figure 9.7: Example of the Retrieve User Space (QUSRTVUS) API

```
     IGENDS        DS
     I             DS                            140
     I                                  B    1   40STRPOS
     I                                  B    5   80STRLEN
     I                                      28  47 USRSPC
     I                                      28  37 SPCNAM
     I                                      38  47 SPCLIB
     C             Z-ADD1         STRPOS
     C             Z-ADD140       STRLEN
     C             MOVEL'SPACE'   SPCNAM
     C             MOVEL'QTEMP'   SPCLIB
     C             CALL 'QUSRTVUS'              RETRIEVE USER SPACE
     C             PARM           USRSPC
     C             PARM           STRPOS
     C             PARM           STRLEN
     C             PARM           GENDS
```

LIST APIS

The List APIs generate list information and output into a user space. You must create and maintain the user space yourself (see "User Spaces" in this chapter). The challenge when using List APIs lies in extracting the generated list from the user space because it sometimes requires several steps to retrieve the correct fields and data structures you need to get the list. It is not uncommon to have to step through several data structures to get to the information retrieved with the List APIs.

Each List API follows the same general format when putting data into a user space. For each of the List APIs, there is an input section, a general header section, and a list section.

General Header Section

The general header section is the same for each List API. It contains general information about the objective of the API, but more importantly, it contains pointers to information about the list data within the user space. In other words, the header section serves as the information directory for the information you request.

The data structure in Figure 9.8 shows the field definitions required to find the data in the user space. Table 9.13 shows all of the fields included in the general header section.

Figure 9.8: Data Structure Including Primary Fields for the General Header of the List APIs

```
IGENDS      DS
I                                          B 113 1160SIZINP
I                                          B 125 1280OFFLST
I                                          B 133 1360NUMLST
I                                          B 137 1400SIZENT
```

Table 9.13: General Header of the List APIs—All Fields

Dec	Type	Field
0	Char(64)	User area
64	Binary(4)	Size of generic header
68	Char(4)	Structure's release and level
72	Char(8)	Format name
80	Char(10)	API used
90	Char(13)	Date and time used
103	Char(1)	Information status
104	Binary(4)	Size of user space used
108	Binary(4)	Offset to input parameter section

Dec	Type	Field
112	Binary(4)	Size of input parameter section
116	Binary(4)	Offset to header section
120	Binary(4)	Size of header section
124	Binary(4)	Offset to list data section
128	Binary(4)	Size of list data section
132	Binary(4)	Number of list entries
136	Binary(4)	Size of each entry

As you can see, the RPG input specifications in Figure 9.8 differ from the chart definition in Table 9.13 by one character. This is because the chart starts at offset 0 while the input specifications must start at position 1. This is very common in most of the API charts in the SPI manual, so be aware. You will also notice that the data type is specified as a B, indicating that the data is stored in a binary format.

List Section

The list section begins in the user space at the position indicated by the field OFFLST in Figure 9.8. The number of entries in the list is indicated in NUMLST and the size of each entry is in SIZENT. Generally speaking, when using these fields, you set up a DO LOOP to step through the user space extracting an item on the list for each step.

The data residing in the list section varies, depending on the API used. Its structure is defined in the aforementioned SPI manual for each API. In general, the lists are extracted with the Retrieve User Space (QUSRTVUS) API and moved to the data structure describing the information retrieved.

Handles—Internal Identification

Some APIs require (as input) information that can only be gotten from other APIs. This type of parameter information is usually referred to as a *handle*. A handle is a temporary, system-generated, identification number used by the system to decrease the time it takes to locate information. You can think of a handle as an address that the system places in its own temporary system address book.

DISPLAY ACCESS PATH COMMAND

Now let's examine one of our favorite utilities that uses many of the different types of APIs, including a List API—the List Database Relations (QDBLDBR) API. This utility is an enhanced form of the Display Database Relations command.

To find the existing data paths that are available over a physical file on the AS/400, you generally perform the following steps:

1. Run the Display Database Relations (DSPDBR) command over the physical file in question.

2. Write down the file and library names of each logical file found on the DSPDBR display.

3. Run the Display File Description (DSPFD) command over each logical file to see if the data path you need already exists.

These steps are time-consuming and cut into your productivity as a programmer. We have written the DSPPATH command to combine those steps for you.

The DSPPATH command output looks like the example in Figure 9.9 (the code for the command is in Figure 9.12). The path for the physical file is listed first. Key fields and sequence (ascending or descending) are shown, followed by any select omit statements used. Then the path information is listed for each logical file built over the physical (even if the logical file is built in a different library than where the physical file resides).

Figure 9.9: Output from the DSPPATH Command

```
                          Display Access Paths

Physical File  . . . . . . . .:  CUSTOMER    Number of logicals. . . . .:   0013
Library  . . . . . . . . . . .:  *LIBL

Library     File       Format     Key Field Seq Select/Omit Values
FILES       CUSTOMER   CUSREC     CUSTNO    A   CUSTOMER NUMBER

FILES       CLACT3     JBYCLS     FMCLAS    A   FINANCIAL CLASS

FILES       CUSTL      CSTREC     CUSNAM    A   CUSTOMER NAME
                                  CUSDLT          O EQ '*'

FILES       CUSTLA     CSTREC     CUSNAM    A   CUSTOMER NAME
                                  CUSNUM    A   CUSTOMER NUMBER
                                  CUSDLT          O EQ '*'

FILES       CUSTLO     CSTREC     CULPMT    A   DATE OF LAST PAYMENT
                                                                  More...


    F3=Exit        F12=Previous
```

Breaking Down the Code in the DSPPATH Program

Examine the code in Figures 9.10, 9.11, and 9.12. After creating some work fields, including a user space, the program calls the GETFIL subroutine to retrieve the key field information for the physical file.

Figure 9.10: DSPDBA RPG Program

```
    FDSPDBADSCF   E                    WORKSTN
    F                                            RRN    KSFILE SFLRCD
    E              AR      4096  1
    E              A2        28  1
    E              ARYF    1000 10
    E              ARYT    1000 40
    IGENDS     DS
    I                             B 113 1160SIZINP
    I                             B 125 12800FFLST
    I                             B 133 1360NUMLST
    I                             B 137 1400SIZENT
    IINPUT     DS
    I                                1  20 USRSPC
    I                                1  10 SPCNAM
    I                               11  20 SPCLIB
    I                               21  28 OUTFMT
    I                               29  48 FILLII
    I                               29  38 FILNAI
    I                               39  48 FILLBI
    I                               49  58 RCDFMI
    ILIST      DS
    I                                1  20 MAINFL
```

```
I                               1   10 MNFILE
I                              11   20 MNLIB
I                              21   30 DEPFIL
I                              31   40 DEPLIB
I                              41   41 DEPTYP
I                              42   44 DEPRSR
I               DS          B  45  480BINREF
I                               1   20 FLDSPC
I                               1   10 FSPNAM
I                              11   20 FSPLIB
IERROR         IDS
I                           B   1   40BYTPRV
I                           B   5   80BYTAVA
I                               9   15 MSGID
I                              16   16 ERR###
I                              17  116 MSGDTA
IRCVVAR        DS             4096
I                           B  62  630FMTNUM
I                           B 317 3200QDBFOS
I                             337  338 ACCTYP
I               DS
I                           B   1   40STRPOS
I                           B   5   80STRLEN
I                           B   9  120LENSPC
I                           B  13  160RCVLEN
I                           B  17  200MSGKEY
I                           B  21  240MSGDLN
I                           B  25  280MSGQNB
I                           B  29  320FSTRPS
I                           B  33  360FSTRLN
IKEYDTA        DS
I                               1   10 DEPKEY
I                              14   14 ASEDES
IFNDSEL        DS              150
I                              70   79 FNDFMT
I                           B 117 1180NUMKEY
I                           B 130 1310SOON
I                           B 132 1350SOOF
I                           B 136 1390OFFSET
IKEYSEL        DS              150
I                               3    3 RULE
I                               4    5 COMP
I                               6   15 CMPNAM
I                           B  16  170NUMSO
I                           B  29  320SOSO
IKEYSOS        DS              150
I                           B   1   40POFSET
I                           B   5   60NL
I                              21   48 SELVAR
I               DS
I                               1   20 FFILLI
I                               1   10 FFILNM
I                              11   20 FFILLB
IFGENDS        DS
I                           B 113 1160FSIZIN
I                           B 117 1200FOFFHD
I                           B 121 1240FSIZHD
I                           B 125 1280FOFFLS
I                           B 133 1360FNUMLS
I                           B 137 1400FSIZEN
IFLIST         DS
I                               1   10 FFLDNM
I                              33   82 FFLDTX
```

```
I              DS
I**                                      1  35 SFTEXT
I                                        1   1 SFASND
I                                        3   3 SFRULE
I                                        5   6 SFCOMP
I                                        8  35 SFVALU
I             '*REQUESTER*LIBL'  C          REQSTR
C       *ENTRY  PLIST
C               PARM             FILLIB 20
C               MOVELFILLIB      OUTFIL 10
C               MOVE FILLIB      OUTLIB 10
C               MOVEL'USRSPC'    SPCNAM
C               MOVEL'QTEMP'     SPCLIB
C               MOVELOUTFIL      FILNAI
C               MOVELOUTLIB      FILLBI
C               Z-ADD116         BYTPRV
C       'QCPFMSG' CAT  'QSYS':3  MSGF
C               SETON                     53    MORE/BOTTOM
C               CALL 'QUSCRTUS'                 CREATE USER SPACE
C               PARM             USRSPC
C               PARM *BLANKS     ATRSPC 10
C               PARM 1024        LENSPC
C               PARM *BLANKS     VALSPC  1
C               PARM '*CHANGE'   AUTSPC 10
C               PARM *BLANKS     TXTSPC 50
C               PARM '*YES'      RPLSPC 10
C               PARM             ERROR
C  *
C               CALL 'QUSROBJD'                 ATTEMPT TO RETRIEVE
C               PARM             RCVVAR         OBJECT DESC
C               PARM 100         RCVLEN
C               PARM 'OBJD0100'FILFMT  8
C               PARM             FILLIB
C               PARM '*FILE'     OBJTYP  8
C               PARM             ERROR
C       MSGID   IFNE *BLANKS                    FILE DOESN'T EXIST
C               EXSR SNDMSG                     SEND MESSAGE AND
C               GOTO END                        GET OUT
C               ENDIF
C  *
C               EXSR SPACE1                     CREATE FIELDS USRSPC
C  *
C               MOVE FILLIB      SFILLB
C               MOVE *ON         FIRST   1
C               EXSR GETFIL                     WRITE ACCESS PATH
C       MSGID   CABEQ'CPF5715'   NORECS
C       MSGID   CABEQ'CPF3210'   END
C               MOVE *OFF        FIRST
C  *
C               CALL 'QDBLDBR'                  LIST DATABASE
C               PARM             USRSPC         RELATIONS TO THE
C               PARM 'DBRL0100'OUTFMT  8        USER SPACE
C               PARM             FILLII
C               PARM '*FIRST'    RCDFMI
C               PARM *BLANKS     IGNORE 10
C               PARM             ERROR
C       MSGID   CABEQ'CPF5715'   NORECS
C               Z-ADD1           STRPOS
C               Z-ADD140         STRLEN
C               CALL 'QUSRTVUS'                 RETRIEVE USER SPACE
C               PARM             USRSPC         GENERAL INFORMATION
C               PARM             STRPOS
C               PARM             STRLEN
C               PARM             GENDS
```

```
      C                    Z-ADD1         STRPOS
      C                    Z-ADDSIZINP    STRLEN
      C                    CALL 'QUSRTVUS'                    RETRIEVE USER SPACE
      C                    PARM           USRSPC              DETAIL INFORMATION
      C                    PARM           STRPOS
      C                    PARM           STRLEN
      C                    PARM           INPUT
      C                    MOVEL'USRSPC'  SPCNAM
      C                    MOVEL'QTEMP'   SPCLIB
      C         OFFLST     ADD  1         STRPOS
      C                    Z-ADDSIZENT    STRLEN
      C                    Z-ADDNUMLST    OUT#
B1    C         DO   NUMLST                                  DO FOR NUMBER OF
      C                    CALL 'QUSRTVUS'                    RETRIEVE THE LIST
      C                    PARM           USRSPC              BY WALKING THROUGH
      C                    PARM           STRPOS              THE USER SPACE.
      C                    PARM           STRLEN
      C                    PARM           LIST
      C         DEPFIL     CABEQ'*NONE'   NORECS
      C                    MOVELDEPFIL    SFILLB
      C                    MOVE DEPLIB    SFILLB
      C                    EXSR GETFIL
      C                    EXSR CLEAR
      C                    ADD  SIZENT    STRPOS
E1    C                    ENDDO
      C         NORECS     TAG
B1    C         RRN        IFGT 0
      C                    SETON                          21
E1    C                    ENDIF
      C                    WRITEFORMAT1
      C                    EXFMTSFLCTL
      C         END        TAG
      C                    SETON                          LR
      *
      C         SNDMSG     BEGSR
      C                    CALL 'QMHSNDPM'                    SEND ERROR MESSAGE
      C                    PARM           MSGID
      C                    PARM           MSGF   20
      C                    PARM           FILLIB
      C                    PARM 20        MSGDLN
      C                    PARM '*DIAG'   MSGTYP 10
      C                    PARM '*'       MSGQ   10
      C                    PARM 1         MSGQNB
      C                    PARM           MSGKEY
      C                    PARM           ERROR              ERROR CODE
      C                    ENDSR
      *
      C         GETFIL     BEGSR
      C                    CALL 'QDBRTVFD'                    GET KEY FIELD INFO
      C                    PARM           RCVVAR              FOR EACH LOGICAL
      C                    PARM 4096      RCVLEN              INTO RCVVAR
      C                    PARM           RFILLB 20
      C                    PARM 'FILD0100'FILFMT  8
      C                    PARM           SFILLB 20
      C                    PARM           RCDFMT 10
      C                    PARM '0'       OVRRID  1          NO OVERRIDES
      C                    PARM '*LCL'    SYSTEM 10          WHAT SYSTEM FILE ON
      C                    PARM '*EXT'    FMTTYP 10          INTERNAL/EXTERNAL
      C                    PARM           ERROR              ERROR CODE
      C         MSGID      CABEQ'CPF5715' ENDGET
      C                    MOVEARCVVAR    AR,1
B1    C         FIRST      IFEQ *ON
      C                    MOVE AR,9      TSTTYP  1           FOR PHYSICAL
      C                    TESTB'2'       TSTTYP             01FILE MUST BE PHYSICAL
```

```
B2   C           *IN01     IFEQ *ON
     C                     MOVE 'CPF3210' MSGID
     C                     EXSR SNDMSG
     C                     GOTO ENDGET
E2   C                     ENDIF
E1   C                     ENDIF
     *
     C                     Z-ADDQDBFOS    I         40          FILE HEADER OFFSET
B1   C                     DO   FMTNUM
     C                     MOVEAAR,I      FNDSEL
     C           OFFSET    ADD  1         S         40
B2   C           FIRST     IFEQ *OFF
     C                     EXSR CLEAR
     C                     ADD  1         RRN
     C                     WRITESFLRCD                          WRITE BLANK LINE
E2   C                     ENDIF
     C                     MOVE RFILLB    SFLIB                 FOR CLARITY
     C                     MOVELRFILLB    SFFILE
     C                     MOVELFNDFMT    SFFMT
     C                     EXSR GETTXT
B2   C                     DO   NUMKEY                          NUMBER OF KEY FIELDS
     C                     MOVEAAR,S      KEYDTA
     C                     TESTB'0'       ASEDES          79 ASCENDING/DESCENDING
B3   C                     SELEC
     C           *IN79     WHEQ *OFF
     C                     MOVE 'A'       SFASND
     C           *IN79     WHEQ *ON
     C                     MOVE 'D'       SFASND
E3   C                     ENDSL
     C                     MOVE DEPKEY    SFKEY
     C                     DO   B         C         40
B3   C           ARYF,C    IFEQ DEPKEY
     C                     MOVELARYT,C    SFVALU    P
     C                     LEAVE
     C                     ENDIF
E3   C                     ENDDO
     C                     MOVELSFVALU    SFTEXT    P
     C                     ADD  1         RRN       40
     C                     WRITESFLRCD
     C                     MOVE *BLANKS   SFLIB
     C                     MOVE *BLANKS   SFFILE
     C                     MOVE *BLANKS   SFFMT
     C                     MOVE *BLANKS   SFVALU
     C                     ADD  32        S
E2   C                     ENDDO
B2   C           SOON      IFNE *ZEROS                          SELECT/OMIT EXISTS
     C                     EXSR SELOMT
E2   C                     ENDIF
     C                     MOVE *BLANKS   SFCOMP
     C                     MOVE *BLANKS   SFRULE
     C                     ADD  160       I
E1   C                     ENDDO
     C           ENDGET    TAG
     C                     ENDSR
     *
     C           SELOMT    BEGSR
     C           SOOF      ADD  1         I1        40          OFFSET TO SEL/OMIT
B1   C                     DO   SOON
     C                     MOVEAAR,I1     KEYSEL
B2   C           COMP      IFEQ 'AL'
     C                     ITER
E2   C                     ENDIF
     C                     MOVE COMP      SFCOMP                KEY FIELD
     C                     MOVE RULE      SFRULE
```

```
     C          SOSO      ADD  1          I2        40
     C                    DO   NUMSO
     C                    MOVEAAR,I2       KEYSOS              OFFSET TO VARIABLE
     C                    MOVEASELVAR      A2
     C                    SUB  19          NL
     C          NL        IFGT *ZEROS
     C                    MOVEA*BLANKS     A2,NL
     C                    ENDIF
     C                    MOVEAA2,1        SFVALU              PART OF SEL/OMIT
     C                    MOVE CMPNAM      SFKEY
     C                    ADD  1           RRN       40
     C                    MOVE *BLANKS     SFASND
     C          SFRULE    CAT  SFCOMP:1    SFTEXT     P
     C                    CAT  SFVALU:1    SFTEXT
     C                    SETON                                59
     C                    WRITESFLRCD
     C                    SETOF                                59
     C          POFSET    ADD  1           I2
     C                    ENDDO
     C                    ADD  32          I1
  E1 C                    ENDDO
     C                    ENDSR
        *
     C          CLEAR     BEGSR
     C                    MOVE *BLANKS     SFLIB
     C                    MOVE *BLANKS     SFFILE
     C                    MOVE *BLANKS     SFFMT
     C                    MOVE *BLANKS     SFKEY
     C                    MOVE *BLANKS     SFTEXT
     C                    MOVE *BLANKS     SFCOMP
     C                    MOVE *BLANKS     SFRULE
     C                    MOVE *BLANKS     SFASND
     C                    ENDSR
       ** GET TEXT FOR EACH FIELD
     C          GETTXT    BEGSR
     C                    MOVE SFFILE      FFILNM
     C                    MOVE SFLIB       FFILLB
     C                    MOVEL'FLDSPC'    FSPNAM     P
     C                    MOVEL'QTEMP'     FSPLIB     P
     C                    CALL 'QUSLFLD'                       LIST FIELDS TO
     C                    PARM             FLDSPC                USER SPACE
     C                    PARM 'FLDL0100'LSTFMT    8
     C                    PARM             FFILLI
     C                    PARM SFFMT        RCDFMI
     C                    PARM '1'          OVRRID  1
     C                    Z-ADD1           FSTRPS
     C                    Z-ADD140         FSTRLN
     C                    MOVEL'FLDSPC'    FSPNAM     P
     C                    MOVEL'QTEMP'     FSPLIB     P
     C                    CALL 'QUSRTVUS'                      RETRIEVE USER SPACE
     C                    PARM             FLDSPC               GENERAL INFORMATION
     C                    PARM             FSTRPS
     C                    PARM             FSTRLN
     C                    PARM             FGENDS
     C          FOFFHD    ADD  1           FSTRPS
     C                    Z-ADDFSIZHD      FSTRLN
     C                    MOVEL'FLDSPC'    FSPNAM     P
     C                    MOVEL'QTEMP'     FSPLIB     P
     C          FOFFLS    ADD  1           FSTRPS
     C                    Z-ADDFSIZEN      FSTRLN
  B1 C                    DO   FNUMLS                          DO FOR NUMBER OF
     C                    MOVEL'FLDSPC'    FSPNAM     P
     C                    MOVEL'QTEMP'     FSPLIB     P
     C                    CALL 'QUSRTVUS'                      RETRIEVE THE LIST
```

```
      C                        PARM              FLDSPC             BY WALKING THROUGH
      C                        PARM              FSTRPS             THE USER SPACE.
      C                        PARM              FSTRLN
      C                        PARM              FLIST
      C                        ADD  1            B        40
      C                        MOVELFFLDNM       ARYF,B
      C                        MOVELFFLDTX       ARYT,B
      C                        ADD  FSIZEN       FSTRPS
E1    C                        ENDDO
      C                        ENDSR
        ** CREATE USER SPACE FOR LISTING FIELDS
      C          SPACE1        BEGSR
      C                        MOVEL'FLDSPC'     FSPNAM   P
      C                        MOVEL'QTEMP'      FSPLIB   P
      C                        CALL 'QUSCRTUS'                      CREATE USER SPACE
      C                        PARM              FLDSPC
      C                        PARM *BLANKS      ATRSPC 10
      C                        PARM 1024         LENSPC
      C                        PARM *BLANKS      VALSPC  1
      C                        PARM '*CHANGE'    AUTSPC 10
      C                        PARM *BLANKS      TXTSPC 50
      C                        PARM '*YES'       RPLSPC 10
      C                        PARM              ERROR
      C                        ENDSR
```

Figure 9.11: DSPDBADS Display File

```
      A                                          CF03    CF12
      A          R SFLRCD                        SFL
      A            SFLIB       10A  O  7  2
      A            SFFILE      10A  O  7 13
      A            SFKEY       10A  O  7 35
      A            SFFMT       10A  O  7 24
      A            SFASND       1   O  7 46
      A            SFTEXT      32   O  7 48
      A 59                                        DSPATR(HI)
      A          R SFLCTL                         SFLCTL(SFLRCD)
      A                                         . SFLSIZ(0024)  SFLPAG(0012)
      A                                           OVERLAY
      A 21                                         SFLDSP
      A                                            SFLDSPCTL
      A 53                                         SFLEND(*MORE)
      A                                        1 29'Display Access Paths' DSPATR(HI)
      A                                        3  2'Physical File . . . . . . . . .:'
      A            OUTFIL      10A  O  3 35DSPATR(HI)
      A                                        4  2'Library . . . . . . . . . . .:'
      A            OUTLIB      10A  O  4 35DSPATR(HI)
      A                                        6  2'Library   '     DSPATR(HI)
      A                                        6 13'File      '     DSPATR(HI)
      A                                        6 35'Key Field'      DSPATR(HI)
      A                                        6 49'Select/Omit Values'  DSPATR(HI)
      A                                        6 24'Format'         DSPATR(HI)
      A                                        6 45'Seq'            DSPATR(HI)
      A                                        3 47'Number of logicals. . . . .:'
      A            OUT#         4  OO  3 77DSPATR(HI)
      A          R FORMAT1
      A                                       23  4'F3=Exit'    COLOR(BLU)
      A                                       23 18'F12=Previous'  COLOR(BLU)
```

Figure 9.12: DSPPATH Command

```
             CMD       PROMPT('DISPLAY ACCESS PATH')
             PARM      KWD(NAME) TYPE(QUAL1) MIN(1) +
                         PROMPT('FILE NAME:')
QUAL1:       QUAL      TYPE(*NAME) LEN(10) MIN(1)
             QUAL      TYPE(*NAME) LEN(10) DFT(*LIBL) +
                         SPCVAL(*LIBL) CHOICE('NAME, +
                         *LIBL') PROMPT('LIBRARY NAME:')
```

The GETFIL subroutine calls the Retrieve File Description (QDBRTVFD) API to return all of the needed information in one variable, called RCVVAR. This variable contains different data structures, which can be in a different offset each time you run the command. The variable also contains offset pointers to indicate where each data structure is located. The RCVVAR field data is loaded into one long, generic array and then (using the offset pointer fields) parts of the array are moved into the correct data structure.

Two loops are established to get all the key field information. The first loop uses FMTNUM, which is the number of formats in the file (logical files can have more than one format). The field QBDFOS contains the offset location to key field information defined in the FNDSEL data structure.

Before we use the information in the FNDSEL data structure, we need to go and get the text description of each field in the file. This is not included in any API we have yet used, but the List Fields API (QUSLFLD) does allow us to get at this information. So, we call subroutine GETTXT, which lists the fields in the file into another user space. We walk through and load the file names and descriptions into two arrays. When it's time to write the subfile record, these arrays are used to retrieve the field descriptions. Then we use the FNDSEL structure information.

The FNDSEL structure contains the Offset (OFFSET) field, which points to an array of key field names. The field NUMKEY indicates how many key fields exist, and is used as the index for the second loop. One subfile record is written for each key field in the array.

The next step is to determine whether or not there are any select or omit statements used in the path. The FNDSEL structure also contains pointers to get at this information. SOON is the number of select/omit statements while SOOF is the offset to the array.

To get a list of all of the logicals over the physical file, the program uses the List Database Relations (QDBLDBR) API. This API produces its list in the user space that was created earlier. The Retrieve User Space (QUSRTVUS) API is then used to extract the file information for each of the logical files. This is done by first retrieving a generic header structure, which contains pointers to the space that has the file information, and then walking through the list stored in the user space until each file has been processed. For each file in the list, the GETFIL subroutine is called to perform the same functions as those performed on the physical file. Once the entire list has been processed, the information is written to the screen.

As you see when you run this command, you now have in instant "road map" of all of the paths that exist over any physical file on your system. This tool can be a real time saver when you are designing new programs.

OfficeVision/400 APIs

IBM Office programs put a great deal of functionality at your fingertips. You can send E-mail, maintain calendars, send notes, do word processing—in short, you can do almost anything a small office needs to do. And, with the wealth of APIs available, you can integrate these functions into your application seamlessly.

Controlling OfficeVision/400 Services

If you have integrated any of the office functions into your applications, you need to know about the Control Office Services (QOCCTLOF) API. This API makes requests of the office services and indicates that several office tasks will be performed. This means that, when you complete an office function (such as display a document), all of the office files and work spaces can be left open, thereby providing a significant performance improvement.

Table 9.14 shows the required input parameter group for this API. QOCCTLOF is a very simple API. You provide the request type, which can be *START, *END, or *CHECK. You also can specify the standard Optional Error Code Data Structure.

Table 9.14: QOCCTLOF—Control Office Services Input Parameters

Parameter	Description	Type	Size
1	Request type	Input	Char(10)
2	Error code	Both	Char(*)

Parameter Definitions:

Request type: Indicate the type of control you are requesting. Valid values are *START, *END, and *CHECK:

*START   Start a service block. This indicates that more office commands will be used. Office services leaves the job in such a state as to maximize the performance of subsequent office service functions. This includes leaving office files open (and you know the performance impact of opening and closing files—see Chapter 1) and leaving work spaces created and already initialized. It is your responsibility to end the service block when you are finished.

*END   End a service block. This indicates that no more office functions will be used, the office files will be closed, and the work space deleted.

*CHECK   Check to see if a service block is active. An error will be returned if a service block is not active.

Error code: The standard Optional Error Code Data Structure.

Your application should call the Control Office Services API when the application starts up, telling Office Services to power up and stay up. When your application finishes, it should call the Office Services API again, telling it to clean up and go home. These two simple calls can cut down significantly on the system overhead required to initiate OfficeVision/400.

Hierarchical File System

The first question that comes to your mind about a *hierarchical file system* is probably, "What is it?" In basic terms, it is the operating system's method of controlling the format of information that it processes.

In a relational database, information is stored in data files. These files contain records, each of which is formatted in exactly the same way. In a hierarchical file system, these files are called *stream files* because they consist of a stream of bytes with no consistent record structure.

Instead of fixed-length records, each record contains pointers that point to where information is stored in the file. In OfficeVision/400, these stream files are called *documents* because they are used to hold text. A stream file is basically a series of data structures that can be accessed using a series of pointers.

These stream files are then arranged in a multilevel structure. Data is grouped into files and files are grouped into larger units, called *directories*. In OfficeVision/400, a directory is called a *folder*. A directory does not contain data, it is simply a named grouping of files. This combination of directories and files in OfficeVision/400 is a good example of a hierarchical file system.

Processing OfficeVision/400 Documents

Let's look at how to read an OfficeVision/400 directory of all documents in a folder, read the document, and then clean up the environment when you are finished. The programming example provided (Figure 9.13) reads all of the documents in a given folder and returns the accumulated collective size.

Figure 9.13: Program to Retrieve and Accumulate the Size of All Documents in a Folder

```
    E                   AB      2000  1
    I           DS
    I                           B    1    40TABLEN
    I                           B    5    80DIRBLN
    I                           B    9   120NUMDIR
    I                           B   13   160NUMDRD
    I                           B   17   200LENDIR
    I                           B   21   240DIRPLN
    IDIRBUF     DS                      2000
    IBINARY     DS                        40
    I                           B    1    40O
    IBIN1       DS                        40
    I                           B    1    40AO
```

```
       IATRIBS      DS                           40
       I                              13   20 ANAME
       IERR         DS                           116
       I I                           B    1   40VAR1
       I              '10    '        C          DIROCN
       *
       C           *ENTRY    PLIST
       C                     PARM            FOLDER  8
       C                     PARM            SIZEA  12
       C           '/QDLS/'  CAT   FOLDER:0  DIRPAT 16 P
       C                     MOVE DIROCN     DIROIF
       C                     Z-ADD116        VAR1
       C                     Z-SUB1          TABLEN
       C                     CALL 'QHFOPNDR'             OPEN DIRECTORY
       C                     PARM            DIRHND 16
       C                     PARM            DIRPAT
       C                     PARM 16         DIRPLN
       C                     PARM            DIROIF  6
       C                     PARM ' '        TABSPC200
       C                     PARM            TABLEN
       C                     PARM            ERR
B1     C           NUMDRD    DOUEQ0
       C                     CALL 'QHFRDDR'             READ DIR ENTRIES
       C                     PARM            DIRHND
       C                     PARM            DIRBUF
       C                     PARM 2000       DIRBLN
       C                     PARM 10         NUMDIR
       C                     PARM            NUMDRD
       C ·                   PARM            LENDIR
       C                     PARM            ERR
       C                     MOVEADIRBUF     AB,1
       C                     MOVEAAB,1       BINARY
       C                     Z-ADDO          NUMENT 40
       C                     Z-ADD1          X      40
B2     C                     DO    NUMENT               FOR NUMBER OF DIR
       C                     ADD  4          X          ENTRIES FOUND, GET
       C                     MOVEAAB,X       BINARY     ATTRIBUTE INFORMATION
       C                     ADD  1          O          TABLE
       C                     Z-ADDO          P      40
       C           P         ADD  4          I      40
       C                     MOVEAAB,O       BINARY     # OF ATTRIBUTES IN
       C                     Z-ADDO          AT#    40  TABLE
B3     C                     DO    AT#
       C                     MOVEAAB,I       BIN1       ATTRIBUTE OFFSET
       C                     ADD  P          AO
       C                     MOVEAAB,AO      ATRIBS
B4     C           ANAME     IFNE 'QALCSIZE'
       C                     ADD  4          I
       C                     ITER
E4     C                     ENDIF
       C                     ADD  20         AO
       C                     MOVEAAB,AO      BINARY
       C                     Z-ADDO          SIZE   90
       C                     ADD  SIZE       TOTSIZ 120
       C                     LEAVE
E3     C                     ENDDO
E2     C                     ENDDO
E1     C                     ENDDO
       C                     CALL 'QHFCLODR'            CLOSE DIRECTORY
       C                     PARM            DIRHND
       C                     PARM            ERR
       C                     MOVE TOTSIZ     SIZEA
       C                     SETON                 LR
```

The first thing this program does is to create a path to get at the requested folder. While a path can serve basically the same function as a library list (after all, it does the same function of listing search objects), it must follow the format /QDLS/Folder name. The program then uses the path retrieved in the QHFOPNDR API to open the directory (folder).

Table 9.15 shows the required parameter group for the Open Directory (QHFOPNDR) API. One of the parameters is the attribute table, followed by a parameter defining the table length. This parameter is where you describe the information that you receive when you read the directory.

Table 9.15: Required Input Parameters for QHFOPNDR

Parameter	Description	Type	Size
1	Directory handle	Output	Char(16)
2	Path name	Input	Char(*)
3	Length of path	Input	Binary(4)
4	Open information	Input	Char(6)
5	Attribute selection table (Table 9.16)	Input	Char(*)
6	Length of attribute selection table	Input	Binary(4)
7	Error code	Both	Char(*)

Parameter Definitions

Directory handle: Handle returned by the API, to be used in other APIs. An example of this is opening and closing the directory.

Path name: Tells the system which objects to open. If the last name in the path is a specific name, then that folder is opened and all documents in that folder are read (using other APIs). If the last name in the path is a generic name, then the next-to-the-last entry in the path is presumed to be the folder name. Only documents that meet the generic entry in that folder are read.

<u>Length of path</u>: Tells the system the length of the path name.

<u>Open information</u>: A 6-byte field where each byte tells the system something about how to perform the open. Character positions and their meanings are:

Position 1 - Lock mode indicating how other jobs can access the directory.

> 0 - No lock. Other jobs can do whatever they are authorized to do.

> 1 - Deny none. Other jobs can read or change but not rename/delete.

> 2 - Deny write. Read only; no change, rename, or delete.

Position 2 - Type of open to perform.

> 0 - Normal open.

> 1 - Permanent open. End Request and Reclaim Resources do not close the directory. Directory is closed when job ends or close API in run.

Position 3 - Reserved; must be blank.

Position 4 - Reserved; must be blank.

Position 5 - Reserved; must be blank.

Position 6 - Reserved; must be blank.

<u>Attribute selection table</u>: This is where you indicate what information should be returned when reading the directory. See Table 9.4 for a complete listing of the standard attributes that you can request with this parameter.

<u>Length of attribute selection table</u>: Indicate the length of attribute selection table. If length is -1, then all attributes are returned and the attribute selection table can be blank.

<u>Error code</u>: Optional Error Code Data Structure.

Table 9.16: Attribute Selection Table

Attribute Name	Size	Description
QNAME	CHAR(*)	Current name of file or directory. Not needed with the QHFRDDR API and not allowed with the QHFCHGAT API.
QFILSIZE	BINARY(4)	The number of bytes of a file's data. This entry is ignored for directories; it is only used for files.
QALCSIZE	BINARY(4)	The number of bytes allocated for a file. It is ignored for directories.
QCRTDTM	CHAR(13)	Date and time the file or directory was created, in CYYMMDDHHMMSS format. Not allowed when creating a directory or file, only when retrieving or changing.
QACCDTTM	CHAR(13)	Date and time last accessed, in CYYMMDDHHMMSS format.
QWRTDTTM	CHAR(13)	Date and time file or directory was last written to, in CYYMMDDHHMMSS format.

Attribute Name	Size	Description
QFILATR	CHAR(10)	The type of item the directory entry is for. Positions 6 to 10 must be blank and positions 1 to 5 must be 0 (no) or 1 (yes).

Positions:

1 = Read-only file. File can not be accessed in write mode and can not be deleted.

2 = Hidden file or directory

3 = System file or directory.

4 = Entry is a directory (not a file).

5 = Changed file. |
| QERROR | CHAR(7) | An attribute returned by the QHFRDDR API when an error is encountered in retrieving the attributes of a directory entry. It contains a CPF error message ID. |

In our example, we are specifying a blank table with a length of negative 1. This is a rather dubious method of telling the API to return every possible attribute (field) that is defined for the directory. While this method is, admittedly, less efficient than specifying only the attributes in which you are interested, it does save quite a few headaches when trying to format the attribute table. This method, in turn, makes maintenance of the program far easier.

Now that the directory is open, our program needs to read it. Our example uses the Read Directory (QHFRDDR) API to accomplish this task. With this API, you give it the handle of the directory that was opened with the QHFOPNDR API. As we stated in the previous section, a handle is simply a temporary internal name given to an object. Some APIs (such as this one) require the use of handles.

The next step in our example is to tell the API how many directory entries to read at one time and then to return information on how many it actually read. When that number is 0, all of the entries in the directory have been read. Table 9.17 shows the required parameter group for the Read Directory (QHFRDDR) API.

Table 9.17: Required Parameter Group for Read Directory (QHFRDDR) API

Parameter	Description	Type	Size
1	Open directory handle	Input	Char(16)
2	Data buffer	Output	Char(*)
3	Length of data buffer	Input	Binary(4)
4	Number of directory entries to read	Input	Binary(4)
5	Number of directory entries read	Output	Binary(4)
6	Length of data returned	Output	Binary(4)
7	Error code	Both	Char(*)

Parameter Definitions

Open directory handle: The field returned from the QHFOPNDR API.

Data buffer: The name of the field where the API puts the requested information. See Figure 9.2 for the format of this data. What information gets returned in this field is dependent upon the attributes selected in the attribute selection table when the directory was opened. The QNAME attribute is always returned, but never specified, in the table thereby ensuring that there is always at least one attribute returned for every directory entry found.

Length of data buffer: The length of the field in parameter 2. It must be large enough to hold at least one directory entry. If it is not, an error is returned.

However, the Length of Data Returned parameter (parameter 6) contains the size of the data the system tried to return. You can use this field to try and correct any problem.

Number of directory entries to read: The number of directory entries to place in the data buffer.

Number of directory entries read: The actual number of directory entries placed in the data buffer. This field is 0 when there are no more entries to read.

Length of data returned: The total number of bytes returned in the buffer if the read was successful. If it was not successful because the field was not large enough to contain at least one directory entry, then this field contains the number of bytes required to hold the next directory entry.

Error code: The standard Optional Error Code Data Structure.

The field DIRBUF is loaded with as many directory entries as it can handle, within the limits of the number of buffers we requested. We ask that 10 directory entries be returned (NUMDIR = 10) with each call to the API. However, the length of the data buffer (2000) can only hold three directory entries, so that is actually how many directory entries are returned with each call to the API. If you need to improve the performance of this utility, this is the place to do it. Increasing the length of the data buffer decreases the number of calls to the API to read all of the directory entries. However, the Catch 22 is that doing this requires more memory for the program to run.

The actual number of directory entries returned from the API is stored in binary form in the first 4 bytes of the buffer. We get that number and use it to establish another loop to read the buffer. The format of the buffer is shown in Tables 9.18, 9.19, and 9.20. We then search through the buffer, looking for the attribute name QALCSIZE (Allocated Size). When we find it, we accumulate the value retrieved to calculate the size of the folder.

The last thing the program does is close the directory using the Close Directory (QHFCLODR) API. You simply supply this API with the handle that was returned in the Open Directory API and also provide it with the standard Optional Error Code Data Structure.

Table 9.18: Format of Data Buffer from QHFRDDR

Type	Field
BINARY(4)	Number of directory entries returned.
BINARY(4)	Offset to directory entry. This field is repeated for each directory entry that is returned.
Directory entry	Attribute information table for this directory entry. See Figure 9.3 for layout of attribute information table. (**Note**: Any offsets given within this table are from the beginning of the directory entry, not from the beginning of the data buffer.)

Table 9.19: Attribute Information Table

Type	Field
BINARY(4)	Number of attributes defined in the table.
BINARY(4)	Offset to the attributes. This field repeats for every attribute being defined or retrieved.

Table 9.20: Attribute Description Table

Type	Description
BINARY(4)	Length of attribute name
BINARY(4)	Length of the data returned for this attribute
BINARY(4)	Reserved
CHAR(*)	Attribute name
CHAR(*)	Attribute value
Note: The attribute descriptions repeat for every attribute in the table, as does the offset to the attribute descriptions.	

SPOOL FILE APIS

The Spool File APIs allow you to manipulate spool files. Use them to generate a list of spool files based on a given selection criteria. You can access a specific spooled file and get the attribute or data within it.

A chart of all spool files and descriptions of their functions are shown in Table 9.21. We use some of the spool file APIs in a utility that moves all spool file entries from one spool file to another.

Table 9.21: Spool File APIs and Their Functions

Name	Title	Description
QSPCLOSP	Close Spooled File	Close an open spool file.
QSPCRTSP	Create Spooled File	Create a spool file. When it is created, it does not contain any data.

Name	Title	Description
QSPGETSP	Get Spooled File	Get data from an existing spool file, previously opened by the QSPOPNSP API.
QUSLSPL	List Spooled File	Generate a list of spooled files into a user space. Selection criteria can be specified to filter the list.
QSPMOVSP	Move Spooled File	Move the spooled file to a different position within the output queue, or move it to another output queue.
QSPOPNSP	Open Spooled File	Open an existing spooled file for the QSPGETSP API, which puts the data in a user space.
QSPPUTSP	Put Spooled File	Put the data into a spooled file that was created using the QSPCRTSP API.
QUSRSPLA	Retrieve Spooled File Attributes	Put specific information about a spooled file into a field. The bigger the field, the greater the amount of information returned.

Moving Spool Files

Why would you want to do this? Because you can. But, aside from that, such spool file manipulation can be used to help ensure that all spool files for a particular job are kept together. This is a feature (Figure 9.14) that you may find handy.

Figure 9.14: Move Spool File Utility

```
E                      ARY      200  1
IGENHDR     DS
I                                 B   1    40OFFSET
I                                 B   9   120NUMLST
I                                 B  13   160SIZENT
I           DS
I                                     1   20 USRSPC
I                                     1   10 SPCNAM
I                                    11   20 SPCLIB
I                                    21   40 OUTSPL
```

```
          I                                      21   30 OUTQUE
          I                                      31   40 OUTLIB
          I                                    B 41  440STRPOS
          I                                    B 45  480LENSPC
          I                                    B 49  520NBRKEY
          I                                    B 53  560MOVLEN
          IRCVVAR     DS
          I                                    B  1   40NBRRTN
          I                                       5  204 DATAR
          IKEYDTA     DS
          I                                    B  1   40FLDRLN
          I                                    B  5   80KEYRTN
          I                                      17   26 KDATA
          I          DS
          I                                       1   10 KDATA1
          I                                    B  1   40SFLNBR
          IERROR      IDS
          I                                    B  1   40BYTPRV
          I                                    B  5   80BYTAVL
          I                                       9   15 MSGID
          I                                      16   16 ERR###
          I                                      17  116 MSGDTA
          IKEYS       DS
          I                                    B  1   40KEY1
          I                                    B  5   80KEY2
          I                                    B  9  120KEY3
          I                                    B 13  160KEY4
          I                                    B 17  200KEY5
          IMOVEDS     DS
          I                                       1   10 MSJOBN
          I                                      11   20 MSJUSR
          I                                      21   26 MSJNBR
          I                                      27   42 MSJHND
          I                                      43   58 MSSHND
          I                                      59   68 MSSNAM
          I                                    B 69  720MSSNBR
          I                                      73   82 MSOUTQ
          I                                      83   92 MSOUTL
          C          *ENTRY    PLIST
          C                    PARM           FRMQUE 10
          C                    PARM           FRMLIB 10
          C                    PARM           FRMUSR 10
          C                    PARM           TOQUE  10
          C                    PARM           TOLIB  10
          C                    MOVEL'SPLSPACE'SPCNAM      P
          C                    MOVEL'QTEMP'   SPCLIB      P
          C                    Z-ADD116       BYTPRV
     B1   C          FRMUSR    IFEQ *BLANKS
          C                    MOVEL'*ALL'    FRMUSR      P
     E1   C                    ENDIF
          C                    EXSR SPACE
          C                    MOVELFRMQUE    OUTQUE      P
          C                    MOVELFRMLIB    OUTLIB      P
          C                    MOVELTOQUE     MSOUTQ      P
          C                    MOVELTOLIB     MSOUTL      P
          C                    Z-ADD201       KEY1
          C                    Z-ADD202       KEY2
          C                    Z-ADD203       KEY3
          C                    Z-ADD204       KEY4
          C                    Z-ADD205       KEY5
          C                    Z-ADD5         NBRKEY
          C                    CALL 'QUSLSPL'            LIST SPOOL ENTRIES
          C                    PARM           USRSPC
          C                    PARM 'SPLF0200'FMTNAM  8
```

```
C                        PARM FRMUSR    USRNAM 10
C                        PARM          OUTSPL
C                        PARM '*ALL'    FORMTY 10
C                        PARM '*ALL'    USRDTA 10
C                        PARM          ERROR
C                        PARM          JOBNAM 26
C                        PARM          KEYS
C                        PARM          NBRKEY
C                        Z-ADD125      STRPOS
C                        Z-ADD116      LENSPC
C                        MOVEL'SPLSPACE'SPCNAM     P
C                        MOVEL'QTEMP'   SPCLIB     P
C                        CALL 'QUSRTVUS'                  RETRIEVE USER SPACE
C                        PARM          USRSPC             FIRST BUFFER POINTER
C                        PARM          STRPOS
C                        PARM          LENSPC
C                        PARM          GENHDR
C            OFFSET      ADD  1        STRPOS
C                        Z-ADDSIZENT   LENSPC
C                        DO   NUMLST
C                        MOVEL'SPLSPACE'SPCNAM     P
C                        MOVEL'QTEMP'   SPCLIB     P
C                        Z-ADD116      BYTPRV
C                        CALL 'QUSRTVUS'                  RETRIEVE USER SPACE
C                        PARM          USRSPC             JOB NAME INFORMATION
C                        PARM          STRPOS
C                        PARM          LENSPC
C                        PARM          RCVVAR
C .                      PARM          ERROR
C                        MOVEADATAR    ARY,1
C                        Z-ADD1        I       30
C                        DO   5
C                        MOVEAARY,I    KEYDTA
C                        SELEC
C            KEYRTN      WHEQ 201
C                        MOVELKDATA    MSSNAM     P
C            KEYRTN      WHEQ 202
C                        MOVELKDATA    MSJOBN     P
C            KEYRTN   ·  WHEQ 203
C                        MOVELKDATA    MSJUSR     P
C            KEYRTN      WHEQ 204
C                        MOVELKDATA    MSJNBR     P
C            KEYRTN      WHEQ 205
C                        MOVELKDATA    KDATA1
C                        MOVE SFLNBR   MSSNBR
C                        ENDSL
C                        ADD  FLDRLN   I
C                        ENDDO
C                        CALL 'QSPMOVSP'
C                        PARM          MOVEDS
C                        PARM 92       MOVLEN
C                        PARM 'MSPF0100'MOVFMT  8
C                        PARM          ERROR
C                        ADD  SIZENT   STRPOS
C                        ENDDO
C                        SETON                    LR
C *
C            SPACE       BEGSR
C                        CALL 'QUSCHGUS'                  ATTEMPT TO CHANGE
C                        PARM          USRSPC             USER SPACE TO ALL
C                        PARM 1        STRPOS             'X00' IF IT EXISTS
C                        PARM 4096     LENSPC
C                        PARM *BLANKS  VALSPC  1
C                        PARM '0'      STORAG  1
```

```
C                    PARM              ERROR
C         MSGID      IFEQ 'CPF9801'                       DOESNT EXIST
C                    CALL 'QUSCRTUS'                      CREATE USER SPACE
C                    PARM              USRSPC
C                    PARM *BLANKS      ATRSPC 10
C                    PARM 4096         LENSPC
C                    PARM *BLANKS      VALSPC  1
C                    PARM '*CHANGE'    AUTSPC 10
C                    PARM *BLANKS      TXTSPC 50
C                    PARM '*YES'       RPLSPC 10
C                    PARM              ERROR
C                    ENDIF
C                    ENDSR
```

Take a look at the code in the program we use to move all spool file entries from one output queue to another. The program appears in Figure 9.14.

The program accepts the output queue name and output queue library from which to do the move. It also accepts the user name that can be used to filter the selection. It then executes the space subroutine to create a user space into which the List Spooled File API can put its data. See "User Space" in this chapter for a detailed description of these APIs.

Next, we create a data structure of codes that indicate to the QUSLSPL API exactly which pieces of information about the spool file we want to put into the user space. (See Table 9.22 for a list of all of the codes that can be used.) The List Spooled File (QUSLSPL) API is then called to get the information.

Table 9.22: Code Table for Spool File APIs

Code	Type	Description
201	Char(10)	Spooled file name
202	Char(10)	Job name
203	Char(10)	User name
204	Char(6)	Job number
205	Binary(4)	Spooled file number
206	Char(10)	Output queue name

Code	Type	Description
207	Char(10)	Output queue library name
208	Char(10)	Device name
209	Char(10)	User-specified data
210	Char(10)	Status
211	Binary(4)	Total number of pages
212	Binary(4)	Current page printing
213	Binary(4)	Number of copies left to print
214	Char(10)	Form type
215	Char(2)	Priority code
216	Char(7)	Date file was opened
217	Char(6)	Time file was opened
218	Char(16)	Internal job name (handle)
219	Char(16)	Internal spooled file identifier (handle)
220	Chart(10)	Device type

The input parameter group for the QUSLSPL API is shown in Table 9.23. All spooled files in the designated output queue are included in the list. Only the spooled file name (201), job name (202), user name (203), job number (204), and spooled file number (205) are returned for each spooled file.

Table 9.23: Input Parameter Group for List Spooled File (QUSLSPL) API

Parameter	Description	Type	Size
1	User space name	Input	Char(20)
2	Format name	Input	Char(8)
3	User name	Input	Char(10)
4	Output queue name	Input	Char(20)
5	Form type	Input	Char(10)
6	User-specified data	Input	Char(10)

Optional Parameter Group 1:

Parameter	Description	Type	Size
7	Error code	Both	Char(*)

Optional Parameter Group 2:

Parameter	Description	Type	Size
8	Job name	Input	Char(26)
9	Array of codes for return data	Input	Array(*) of Binary(4)
10	Number of fields in array in parameter 9	Input	Binary(4)

Parameter Definitions:

User space name: Object name and library name of the user space to receive the generated list. Special values for library name are Current Library (*CURLIB) or Library List (*LIBL).

Format name: The format name of the system data structure that defines the format of the returned data. Valid format name values are: SPLF0100 or SPLF0200.

User name: The name of the user whose spooled files should be included in the list. Part of the filtering criteria to generate the list. It must be blank if the job name parameter is specified. Special values are: All Users (*ALL) or the Current User ID (*CURRENT).

Output queue name: Object name and library name of the output queue whose files are to be searched to determine if they are to be included in the list. These values are used as part of the filtering criteria to generate the list. Special values are: *ALL (then library part must be blank), Current Library (*CURLIB), or Library List (*LIBL) for library part of output queue name.

Form type: All files whose form type attribute matches this are to be included in the list. This field is also used as part of the filtering criteria to generate the list. Special values are: *ALL (all form types) or *STD (the system default form type).

User-specified data: All files whose user-specified data attribute matches this are included in the list. Again, this value can be part of the filtering criteria to generate the list. Special value is *ALL.

Error code: The standard Optional Error Code Data Structure.

Job name: All files whose job name matches this value are to be included in the list. Job name can also be used as part of the filtering criteria to generate the list. This parameter must be blank if the user name, output queue name, form type, or user-specified data are not blank. The job name comprises three parts:

* Job Name: Char(10) - specific name or * (indicates current job).

* User ID: Char(10) - user profile name or blanks if job name is *.

- Job Number: Char(6) - specific job number or blanks if job name is specified as *.

Array of codes for return data: Array of codes indicating which attributes to return in format SPLF0200. Only the data represented by the codes are returned by the API. The valid codes are represented in Table 9.6. If the number of keys parameter is 0, this parameter is ignored.

Number of fields in array in parameter 9: The number of entries in the array of codes parameter. Must be 0 if the SPLF0100 format is being used. If this parameter is omitted, 0 is assumed.

After the call to the QUSLSPL API, the user space contains the information we are looking for. We need to use Retrieve User Space (QUSRTVUS) API, to get the information. As with all List APIs, the format of the data contains a generic header, an input parameter section, a specific header section, and, finally, the list data section. The generic header section contains pointers to the other sections. See List APIs in Table 9.13 for a complete description of this section.

The Retrieve User Space (QUSRTVUS) API gets us the generic header, which points us to the list section and also tells us how many entries are in the list. We use that number, NUMLST, to establish a loop to walk through the user space extracting each entry in the list. See Table 9.24 for the format of the list section. Each entry in the list contains the five fields we are looking for, so we extract each field separately.

Table 9.24: Format of Lists from List Spooled File (QUSLSPL)

SPLF0100:

Offset	Type	Description
0	Char(10)	User name
10	Char(10)	Output queue name
20	Char(10)	Library name
30	Char(10)	Form type

Offset	Type	Description
40	Char(10)	User specified data
50	Char(16)	Internal job identifier (handle)
66	Char(16)	Internal spooled file identifier (handle)

SPLF0200:

Offset	Type	Description
0	Binary(4)	Number of fields returned

These fields repeat for each code requested, so the offsets varies.

Offset	Type	Description
	Binary(4)	Length of field information returned
	Binary(4)	Code for data returned
	Char(1)	Type of data
	Char(3)	Reserved
	Binary(4)	Length of data returned
	Char(*)	Data returned for specified code
	Char(*)	Reserved

Having obtained all the fields necessary to move a spool file, we now call the Move Spool File (QSPMOVSP) API to actually move the spool file to the target output queue. The required input parameters for this API are shown in Table 9.25.

Table 9.25: Input Parameter Group for Move Spool File (QSPMOVSP)

Parameter	Description	Type	Size
1	Move information data structure	Input	Char(20)
2	Length of move data structure	Input	Binary(4)
3	Format name of data structure	Input	Char(8)
4	Standard error code data structure	Both	Char(*)

Parameter Definitions

Move information data structure: The information required by the system to perform the move. It must be specified in either MSPF0100 or MSPF0200 format. See Table 9.10 for more information on these data structures.

Length of move data structure: The length of the information data structure. The minimum length for MSPF0100 is 92 and 144 for the MSPF0200 format.

Format name of data structure: The name of the format that describes the information data structure. Specify either MSPF0100 or MSPF0200 (see Table 9.26).

Standard error code data structure: The standard Optional Error Code Data Structure.

Table 9.26: Information Formats for Move Spooled File (QSPMOVSP)

MSF0100 Format:

Offset	Type	Description
0	Char(10)	From job name
10	Char(10)	From job user name

Offset	Type	Description
20	Char(6)	From job number
26	Char(16)	From internal job identifier (handle)
42	Char(16)	From internal spooled file identifier (handle)
58	Char(10)	From spooled file name
68	Binary(4)	From spooled file number
72	Char(10)	To output queue name
82	Char(10)	To output queue library name

MSF0200 Format:

Offset	Type	Description
0	Char(10)	From job name
10	Char(10)	From job user name
20	Char(6)	From job number
26	Char(16)	From internal job identifier (handle)
42	Char(16)	From internal spooled file identifier (handle)
58	Char(10)	From spooled file name
68	Binary(4)	From spooled file number
72	Char(10)	To job name
82	Char(10)	To job user name

Offset	Type	Description
92	Char(10)	To job number
98	Char(16)	To internal job identifier (handle)
114	Char(16)	To internal spooled file identifier (handle)
130	Char(10)	To spooled file name
140	Binary(4)	To spooled file number

We choose to use the MSPF0100 format, which provides the function of moving the spooled file ahead of all other spooled files on the target output queue. We are reading the source output queue in one order and moving each spooled file to the top of the target output queue, so this has the net effect of reversing the order of the spooled files on the target output queue.

If the order of the spooled files is of importance, we use the MSPF0200 format, which puts the spooled files *after* the target spooled file, thus keeping the original sequence of spooled files.

Restrictions on Moving a Spooled File

There are a number of restrictions you must consider when moving a spooled file. These are:

- You can not move a spooled file that is being held by the HLDJOB SPLFILE(*YES) command.

- A spooled file that is already printing can not be moved.

- You can not move a spooled file to follow a spooled file with an open status.

- You can not move a spooled file to follow a spooled file with a closed status, unless both spooled files are part of the same job.

- You can not move a spooled file to follow a spooled file with a deferred status, unless both spooled files are part of the same job.

- The target output queue must be defined as *FIFO (first in, first out).

- You can not move a spooled file to follow a spooled file that is printing, unless the target spooled file is the last spooled file selected by the writer. The system considers a spooled file to be printing if it is in any of the following status conditions: PND (pending), WTR (at the writer), PRT (printing), SND (being sent), or MSGW (message waiting).

- A spooled file that is at the ready, open, closed, or deferred status is changed to the held status if it is moved to follow a spooled file that is held or saved.

- A spooled file that has a status of held, open, closed, or saved is changed to ready status when it is moved to the top of an output queue.

- A spooled file that has a status of held, open, closed, or saved is changed to ready status when it is moved to follow a spooled file that has a ready status.

API Summary

Application programming interfaces provide a wide variety of functions not normally available to the RPG programmer. As with all things in life, variety breeds complexity, but that should not deter you from using these valuable tools. If you do your homework and become proficient in using APIs, you become a much better programmer in the process.

This chapter provides you with some tools, Display Path (DSPPATH) and Move Spooled Files (MOVSPL), that can help you in your everyday tasks. Using DSPPATH improves functions already provided by the operating system. Using MOVSPL provides a new tool. As you become proficient in using APIs, you will generate your own tools. When you do, feel free to contact us. We would love to hear from you.

Chapter 10

Tracking Down Problems

If none of your programs ever have bugs, you probably do not need to read this chapter...

but the fact that you are still reading means you probably are in the same boat as the rest of us.

No matter how long you have been programming, how smart you are, or how carefully you code your programs, you are going to make mistakes. We are not stating anything that you do not already know, and it should not be that discouraging to find out that you are only human.

One of the things that separates good programmers from those who go through their professional lives in mediocrity, is how quickly they can find and fix the problems that inevitably occur. The topics covered in this chapter include learning how to debug interactive and batch jobs, using journaling as a debug tool, and how to interpret and change the amount of information written to your job logs.

FINDING DEBUG IN DEPROGRAM

Debug is often the last place a programmer goes when trying to solve a problem in their RPG program. They look at the data and the code until their eyes are bugging out trying to solve the problem before going to that *last* resort.

We are here to tell you that this is the worst possible approach you can take. You need to make Debug your best friend. It should be the *first* step you take when trying to solve a programming problem. As a matter of fact, it is sometimes a good idea to place a brand new program under Debug the very first time you run it so you can step through the code and make sure the program is doing what was intended.

Have you ever heard the expression "an ounce of prevention is worth a pound of cure?" Nothing could hit closer to home than that old adage as it applies to RPG programming. Solving a problem in a program is usually 10 times harder once the program is in production. This is especially true if the program with the error happens to update database files.

The amount of programming time lost to pride and stubbornness is simply staggering. And, if your excuse has been that you did not know how to use Debug, you are just going to have to find a new one.

DEBUG 101

AS/400 Debug is a process whereby you take a program or programs and place them under a microscope while they run. You can define points in the program where the program must take a break (cleverly called breakpoints) and give you time to examine and change variables within your program while it is running. You may also add, modify, or remove breakpoints, depending upon your needs at the time. You can establish *trace* ranges where the progress of your program is recorded. You can even run Debug on programs that run in batch.

Before we get too carried away, let's lay out the various Debug commands that may be run. Table 10.1 is a list of the Debug commands and their functions.

Table 10.1: Debug Commands

Debug Command	Function
ADDBKP	Add Breakpoint tells your program when you would like it to take a break. You indicate the source statement number where you want the break to occur and what, if any, variables you want displayed at that time.
ADDPGM	Add Program allows you to put more than one of the programs in your job stream into Debug at the same time.
ADDTRC	The Add Trace command invites the system to begin recording trace data that records what is happening within your RPG program. You can specify which variables you want to trace within your program as well as the range of the source statement numbers you want the trace to include.
CHGDBG	Change Debug is used to change parameters that are specified when the Debug session is initiated.
CHGPGMVAR	The Change Program Variable command does exactly what its name states. It allows you to change variables from within your program while your program is running but is at a breakpoint.
CLRTRCDTA	The Clear Trace Data command clears out trace data that accumulates during your Debug session.
DSPDBG	The Display Debug command displays the names of the various programs that are currently under Debug as well as what the current invocation stack is.
DSPPGMVAR	The Display Program Variable command is used to see the values in your program variables. Note that you may not use parameters (PARMS) or key lists (KLIST) with this command. The system does not recognize these as valid variables, so you must specify the subfields within these elements.

Debug Command	Function
DSPTRC	Display Trace displays the various trace ranges that are currently in effect.
DSPTRCDTA	Display the Trace Data that has been accumulated so far. This data consists of the program statement numbers that were executed while the trace was in effect.
ENDDBG	The End Debug command is used to terminate the Debug environment.
ENDSRVJOB	End the Service Job. This is used when you have completed using Debug on a batch job or an interactive job running in another session.
RMVBKP	The Remove Breakpoint command removes the breakpoint assigned to the statement(s) you specify.
RMVPGM	Remove Program. Removes a program from the list of programs currently under Debug.
RMVTRC	Remove Trace removes the trace environment from all or a specific range of source statements.
STRDBG	The Start Debug command initiates the Debug environment. You specify the program name to place under Debug and whether or not you want the program to update production files or not.
STRSRVJOB	Start Service Job sets up an environment where you can debug batch jobs or interactive jobs run on other workstation sessions.

IN DEBEGINNING

Like most things in life, you can make the debugging process as simple or as complicated as you want to make it. But even the most simple Debug functions can offer you a tremendous amount of information and insight into the function of your programs.

You begin the Debug process by running the Start Debug (STRDBG) command. In it, you indicate the name of the program(s) you want to place under Debug and whether or not you want the program to be able to update production files while the program is in the Debug environment.

While it is possible to indicate more than one program name in the Start Debug (STRDBG) command, usually we do not because you can always add a program to the Debug environment using the Add Program (ADDPGM) command at some future breakpoint.

The following command starts Debug on a program named TESTPGM (specifying that production files are updated when the program runs). Note that we did not qualify the program name, so the current library list is used to find the program named TESTPGM.

```
STRDBG TESTPGM UPDPROD(*YES)
```

Unless you have test libraries on your system that were built with the type of *TEST, you should probably initiate your Debug session with the parameter of UPDPROD(*YES) so production files may be updated when the program is run. Failure to do so results in an error the first time your program tries to update a file. Obviously, the value placed in this parameter does not matter if your program(s) does not update any files or if the files being updated exist in a *TEST library.

Now our program runs under the Debug environment, but we have not indicated the functions that we want Debug to perform. If we run the program now, we do not see any results at all. We must decide if we want Debug to take a break at specified breakpoints or if we want the progress of our program to be recorded in the form of trace data, which records the sequence of the source statements that are executed. Now that we have initiated our Debug environment, we can add our breakpoint.

ADDING DEBREAKPOINT

As a general rule, most programmers that do use Debug prefer to use breakpoints as opposed to trace data (even though both may be used to complement each other). The principle reason for this is that breakpoints give the programmer more control to look at or change different variables as well as to establish different breakpoints or add other programs while the program is still running. So let us add a breakpoint prior to executing the program.

The first step in defining a breakpoint is to identify the exact source statement where you want the breakpoint to occur. To do this, the compiled program must identically match the source member you are using to identify the source statement number where the break is to occur.

If you are not sure that your program matches the source, either use the Display Program (DSPPGM) command to find out, or simply recompile the program. If you do decide to recompile and you already started Debug on the program, use the ENDDBG command to end Debug prior to compiling, or Debug will not be running on the copy of the program that you think it is testing. Once you are sure that the source member and the program match, you can go about selecting the source statement number where you want your program breaks to occur.

When selecting a source statement for your breakpoint, select a source statement that you *know* will be executed. Selecting a statement that does not get executed results in no breakpoint. It is easy to add, change, or remove breakpoints later while the program is running (provided you are at a breakpoint). Also note that the breakpoint event always occurs just *prior* to the execution of the statement where you are adding the breakpoint.

Statement numbers used when running the Add Breakpoint (ADDBKP) command need to include the positions to both sides of the decimal point. In other words, statement 84 would be specified as 8400. The SEU does not automatically resequence all source members upon exiting an edit session (depending upon your personal configuration), so there may be statement numbers in your source member that are not whole numbers.

To add a breakpoint at statement 84 of our program, specify the ADDBKP command below. In this example, we elect to display the value of the variable named FIELD at the same time the breakpoint is executed.

```
ADDBKP 8400 FIELD
```

For the purposes of brevity, the commands we use as examples in this chapter are in the most abbreviated forms that are practical. If you are curious about other parameters that may be specified in these commands, simply press F4 to prompt for the commands in lieu of pressing the Enter key.

Because we only have one program running under Debug, we do not need to worry about indicating to which program the breakpoint is added. If we have multiple programs under Debug in the same session, the breakpoint is applied against the default program unless we specify otherwise.

Our program is now in Debug and the breakpoint is set. We can add additional breakpoints, put additional programs in our call stack in Debug, or initiate a trace process (discussed later in the chapter when we cover the trace feature of Debug). But all of these actions can be performed once the Debug process is underway.

All that is left to do now is to call our program. When the program reaches a point of execution where the source statement specified in our breakpoint is about to be executed, the breakpoint display appears on our screen. It looks similar to the screen in Figure 10.1.

Figure 10.1: Breakpoint Display

```
                    Display Breakpoint

    Statement/Instruction . . . . . . . . . :  8400 /00C0
    Program . . . . . . . . . . . . . . . . :  TESTPGM
    Recursion level . . . . . . . . . . . . :  1
    Start position  . . . . . . . . . . . . :  1
    Format  . . . . . . . . . . . . . . . . :  *CHAR
    Length  . . . . . . . . . . . . . . . . :  *DCL

    Variable  . . . . . . . . . . . . . . . :  FIELD
      Type  . . . . . . . . . . . . . . . . :    CHARACTER
      Length  . . . . . . . . . . . . . . . :    2
        *...+....1....+....2....+....3....+....4....+....5
     'XX'




    Press Enter to continue.

    F3=Exit program    F10=Command entry
```

In Figure 10.1, we see that the value of our variable named FIELD is XX. Our next step probably depends upon the value of our variable. We have a number of choices. We may want to:

• Invite another program into the Debug session.

• Display other program variables.

• Add, change, or remove breakpoints.

• Change program variables.

- Start a trace on program variables or a range of program statements.

- Display our job to review the job log or see what kind of I/O activity has taken place on the files we have open.

No matter which option we pursue, the first step is getting to a command line. As you can see in Figure 10.1, pressing F10 from the Display Breakpoint screen accomplishes this goal. The command entry display appears, as seen in Figure 10.2.

Figure 10.2: Command Entry Display While Running Debug

```
                            Command Entry                          CPU
                                                    Request level:    4
 Previous commands and messages:
   > /* Breakpoint at Statement/Instruction 8400 /00C0 Program TESTPGM Recursio
     n level 1 */










                                                                   Bottom
 Type command, press Enter.
 ===> _____
      _____
      _____

 F3=Exit    F4=Prompt    F9=Retrieve    F10=Include detailed messages
 F11=Display full        F12=Cancel     F13=Information Assistant    F24=More keys
```

From the command entry screen, our options are wide open. We can basically run any command we want. One of the more likely options is to display a program variable. To display the contents of a field named CITY, you key:

        DSPPGMVAR CITY

and the value of the field appears. It looks similar to the Display Breakpoint screen in Figure 10.1.

If we want to change the value of the variable named CITY to Carlsbad, we key:

```
CHGPGMVAR CITY CARLSBAD
```

If you think about it, the ability to change variables is a very powerful feature of the Debug tool. If you isolate a problem in your program where a variable has the incorrect value, you can correct the variable while you are at a program breakpoint and then let the rest of the program run to see if you attain your desired results.

You can also use the Display Program Variable (DSPPGMVAR) and Change Program Variable (CHGPGMVAR) commands to work with arrays and indicators. For example, if you want to see the status of indicator 68, simply key:

```
DSPPGMVAR *IN68
```

The value of the indicator is displayed as a 1 if the indicator is on, or a 0 if the indicator is off.

You see the value of all indicators by keying:

```
DSPPGMVAR *IN
```

The values of all of the indicators display on the screen as if they were in an array. Figure 10.3 is an example of the display. In the example, indicators 21 and 22 are on, while the rest of the indicators (at least up through indicator 60) are off. As indicated by the plus sign (+) in the lower right corner, pressing the Page Down key reveals the values of the remaining indicators.

Figure 10.3: Displaying Program Variables While Running Debug

```
                        Display Program Variables

Program . . . . . . . . . . . . . . . . . :  TESTPGM
Recursion level . . . . . . . . . . . . . :  1
Start position  . . . . . . . . . . . . . :  1
Format  . . . . . . . . . . . . . . . . . :  *CHAR
Length  . . . . . : . . . . . . . . . . . :  *DCL

Variable  . . . . . . . . . . . . . . . . :  *IN
  Lower/upper bounds  . . . . . . . . . :    (1:99)
  Type  . . . . . . . . . . . . . . . . :    CHARACTER
  Length  . . . . . . . . . . . . . . . :    1
  Element        --------------------Values--------------------
          1   '0'   '0'   '0'   '0'   '0'   '0'   '0'   '0'   '0'   '0'
         11   '0'   '0'   '0'   '0'   '0'   '0'   '0'   '0'   '0'   '0'
         21   '1'   '1'   '0'   '0'   '0'   '0'   '0'   '0'   '0'   '0'
         31   '0'   '0'   '0'   '0'   '0'   '0'   '0'   '0'   '0'   '0'
         41   '0'   '0'   '0'   '0'   '0'   '0'   '0'   '0'   '0'   '0'
         51   '0'   '0'   '0'   '0'   '0'   '0'   '0'   '0'   '0'   '0'                    +

Press Enter to continue.

F3=Exit    F12=Cancel
```

Use the CHGPGMVAR command to change the status of indicators, just like you can any other variable. To turn on indicator 55, key:

```
CHGPGMVAR *IN55 '1'
```

From the command entry lines we may also want to add breakpoints using the ADDBKP command or remove breakpoints using the RMVBKP command. If your breakpoints fall within a logical program loop, you may not need to see your results over and over again.

USING DEBUG TO DECIPHER I/O PROBLEMS

If your questions or problems involve I/O processing, you may find that running the Display Job (DSPJOB) command is useful while you are at a breakpoint. Key the DSPJOB command from the command entry line and then see the familiar Display Job menu of options. If you choose option 14 (Display Open Files, if active), you see all of the files that are open in your job stream.

By pressing a function key, you can see all of the I/O details for each file that is currently open (this includes your display files too!). These details include the file type, the I/O count (how many reads and writes), how the file was opened (e.g., input only, update), the relative record number of the last record read (indicating where the current file pointer is), and whether or not the file was opened with a shared data path.

Depending upon where your breakpoint is set, this information can often lead to helping you solve a number of problems in your program. If the I/O count looks unusually high, you may be reading records that you did not intend to read. If the file was opened with a shared data path, you may have forgotten to reset your file pointer prior to your first read. When trying to solve data problems, this technique can often help you in your detective work.

CONDITIONAL DEBUG BREAKPOINTS

Let's talk about one of the more advanced functions of the Debug utility. Conditional breakpoints can be required if you are experiencing problems that are happening within a reiterative logical process (more commonly referred to as a loop).

It may be impractical to add a breakpoint that is happening on every step through a loop if the error you are looking for is intermittent. Instead, set a breakpoint that only occurs when certain conditions are met. A conditional breakpoint may be established using the Add Breakpoint (ADDBKP) command.

If we want a breakpoint to occur at a certain statement, but only if indicator 55 is on, we key the following:

```
ADDBKP 8600 PGMVAR(*IN55) BKPCOND(*PGMVAR1 *EQ '1')
```

In this particular example, a breakpoint occurs just prior to the execution of statement 86, but only if indicator 55 is on.

The Program Variable (PGMVAR) keyword indicates that the variable we want considered in our conditional parameter is indicator 55. The Breakpoint Condition (BKPCOND) parameter indicates that the condition is based upon the first variable (in our variable list specified with the PGMVAR parameter) and we only want the breakpoint executed if the indicator field was a 1 (meaning that it is on).

Another option for conditional breakpoints is the ability to skip iterations of a loop. For example, if you want a loop to be executed 50 times prior to displaying your breakpoint:

```
ADDBKP 8600 PGMVAR(*IN55) SKIP(50)
```

In this example, statement 86 is executed 50 times before the breakpoint appears and the value of indicator 55 is displayed.

Conditioned breakpoints can get more complicated than this by including more variables and more complex conditional equations, but you need to consult the IBM manuals if you want to get that fancy.

USING TRACE TO FOLLOW WHERE YOU HAVE BEEN

As a general rule, where you are going is probably more important to you than where you have been. An obvious exception to this rule is when you are trying to debug a program. If you can see what the program did prior to the error, it is easier to see why the error occurred. The good news, of course, is that you can if you utilize the trace function of Debug.

When you run the ADDTRC command while in the Debug environment, the system begins to accumulate trace data for the statement numbers you specify. This trace data is actually a road map of where the program has been. The source statement number of each statement executed is logged in the trace data and can be displayed via the Display Trace Data (DSPTRCDTA) command.

The trace function is also used to record changes in variables. Depending upon how you set up the trace, you can log the value of your variable every time it is referenced within your trace statement range, or only when the variable is changed.

Before you run the ADDTRC command, however, you need to be aware that the default number of statements within a Debug session is only 200 statements. When Debug is running, your program executes until the maximum number of statements has been logged (200 statements in this case) and the program stops as if a breakpoint has been encountered (Figure 10.4). A message is issued, informing you that the maximum number of trace statements has been recorded. At that point, you may display, clear, or reset your trace data requirements.

Chapter 10—Tracking Down Problems

Figure 10.4: Maximum Number of Debug Trace Statements Reached

```
                        Display Breakpoint

  Statement/Instruction . . . . . . . . . :   L000003 /0CEF
  Program . . . . . . . . . . . . . . . :    TESTPGM
  Recursion level . . . . . . . . . . . :    1

















  Press Enter to continue.

  F3=Exit program    F10=Command entry
Maximum number of traced statements reached.
```

The 200-statement default for maximum number of trace statements is established when you run your Start Debug (STRDBG) command. You could easily set your maximum number of statements to something else by specifying the MAXTRC parameter when starting Debug, or use the Change Debug (CHGDBG) command if Debug is already running. You may even want to set the maximum number of trace statements to one (MAXTRC 1) so the system breaks at each line of the code processed. This allows you to step through the code of your program one statement at a time.

Another trace option that is established when running the Start Debug (STRDBG) and Change Debug (CHGDBG) commands is whether or not the trace data should wrap. As we have already established, a breakpoint is displayed when the maximum number of trace statements is reached, as long as we take the default options. But, if we want the program to continue running when the maximum number of trace statements is reached, we instruct the Debug program to wrap new trace statements over the oldest trace statements.

Let's start a trace using the default settings established when we ran our Start Debug (STRDBG) command. In this example, we let Debug trace all of our source statements and we do not track the contents of any variables:

```
ADDTRC
```

This command begins our trace and logs the statement numbers of all statements executed. When the default maximum number of 200 trace statements is logged, a display appears that looks something like that in Figure 10.4.

We could have specified a statement number range of statements where we wanted the trace data collected. To specify a range, key:

```
ADDTRC STMT(13100 50500)
```

In the example above, trace data is collected for statements between 131 and 505.

When this display appears, the system has logged 200 trace statements, but we need to run the Display Trace Data (DSPTRCDTA) command if we want to see them. We first press F10 to get to our Command Entry screen, and then key:

```
DSPTRCDTA
```

By taking the defaults on this command, the trace data is displayed on the screen. It looks something like Figure 10.5.

Figure 10.5: Displaying Debug Trace Data

```
                         Display Trace Data

                Statement/
Program         Instruction        Recursion Level      Sequence Number
TESTPGM         .ENTRY                  1                     1
TESTPGM         *INIT                   1                     2
TESTPGM         .OPEN                   1                     3
TESTPGM         .OPEN                   1                     4
TESTPGM         .OPEN                   1                     5
TESTPGM         .OPEN                   1                     6
TESTPGM         .OPEN                   1                     7
TESTPGM         .OPEN                   1                     8
TESTPGM         12000                   1                     9
TESTPGM         12100                   1                     10
TESTPGM         12200                   1                     11
TESTPGM         12300                   1                     12
TESTPGM         B0000000                1                     13
TESTPGM         B0000014                1                     14
TESTPGM         12900                   1                     15    +

Press Enter to continue.

F3=Exit    F12=Cancel
```

As you can see, the statements or instructions executed have been logged in the trace data and reflect the sequence the program processed them. In the preceding example, we could have elected to print the trace data instead of bringing it up to the screen. To do so we key:

    DSPTRCDTA OUTPUT(*PRINT)

Our trace data buffer is now full, so we must clear the buffer to continue our trace. There are two ways to do this. We could clear the buffer when we display the trace data by employing the CLEAR parameter:

    DSPTRCDTA CLEAR(*YES)

The data is cleared as we display it. But we may not want to clear the buffer until we have had a chance to review the data. If this is the case, use the CLRTRCDTA (Clear Trace Data) command. There are no parameters on this command, you simply key CLRTRCDTA while you are at a breakpoint and the buffer is cleared.

USING TRACE TO TRACK THE CONTENTS OF VARIABLES

One of the more valuable features of the trace function is the ability to track references and changes in contents of program variables. Doing so is merely a function of the Add Trace (ADDTRC) command.

To log trace data for a variable named FIELD, key:

```
ADDTRC PGMVAR(FIELD)
```

At the beginning of the trace and each time the variable named FIELD is changed, the modification is automatically logged into the trace data. When you run the DSPTRCDTA command, it looks something like the example in Figure 10.6.

Figure 10.6: Tracking Changes in Variables with Debug Trace Data

```
                         Display Trace Data

                  Statement/
Program           Instruction          Recursion Level      Sequence Number
TESTPGM           L000006                    1                      203

  Start position  . . . . . . . . . . . . . : 1
  Length  . . . . . . . . . . . . . . . . . : *DCL
  Format  . . . . . . . . . . . . . . . . . : *CHAR
  Variable  . . . . . . . . . . . . . . . . : FIELD
    Type  . . . . . . . . . . . . . . . . . :   CHARACTER
    Length  . . . . . . . . . . . . . . . . :   5
    *...+....1....+....2....+....3....+....4....+....5


                  Statement/
Program           Instruction          Recursion Level      Sequence Number
TESTPGM           L000007                    1                      204
TESTPGM           L000008                    1                      205   +

Press Enter to continue.

F3=Exit   F12=Cancel
```

The value of the variable named FIELD is logged within the trace data each time the variable is changed. If we wanted to log each time the variable not only is changed, but is referenced at all, we could do so with the OUTVAR parameter of the ADDTRC command:

```
ADDTRC PGMVAR(FIELD) OUTVAR(*ALWAYS)
```

In the preceding example, each and every reference to the variable named field is automatically logged in the trace data.

DEBUGGING BATCH JOBS

Now that we have discussed the basics of starting Debug, setting breakpoints, and displaying program variables, it is time to talk about batch jobs. As you have probably noticed, all of the Debug data we displayed was brought up to the screen. That is great when we are talking about an interactive program, but what do we do when it is a batch program that needs to be diagnosed?

Starting the Service Job

To run Debug on a batch program, you need to use a feature called a *service job*. Before initiating the service job, you need three components that describe the job you are debugging: the job name, the user, and the job number.

Finding this information is easy if the program happens to be at an error message or is already running (does the phrase *in a loop* come to mind?). You can use Work with Active Jobs (WRKACTJOB) or Work with Submitted Jobs (WRKSBMJOB) to find the job in question and then take the option that says "Work with Job." You will find all three parameters you need displayed at the top of the screen as shown in Figure 10.7.

Figure 10.7: Work with Job Display

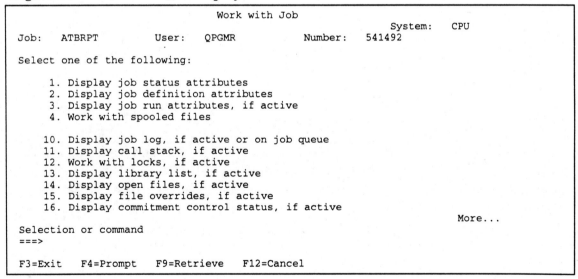

```
                         Work with Job
                                               System:    CPU
  Job:    ATBRPT        User:    QPGMR        Number:    541492

  Select one of the following:

        1. Display job status attributes
        2. Display job definition attributes
        3. Display job run attributes, if active
        4. Work with spooled files

       10. Display job log, if active or on job queue
       11. Display call stack, if active
       12. Work with locks, if active
       13. Display library list, if active
       14. Display open files, if active
       15. Display file overrides, if active
       16. Display commitment control status, if active
                                                          More...
  Selection or command
  ===>

  F3=Exit   F4=Prompt   F9=Retrieve   F12=Cancel
```

If the job is already running, you need to put the job on hold. This is easily accomplished while you are in the WRKACTJOB or WRKSBMJOB commands, by simply following the prompts on the screen.

On the other hand, if the job you want to debug is not already running, you need to go about it a little differently. You do not want the job to begin running until you have initiated the service job.

Place the job queue on hold using the HLDJOBQ command and then submit the job. Placing the job queue on hold does not stop existing programs from running, but it will keep new jobs in the queue from being initiated.

The next step is to submit your job. You can then use the WRKSBMJOB to get the job identification parameters so you can start the service job.

By now, you should have written the job name, user, and number down. Key in:

    STRSRVJOB

and press F4. You should see a screen that looks like Figure 10.8.

Figure 10.8: Starting a Service Job

```
                    Start Service Job (STRSRVJOB)
Type choices, press Enter.
Job name . . . . . . . . . . . JOB          atbrpt
  User . . . . . . . . . . .                qpgmr
  Number . . . . . . . . . .                541492
                                                          Bottom
F3=Exit   F4=Prompt   F5=Refresh   F10=Additional parameters   F12=Cancel
F13=How to use this display       F24=More keys
```

You may want to use a shortcut by keying the STRSRVJOB command while you are on the Work with Job display. The parameters you need to run the STRSRVJOB command are already at the top of your screen and may be entered right to left. For example, if you are at the display seen in Figure 10.7, and you want to start your service job, key:

    STRSRVJOB 541492/QPGMR/ATBRPT

Using this method, you begin your service job from the command line on the Work with Job display. Let's move on to the next step.

Starting Debug on the Batch Job

Now that you have started the service job, you need to put the program into Debug. You may now use the STRDBG command just as if you are putting an interactive program into Debug, but the system will not let you add your breakpoints until the job actually begins.

It is time to release the job queue using the RLSJOBQ command. The system sends a break message when your job is ready to begin. The message looks something like that displayed in Figure 10.9.

Figure 10.9: The Start Serviced Job Display

```
                         Start Serviced Job
                                               System:    CPU
   Job:    ATBRPT         User:    QPGMR        Number:    541580

   The serviced job has been released from the job queue.  Press Enter to
   start the job or F10 to enter debug commands for that job.








   Press Enter to continue.

   F10=Command entry
   (C) COPYRIGHT IBM CORP. 1980, 1993.
```

DEFINING YOUR BREAKPOINTS

At this point, you must key F10 to get to a command entry screen. Your program is in Debug, but you have not told the system where you want it to break. To do that, use the ADDBKP or ADDTRC functions, as previously described, to define where you want your program to stop, just as you would if debugging an interactive job.

Perform the rest of the Debug functions as if the program is interactive. That is all there is to it! When the job is complete, you get another break message informing you that the job being serviced has ended (do not confuse this with ending the service job).

Once the message has been delivered, you need to end both Debug and the service job. This can be accomplished by using ENDDBG and ENDSRVJOB accordingly. Failure to perform these cleanup functions could result in some rather unintentional and undesirable results later in your session.

JOURNALING AS A DEBUG TOOL

Every once in a while, we hear about this data file that is mysteriously changing by itself. There seems to be no rhyme or reason to it. And, because 24 different programs in 7 different libraries are used to update this file, tracking down this anomaly is no small task. But wait! There is hope. You can use journaling to narrow down your search for the culprit.

Journaling is a process that, when employed, records changes made to a physical file in an object called (appropriately enough) a journal receiver. These changes are recorded as journal entries, and are much like the journal entries you would find in a general ledger. The purpose of each is the same: record a path that may be followed if you ever have to go back.

Generally speaking, journaling is used for automatic error recovery and is necessary if you use commitment control. But, for our purposes, we use it to help us track down the source of our wayward data.

Before you get too far into this subject, be aware that this technique can often take quite a bit of disk space. Depending upon how much activity occurs involving the file in question, and how long it is between the intermittent data error you are looking for, the journal of file changes can get quite large. The journal does not only record what has changed in the record, but, in fact, copies the entire record that is changed as well as recording the who, when, and where of the change. You obviously incur additional I/O while journaling is active, which may impact overall system performance. Like most things in life, you need to determine whether the potential benefits outweigh the cost.

Journaling 101

To perform journaling, you need to concern yourself with two principle components: the journal receiver and the journal itself. On the AS/400, it is the journal receiver that actually holds the journal entries (changes to the file, in our case). The journal itself is more like a directory of which file is being journaled, which receivers exist in the journal, and a variety of other information that describes the journal itself. Think of the journal as the header file when you have a system that has a header/detail record relationship (where the receiver is the detail record).

You need to create the journal receiver and then the journal. In the past, it was up to the programmers and operators to maintain the journal receivers. Failure to do so results in a situation where disk space gets gobbled up rapidly.

With the announcement of V3R1 came an improvement to the Create Journal (CRTJRN) command. Now you can elect to have the journal receivers managed by the system itself. If you specify a threshold size when the journal receiver is created, and use the Manage Receiver (MNGRCV) parameter when the journal is created, the system cleans up your journal receivers for you. The operating system checks to see if your receiver has reached its threshold size at system IPL time. If the threshold is reached, the system detaches the active receiver from the journal and automatically creates and attaches a new receiver in its place. Once this action has been performed, the freshly deactivated journal may be saved (if desired) and deleted from the system to free up valuable disk space. Realizing that not everyone is on V3R1 yet, we have elected to use self-managed journal receivers for our examples here.

Before creating the journal, we must first create the receiver that will initially contain our journal entries. In the first example, we create a journal receiver called CUSTRCV in a library called TESTLIB. This is done by keying the following command:

```
CRTJRNRCV JRNRCV(TESTLIB/CUSTRCV)
```

We then create a journal named CUSTJRN in library TESTLIB by keying the following command:

```
CRTJRN JRN(TESTLIB/CUSTJRN) JRNRCV(TESTLIB/CUSTRCV)
```

Note that we have indicated in the Create Journal (CRTJRN) command the name of the initial receiver that is used to store our journal entries.

After those two simple commands, you are ready for your detective work. All you need to do to activate journaling is to run the Start Journal Physical File (STRJRNPF) command. To begin journaling our file named CUSTOMER in library TESTLIB, we simply key:

```
STRJRNPF FILE(TESTLIB/CUSTOMER) JRN(CUSTJRN)
```

Now that journaling is active, our journal records everything that happens to our CUSTOMER file. That includes every time the file is opened, closed, or saved. Every time a record is written, deleted, or updated. Every time the file is touched!

Reading the Journaling Results

Anytime we want to see all of the recorded journal entries for our CUSTOMER file, we key the following command:

```
DSPJRN JRN(TESTLIB/CUSTJRN)
```

A display similar to that in Figure 10.10 appears on screen. For the purposes of our example, though, we see a little too much information. We do not really care when the file was opened, closed, or saved. We are more interested in knowing who, what, and when a program is updating our file. Thankfully, the Display Journal (DSPJRN) command allows us to filter out the journal entries we do not want to see.

Figure 10.10: Output from the Display Journal Entry (DSPJRN) Command

```
Display Journal Entries ·

Journal  . . . . . . :   CUSTJRN        Library  . . . . . . :     TESTLIB

Type options, press Enter.
  5=Display entire entry


Opt    Sequence   Code   Type   Object      Library    Job         Time
             5      R      PT    CUSTOMER    TESTLIB    DEVELOP1    14:33:57
             8      R      PT    CUSTOMER    TESTLIB    DEVELOP1    14:34:10
            11      R      UP    CUSTOMER    TESTLIB    DEVELOP1    14:35:05
            14      R      UP    CUSTOMER    TESTLIB    DEVELOP1    14:36:57
            19      R      PT    CUSTOMER    TESTLIB    DEVELOP2    14:46:26
            22      R      PT    CUSTOMER    TESTLIB    DEVELOP2    14:47:34
            25      R      PT    CUSTOMER    TESTLIB    DEVELOP1    14:49:11
            28      R      PT    CUSTOMER    TESTLIB    DEVELOP2    14:50:33
            32      R      DL    CUSTOMER    TESTLIB    DEVELOP2    14:51:03
            35      R      PT    CUSTOMER    TESTLIB    DEVELOP1    14:51:28



F3=Exit    F12=Cancel
```

To see only journal entries where a record was changed, key the following command:

```
DSPJRN JRN(TESTLIB/CUSTJRN) JRNCDE((R))
```

The output from the DSPJRN command is a screen similar to the one in Figure 10.10. Note that all entries under the Code heading are an R, indicating that we are looking at journal entries where a record has been changed. Under the Type heading, you see the various type codes indicating the type of update that was performed. The PT code indicates that a record was added or posted, the UP code indicates an update, the DL indicates where a record was deleted, and so on. You can place the cursor on the type field and press HELP to get a more complete list of the possible codes.

If you see an entry that piques your interest, you can key a 5 in front of that entry and press Enter to see a more detailed accounting of the journal entry. You are presented with a display that is similar to Figure 10.11.

Figure 10.11: Entry-specific Data Displayed with the DSPJRN Command

```
                          Display Journal Entry

   Object . . . . . . . :   CUSTOMER       Library . . . . . . :   TESTLIB
   Member . . . . . . . :   CUSTOMER.      Sequence . . . . . . :   11
   Code . . . . . . . . :   R  - Operation on specific record
   Type . . . . . . . . :   UP - Update, after-image

               Entry specific data
   Column       *...+....1....+....2....+....3....+....4....+....5
   00001        '0000000004Appleton, Josephine                   '
   00051        '2368 North Avenue          San Diego            '
   00101        '          CA92126000000010'



                                                             Bottom
   Press Enter to continue.

   F3=Exit    F6=Display only entry specific data
   F10=Display only entry details    F12=Cancel    F24=More keys
```

The entry-specific data that is displayed may look scrambled if packed data exists in the record. If you want your detective to tell you who, what, when, and where, simply press F10 (Display only entry details). You are presented with a display similar to Figure 10.12, which tells you all of the above.

Figure 10.12: Entry Details Displayed via the DSPJRN Command

```
                    Display Journal Entry Details

   Journal  . . . . . . :    CUSTJRN         Library  . . . . . . :    TESTLIB
   Sequence . . . . . . :    11

   Code . . . . . . . . :    R  - Operation on specific record
   Type . . . . . . . . :    UP - Update, after-image

   Object . . . . . . . :    CUSTOMER        Library  . . . . . . :    TESTLIB
   Member . . . . . . . :    CUSTOMER        Flag . . . . . . . . :    0
   Date . . . . . . . . :    05/31/95        Time . . . . . . . . :    14:35:05
   Count/RRN  . . . . . :    5               Program  . . . . . . :    MNTCUST

   Job  . . . . . . . . :    600955/CPUPGMR/DEVELOP1
   User profile . . . . :    CPUPGMR         Ref Constraint . . . :    No
   Commit cycle ID  . . :    0               Trigger  . . . . . . :    No



   Press Enter to continue.

   F3=Exit    F10=Display entry    F12=Cancel    F14=Display previous entry
   F15=Display only entry specific data
```

It is entirely possible that your journal contains too many entries to make this particular method practical, or that the data you are looking for is contained in a packed field. If either of these situations is the case, you may want to display the information to an outfile. You could then code an RPG program that processes the outfile and, from there, narrow down your search.

When displaying a journal to an outfile, the Display Journal (DSPJRN) command puts the first 100 bytes per record of your data into a single field that is a default length of 100 bytes. If you need to see more than the first 100 bytes of your file (we need 126 bytes in our CUSTOMER file example), use the ENTDTALEN parameter of the DSPJRN command or your data is truncated automatically.

To send our CUSTOMER file journal entries to an outfile named JOURNOUT in library TESTLIB, key:

```
DSPJRN JRN(TESTLIB/CUSTJRN) JRNCDE((R)) OUTPUT(*OUTFILE)
OUTFILE(TESTLIB/JOURNOUT) ENTDTALEN(126)
```

The *after* picture of the complete record is stored in a single field named JOESD (Journal Entry Specific Data). We could use the substring function of QRYDTA to parse out the data we are looking for. But we have found that looking at individual fields in the after picture is easier if you use an RPG program.

We do this by moving the JOESD field to an external data structure of the same name as the file being journaled. For the example in Figure 10.13, we simply use our CUSTOMER physical file as an external data structure within our program. We did not code a File Specification for the customer file, because our program uses the description of the customer file and not the actual file itself.

Figure 10.13: RPG Code to Process a Display Journal (DSPJRN) Outfile

```
FJOURNOUTIF  E                        DISK
IOUTFMT      E DSCUSTOMER
C                       READ JOURNOUT                   50
C             *IN50     IFEQ *OFF
C                       MOVELJOESD      OUTFMT
C                       ENDIF
```

The RPG program in Figure 10.13 could be used to read and interpret the data from the journal entries. Our example is incomplete, in that you would probably want to perform some sort of selective process to narrow down your search and then either send the data to a database file or to the printer.

Changing Receivers

Receivers can have voracious appetites. If left alone, one receiver can easily eat up your disk space without even belching. You can only curb its appetite by killing it. Before you can kill it (by deleting the journal receiver), you must detach it from the journal. To do so, issue the following command:

```
CHGJRN JRN(CUSTJRN) JRNRCV(*GEN)
```

This command detaches the Current Receiver (CUSTRCV), creates a new journal receiver, and attaches the new receiver to the journal. The name of the new receiver is the name of the old receiver with a four-digit sequence number attached to the end of the name. In our example, the name of the new receiver is CUSTRC0001. Notice that the sequence number automatically replaces the last digit of the receiver name because the original receiver name was seven characters long. If you prefer, make up your own name for the new receiver and enter it instead of *GEN.

You are now free to kill the beast and get back all of the storage it ate. Issue the command:

```
DLTJRNRCV RCV(TESTLIB/CUSTRCV)
```

If you have not saved the receiver, you get the error message:

```
CPA7025 - Receiver CUSTRCV in TESTLIB never fully saved. (I C).
```

Reply to the message with an I to ignore it, and the receiver is deleted.

Remember to Clean Up Your Mess

Once you have isolated your problem, you need to end journaling and clean up your disk. Before you can delete the journal, you must tell the system to stop journaling the file. You do that by issuing the command:

```
ENDJRNPF FILE(TESTLIB/CUSTOMER)
```

You can then delete the journal by issuing the command:

```
DLTJRN JRN(TESTLIB/CUSTJRN)
```

If you have created other receivers, do not forget to delete them.

JOB LOGS AND PROBLEM DETERMINATION

Job streams can get incredibly long and complex. Tracking down problems can become very difficult when dealing with these types of jobs. Sometimes your problem is hidden, and solving it is mostly a matter of figuring out how to retrieve more information from your system than is currently being offered. That is where the job log comes in.

Every job has a job log. If you are signed on and running an interactive session, your job log can keep track of the commands you are running, the messages you get, and the commands that are run within the CL programs you call. The amount of information written to your job log is generally controlled by the job description you are currently running (more on this later in the chapter when we discuss logging levels).

When you are in an interactive session, your job log is maintained while your session is active and then is generally deleted when you sign off (depending upon how your system is configured and the parameters specified when running the Signoff command). A batch job has its own job log that can be seen via the Work with Submitted Jobs (WRKSBMJOB) command when you choose the option to review spooled files.

The job log can be the key to solving a problem that may not result in a visible error message. To see what is in your own job log, simply key Display Job Log (DSPJOBLOG) and press Enter, as we have done in Figure 10.14. Notice that you can display additional detail by pressing F10 to see a screen similar to that in Figure 10.15. You are probably already familiar with these displays, because they are accessible from so many other commands like Work with Submitted Jobs (WRKSBMJOB), Work with Active Jobs (WRKACTJOB), and Display Job (DSPJOB).

Figure 10.14: Output from the DSPJOBLOG Command

```
                           Display Job Log
                                                  System:     CPU
     Job . . :   WORKSTN1      User . . :   QPGMR      Number . . . :    885343

     3>> dspjoblog




                                                                    Bottom
     Press Enter to continue.

     F3=Exit    F5=Refresh    F10=Display detailed messages    F12=Cancel
     F17=Top    F18=Bottom
```

Figure 10.15: Detailed Messages Displayed from the DSPJOBLOG Command

```
                           Display All Messages
                                                  System:     CPU
     Job . . :   WORKSTN1      User . . :   QPGMR      Number . . . :    885343

          QINTER in QSYS. Job entered system on 08/26/95 at 07:38:32.
     > /*        */

     3 > DSPJOBLOG
     3 > CHGJOB
     3 > dspjoblog
     3 > wrkactjob
     3 > wrksbmjob
     3 > SAVLIB LIB(TEST)
     3 > DSPJOBLOG
     3 > wrkactjob
     5 > wrkoutq
     3>> dspjoblog
                                                                    Bottom
     Press Enter to continue.

     F3=Exit    F5=Refresh    F12=Cancel    F17=Top    F18=Bottom
```

The Display Detailed Messages screen (displayed by pressing F10 on the Display Job Log screen) shows the various commands that were run by the job. The job invocation level is also displayed directly preceding each command. The invocation level tells you how deeply nested a command is within a job.

You can also use the DSPJOBLOG command to look at job logs of other users or jobs other than that of your current session (depending upon your security configuration) by specifying additional parameters. You can see the parameters when you press F4 after keying the command.

How Much Information is Being Recorded in My Job Log?

The level of detail recorded in your job log is primarily a function of your message logging level and whether or not your job is recording CL program commands. Most systems are configured to record relatively little information because there is a performance hit that occurs when all commands and messages are being recorded in the job log.

Finding out how much information currently is being recorded in your job log is simple. Just run the Display Job (DSPJOB) command and choose the option to Display Job Definition Attributes. You should see a display similar to Figure 10.16.

Figure 10.16: Determining Message and CL Program Command Logging Levels

```
                     Display Job Definition Attributes
                                                 System:    CPU
     Job:    WORKSTN1       User:    QPGMR        Number:    885343

     Job description . . . . . . . . . . . . . . . . . :   JOBDESC
       Library . . . . . . . . . . . . . . . . . . . . :   QGPL
     Job queue . . . . . . . . . . . . . . . . . . . . :
       Library . . . . . . . . . . . . . . . . . . . . :
     Job priority (on job queue) . . . . . . . . . . . :
     Output priority (on output queue) . . . . . . . . :   5
     End severity  . . . . . . . . . . . . . . . . . . :   30
     Message logging:
       Level . . . . . . . . . . . . . . . . . . . . . :   4
       Severity  . . . . . . . . . . . . . . . . . . . :   0
       Text  . . . . . . . . . . . . . . . . . . . . . :   *SECLVL
     Log CL program commands . . . . . . . . . . . . . :   *NO
     Printer device  . . . . . . . . . . . . . . . . . :   NOPRINT
     Default output queue  . . . . . . . . . . . . . . :   NOPRINT
       Library . . . . . . . . . . . . . . . . . . . . :   QGPL
                                                             More...
     Press Enter to continue.

     F3=Exit   F5=Refresh   F12=Cancel   F16=Job menu
```

As we mentioned before, the information displayed here is a byproduct of the job description (in this case the JOBDESC job description in library QGPL). As is the case with most things on the AS/400, these parameters may be overridden. Our areas of interest for the purposes of this topic are whether or not your job records CL program commands and what the message logging level settings for your jobs happen to be.

Logging Commands within CL Programs

If your job has been defined to log CL program commands, commands within CL programs are recorded in your job log when they are encountered. This is handy because it establishes an audit trail in your job log similar to that of the trace feature of Debug.

Message Logging

The message logging settings are based on three principle components: the message logging level, message severity, and message text level. The relationship of the three components determines which messages to filter from the job log and which ones to leave in.

Message logging level: This parameter is used to tell the system how severe a message should be before it is logged into your job log. The possible values are 0 through 4.

0 - No messages are logged.

1 - Job start, completion, and completion status messages are logged. Also, all messages with a severity level greater than or equal to that indicated in the message severity parameter.

2 - All information recorded at level 1 plus any commands keyed or from within a CL program that result in a message with a severity level greater than or equal to that indicated in the message severity parameter.

3 - All information recorded at level 2, plus any commands keyed or called from within a CL program.

4 - All information recorded at level 3, plus any trace messages as well.

Message severity: This parameter is used in conjunction with the previous message logging level parameter to indicate how severe an error should be before it is logged into the job log.

Message text level: This parameter is used to indicate how much data should be recorded in the job log when an error occurs that meets the criteria specified with the two prior parameters. These are:

*MSG   Only the message text of the error is recorded.

*SECLVL The message text and the help text associated with the error are recorded in the job log.

*NOLIST A job log is not produced unless the job ends abnormally. If a job log is created, the message text and the associated help text are recorded in the job log.

Changing Job Logging Levels

The logging level of a job may be changed on a temporary or permanent basis depending upon your needs. If you want to change the logging level of your interactive session so it will record the most information possible, key:

```
CHGJOB LOG(4 0 *SECLVL) LOGCLPGM(*YES)
```

On the other hand, you can change the logging level permanently by changing the level set in the job description. To find out which job description you are running under, you can use the Display Job (DSPJOB) command, as in Figure 10.16.

Be aware that changing the job description to record more information in the job log affects the jobs of anyone who is running under the job description. System performance ultimately is affected. Obviously, system overhead is required to log additional information. On the other hand, if your system is reasonably stable, you may want to reduce your default logging levels to help enhance performance.

If your desire is for the system to record more information so you can track down problems easier, increasing the logging levels may help. You could change a job description named JOBDESC in QGPL to record the maximum information, by keying:

```
CHGJOBD JOBD(QGPL/JOBDESC) LOG(4 0 *SECLVL) LOGCLPGM(*YES)
```

Another place where you may want to change your job logging levels is with a submitted job. You can actually change them with the Submit Job (SBMJOB) command itself. To submit a job calling program XXX with the maximum logging level, key:

```
SBMJOB CMD(CALL PGM(XXX)) LOG(4 0 *SECLVL) LOGCLPGM(*YES)
```

Job logs for interactive sessions disappear when a user signs off using the default parameters of the Signoff command. The LOG parameter of the Signoff command is usually set to default to *NOLIST, which tells the system that the session job log is not needed after a user signs off. Changing the LOG parameter to *LIST causes the job log to be spooled to the printer.

Unfortunately, it is difficult to train many operators to remember to change the sign-off parameters if they had problems during their session. Consequently, the problems encountered during the session are lost forever. One solution to this problem is to change the default for the Signoff command. But this generates job logs for sessions where no problems are encountered, as well as those sessions with problems.

Perhaps a more sensible solution to this problem is a very useful program found in the *OS/400 Work Management Guide.* The program (Figure 10.17) allows you to set up an initial menu program that only keeps the job logs if errors are encountered in the session. We find this to be a very useful program and well worth publishing again.

Figure 10.17: CL Menu Program to Help Manage Job Logs

```
PGM
            DCLF MENU
            DCL &SIGNOFFOPT TYPE(*CHAR) LEN(7)
               VALUE(*NOLIST)
            .
            .
            .
            MONMSG MSG(CPF0000) EXEC(GOTO ERROR)
   PROMPT:  SNDRCVF RCDFMT(PROMPT)
            CHGVAR &IN41 '0'
            .
            .
            .
            IF (&OPTION *EQ '90') SIGNOFF
               LOG(&SIGNOFFOPT)
            .
            .
            .
            GOTO PROMPT
   ERROR:   CHGVAR &SIGNOFFOPT '*LIST'
            CHGVAR &IN41 '1'
            GOTO PROMPT
            ENDPGM
```

SOLUTIONS ARE BEST FOUND BY THOSE WHO KNOW HOW TO LOOK FOR THEM

It seems painfully obvious, but it is a constant surprise to us how many programmers fail to learn how to use the tools that are at their disposal. Programming is a lot more that just learning a programming language and writing code.

The best programmers are those who know how to use all of the tools in the toolbox. This includes the utilities that are shipped as part of the OS/400 operating system, the programming tools in this book, and the tools that are found within QUSRTOOL. The QUSRTOOL library was sent with the AS/400 operating system for all releases prior to V3R1 (when it became a product available for purchase) and should be required reading for AS/400 RPG programmers.

Take the time to learn how to use all of the tools at hand, and you just may become a master in your trade.

Chapter 11

Tools for the Toolbox

This chapter includes some of our favorite AS/400 utilities that have been developed over the years. We hope that you find them as useful as we have.

We dedicate this chapter to explaining and detailing five of our favorite programmer utilities (Table 11.1). We think that these tools make our job easier and are hopeful that others will find this to be the case as well.

Table 11.1: A Summary of Tools for the Toolbox

Command	Description
DSPPTH	The Display Path command is designed to help you instantly find all of the various keyed access paths that exist for a specific physical file. Specify the name and library of the physical file and a display is presented that shows all of the various access paths that currently exist over the file. The utility displays the number of logical views that exist over the file and the keyed access path of each.
DSPFLD	The Display Field command gives you an instant, online look at all of the fields in a physical or logical file. The record length, number of fields, key fields, and file type are identified as well as detail information on each field. The field-level detail includes field name, buffer positions, description text, size, and data type.
RGZPFFLTR	The Reorganize Physical File Filter command is designed to free up space on your system that is occupied by deleted records. The utility looks at all physical files on your system and automatically runs the Reorganize Physical File Member (RGZPFM) command on any file where the percentage of deleted records in the file exceeds the threshold percentage you set when you run the RGZPFFLTR command.
FNDDSPLF	The Find Displaced Logical Files utility is designed to help you find logical files that do not reside in the same library as the physical file(s) they are over. This condition has the potential to be dangerous, particularly when libraries are saved or restored.
WRKOBJREF	The Work with Object Reference command is designed to allow you to display all references to a specified object in an online display. Some object types that may be displayed are files, programs, and data areas. If the object type happens to be a physical file, references to the logical files over it may be displayed as well.

THE DISPLAY PATH COMMAND

When you sit down to write a new program on the AS/400, one of the first steps is to determine which paths are available for the data you need to process. To find the existing data paths that are available over a physical file on the AS/400, you generally perform the following steps:

1. Run Display Database Relations (DSPDBR) over the physical file in question.

2. Write down the file and library names of each logical file found on the DSPDBR display.

3. Run the Display File Description (DSPFD) command over each logical file to see if the data path you need already exists.

These three steps can be time consuming and cut into your productivity as a programmer. Some creative programmers have developed tools that perform these steps automatically and save much of the time required. These tools write the results of the DSPDBR command to an *outfile* and then either print them or bring them up on a display. Our Display Path (DSPPTH) command, however, goes one step further by using the system APIs discussed in Chapter 9, bringing the information to the screen much more quickly.

The DSPPTH command output looks like the example in Figure 11.1. The path for the physical file is listed first. Key fields and sequence (ascending or descending) are shown, followed by any select omit statements used. Then the path information is listed for each logical file built over the physical (even if the logical file is built in a different library).

Figure 11.1: Output from the Display Path (DSPPTH) Command

```
                              Display Access Paths

Physical File . . . . . . . .:   CUST        Number of logicals. . . . .:   0014
Library  . . . . . . . . . . .:   *LIBL

Library     File       Format      Key Field Seq Select/Omit Values
TESTLIB     CUST       CUSREC      CUSNUM       A CUSTOMER NUMBER

TESTLIB     CUSBYCLS   CUSREC      CUSCLS       A FINANCIAL CLASS

TESTLIB     CUSBYNAM   CUSREC      CUSNAM       A CUSTOMER NAME
                                   CUSDLT       O EQ '*'

PRODLIB     CUSBYCRD   CUSREC      CUSCRD       A CREDIT LIMIT
                                   CUSNAM       A CUSTOMER NAME
                                   CUSDLT       O EQ '*'

PRODLIB     CUSBYPMT   CUSREC      CUSPMT       A DATE OF LAST PAYMENT
                                                                    More...



   F3=Exit        F12=Previous
```

As you can see from the preceding example, the various access paths for a file are found easily using the DSPPTH utility. Three components that make up this utility: the DSPPTH command in Figure 11.2, the DSPPTHDS display file in Figure 11.3, and the DSPPTHRG RPG program in Figure 11.4.

Figure 11.2: Source for the Display Path (DSPPTH) Command

```
/*******************************************************************************/
/*    TO CREATE:                                                             */
/*        CRTCMD CMD(XXXLIB/DSPPTH PGM(XXXLIB/DSPPTHRG)                      */
/*******************************************************************************/
            CMD          PROMPT('DISPLAY PATH')
            PARM         KWD(FILE) TYPE(NAME1) MIN(1) PROMPT('File +
                          Name:')
NAME1:      QUAL         TYPE(*NAME) LEN(10)
            QUAL         TYPE(*CHAR) LEN(10) DFT(*LIBL) SPCVAL((' ' +
                          *LIBL)) CHOICE('Name, *LIBL') +
                          PROMPT('Library Name:')
```

Figure 11.3: Source for the DSPPTHDS Display File

```
     ****************************************************************
     *   TO COMPILE:
     *     CRTDSPF FILE(XXXLIB/DSPPTHDS)
     ****************************************************************
     A                                        CF12
     A                                        CF03
     A          R SFLRCD                       SFL
     A            SFLIB         10A  O  7  2
     A            SFFILE        10A  O  7 13
     A            SFKEY         10A  O  7 35
     A            SFFMT         10A  O  7 24
     A            SFTEXT        35   O  7 46
     A 59                                     DSPATR(HI)
     A          R SFLCTL                      SFLCTL(SFLRCD)
     A                                        SFLSIZ(0024)
     A                                        SFLPAG(0012)
     A                                        OVERLAY
     A 21                                     SFLDSP
     A                                        SFLDSPCTL
     A 53                                     SFLEND(*MORE)
     A                              1 29'Display Access Paths'  DSPATR(HI)
     A                              3  2'Physical File . . . . . . . .:'
     A            OUTFIL        10A  O  3 35DSPATR(HI)
     A                              4  2'Library . . . . . . . . . . .:'
     A            OUTLIB        10A  O  4 35DSPATR(HI)
     A                              6  2'Library    '   DSPATR(HI)
     A                              6 13'File       '   DSPATR(HI)
     A                              6 35'Key Field'     DSPATR(HI)
     A                              6 49'Select/Omit Values'  DSPATR(HI)
     A                              6 24'Format'              DSPATR(HI)
     A                              6 45'Seq'                 DSPATR(HI)
     A                              3 47'Number of logicals. . . . .:'
     A            OUT#           4 00  3 77DSPATR(HI)
     A          R FORMAT1
     A                             23  4'F3=Exit'   COLOR(BLU)
     A                             23 18'F12=Previous'  COLOR(BLU)
```

Power RPG III

Figure 11.4: Source for the DSPPTHRG RPG Program

```
    ************************************************************************
    *   TO COMPILE:
    *      CRTRPGPGM PGM(XXXLIB/DSPPTHRG)
    ************************************************************************
FDSPPTHDSCF  E                   WORKSTN
F                                     RRN   KSFILE SFLRCD
E                 AR      4096  1
E                 A2        28  1
E                 ARYF    1000 10
E                 ARYT    1000 40
IGENDS       DS
I                                 B 113 1160SIZINP
I                                 B 125 12800FFLST
I                                 B 133 1360NUMLST
I                                 B 137 1400SIZENT
IINPUT       DS
I                                     1  20 USRSPC
I                                     1  10 SPCNAM
I                                    11  20 SPCLIB
I                                    21  28 OUTFMT
I                                    29  48 FILLII
I                                    29  38 FILNAI
I                                    39  48 FILLBI
I                                    49  58 RCDFMI
ILIST        DS
I                                     1  20 MAINFL
I                                     1  10 MNFILE
I                                    11  20 MNLIB
I                                    21  30 DEPFIL
I                                    31  40 DEPLIB
I                                    41  41 DEPTYP
I                                    42  44 DEPRSR
I                                 B  45  480BINREF
I            DS
I                                     1  20 FLDSPC
I                                     1  10 FSPNAM
I                                    11  20 FSPLIB
IERROR       IDS
I                                 B   1   40BYTPRV
I                                 B   5   80BYTAVA
I                                     9  15 MSGID
I                                    16  16 ERR###
I                                    17 116 MSGDTA
IRCVVAR      DS           4096
I                                 B  62  630FMTNUM
I                                 B 317 3200QDBFOS
I                                   337 338 ACCTYP
I            DS
I                                 B   1   40STRPOS
I                                 B   5   80STRLEN
I                                 B   9  120LENSPC
I                                 B  13  160RCVLEN
I                                 B  17  200MSGKEY
I                                 B  21  240MSGDLN
I                                 B  25  280MSGQNB
I                                 B  29  320FSTRPS
I                                 B  33  360FSTRLN
IKEYDTA      DS
I                                     1  10 DEPKEY
I                                    14  14 ASEDES
IFNDSEL      DS           150
```

```
I                                        70  79 FNDFMT
I                                      B 117 1180NUMKEY
I                                      B 130 1310SOON
I                                      B 132 1350SOOF
I                                      B 136 1390OFFSET
IKEYSEL     DS                             150
I                                         3   3 RULE
I                                         4   5 COMP
I                                         6  15 CMPNAM
I                                      B  16 170NUMSO
I                                      B  29 320SOSO
IKEYSOS     DS                             150
I                                      B   1  40POFSET
I                                      B   5  60NL
I                                        21  48 SELVAR
I           DS
I                                         1  20 FFILLI
I                                         1  10 FFILNM
I                                        11  20 FFILLB
IFGENDS     DS
I                                      B 113 1160FSIZIN
I                                      B 117 1200FOFFHD
I                                      B 121 1240FSIZHD
I                                      B 125 1280FOFFLS
I                                      B 133 1360FNUMLS
I                                      B 137 1400FSIZEN
IFLIST      DS
I                                         1  10 FFLDNM
I                                        33  82 FFLDTX
I           DS
I                                         1  35 SFTEXT
I                                         1   1 SFASND
I                                         3   3 SFRULE
I                                         5   6 SFCOMP
I                                         8  35 SFVALU
I           '*REQUESTER*LIBL'    C          REQSTR
C           *ENTRY   PLIST
C                    PARM           FILLIB 20
C                    MOVELFILLIB    OUTFIL 10
C                    MOVE FILLIB    OUTLIB 10
C                    MOVEL'USRSPC'  SPCNAM
C                    MOVEL'QTEMP'   SPCLIB
C                    MOVELOUTFIL    FILNAI
C                    MOVELOUTLIB    FILLBI
C                    Z-ADD116       BYTPRV
C           'QCPFMSG' CAT  'QSYS':3 MSGF
C                    SETON                      53    MORE/BOTTOM
C                    CALL 'QUSCRTUS'                  CREATE USER SPACE
C                    PARM           USRSPC
C                    PARM *BLANKS   ATRSPC 10
C                    PARM 1024      LENSPC
C                    PARM *BLANKS   VALSPC  1
C                    PARM '*CHANGE' AUTSPC 10
C                    PARM *BLANKS   TXTSPC 50
C                    PARM '*YES'    RPLSPC 10
C                    PARM           ERROR
 *
C                    CALL 'QUSROBJD'                  ATTEMPT TO RETRIEVE
C                    PARM           RCVVAR            OBJECT DESC
C                    PARM 100       RCVLEN
C                    PARM 'OBJD0100'FILFMT  8
C                    PARM           FILLIB
C                    PARM '*FILE'   OBJTYP  8
C                    PARM           ERROR
```

```
     C          MSGID     IFNE *BLANKS                    FILE DOESN'T EXIST
     C                    EXSR SNDMSG                       SEND MESSAGE AND
     C                    GOTO END                          GET OUT
     C                    ENDIF
      *
     C                    EXSR SPACE1                      CREATE FIELDS USRSPC
      *
     C                    MOVE FILLIB    SFILLB
     C                    MOVE *ON       FIRST   1
     C                    EXSR GETFIL                      WRITE ACCESS PATH
     C          MSGID     CABEQ'CPF5715' NORECS
     C          MSGID     CABEQ'CPF3210' END
     C                    MOVE *OFF      FIRST
      *
     C                    CALL 'QDBLDBR'                   LIST DATABASE
     C                    PARM           USRSPC             RELATIONS TO THE
     C                    PARM 'DBRL0100'OUTFMT  8          USER SPACE
     C                    PARM           FILLII
     C                    PARM '*FIRST'  RCDFMI
     C                    PARM *BLANKS   IGNORE 10
     C                    PARM           ERROR
     C          MSGID     CABEQ'CPF5715' NORECS
     C                    Z-ADD1         STRPOS
     C                    Z-ADD140       STRLEN
     C                    CALL 'QUSRTVUS'                  RETRIEVE USER SPACE
     C                    PARM           USRSPC             GENERAL INFORMATION
     C                    PARM           STRPOS
     C                    PARM           STRLEN
     C                    PARM           GENDS
     C                    Z-ADD1         STRPOS
     C                    Z-ADDSIZINP    STRLEN
     C                    CALL 'QUSRTVUS'                  RETRIEVE USER SPACE
     C                    PARM           USRSPC             DETAIL INFORMATION
     C                    PARM           STRPOS
     C                    PARM           STRLEN
     C                    PARM           INPUT
     C                    MOVEL'USRSPC'  SPCNAM
     C                    MOVEL'QTEMP'   SPCLIB
     C          OFFLST    ADD  1         STRPOS
     C                    Z-ADDSIZENT    STRLEN
     C                    Z-ADDNUMLST    OUT#
 B1  C                    DO   NUMLST                      DO FOR NUMBER OF
     C                    CALL 'QUSRTVUS'                  RETRIEVE THE LIST
     C                    PARM           USRSPC            BY WALKING THROUGH
     C                    PARM           STRPOS            THE USER SPACE.
     C                    PARM           STRLEN
     C                    PARM           LIST
     C          DEPFIL    CABEQ'*NONE'   NORECS
     C                    MOVELDEPFIL    SFILLB
     C                    MOVE DEPLIB    SFILLB
     C                    EXSR GETFIL
     C                    EXSR CLEAR
     C                    ADD  SIZENT    STRPOS
 E1  C                    ENDDO
     C          NORECS    TAG
 B1  C          RRN       IFGT 0
     C                    SETON                      21
 E1  C                    ENDIF
     C                    WRITEFORMAT1
     C                    EXFMTSFLCTL
     C          END       TAG
     C                    SETON                      LR
      *
     C          SNDMSG    BEGSR
```

```
      C                      CALL  'QMHSNDPM'              SEND ERROR MESSAGE
      C                      PARM            MSGID
      C                      PARM            MSGF    20
      C                      PARM            FILLIB
      C                      PARM 20         MSGDLN
      C                      PARM '*DIAG'    MSGTYP  10
      C                      PARM '*'        MSGQ    10
      C                      PARM 1          MSGQNB
      C                      PARM            MSGKEY
      C                      PARM            ERROR               ERROR CODE
      C                      ENDSR
      *
      C            GETFIL    BEGSR
      C                      CALL  'QDBRTVFD'              GET KEY FIELD INFO
      C                      PARM            RCVVAR         FOR EACH LOGICAL
      C                      PARM 4096       RCVLEN          INTO RCVVAR
      C                      PARM            RFILLB  20
      C                      PARM 'FILD0100' FILFMT   8
      C                      PARM            SFILLB  20
      C                      PARM            RCDFMT  10
      C                      PARM '0'        OVRRID   1      NO OVERRIDES
      C                      PARM '*LCL'     SYSTEM  10      WHAT SYSTEM FILE ON
      C                      PARM '*EXT'     FMTTYP  10      INTERNAL/EXTERNAL
      C                      PARM            ERROR           ERROR CODE
      C            MSGID     CABEQ'CPF5715'  ENDGET
      C                      MOVEARCVVAR     AR,1
B1    C            FIRST     IFEQ *ON
      C                      MOVE AR,9       TSTTYP   1        FOR PHYSICAL
      C.                     TESTB'2'        TSTTYP         01FILE MUST BE PHYSICAL
B2    C            *IN01     IFEQ *ON
      C                      MOVE 'CPF3210' MSGID
      C                      EXSR SNDMSG
      C                      GOTO ENDGET
E2    C                      ENDIF
E1    C                      ENDIF
      *
      C                      Z-ADDQDBFOS     I       40     FILE HEADER OFFSET
B1    C                      DO   FMTNUM
      C                 .    MOVEAAR,I       FNDSEL
      C            OFFSET    ADD  1          S       40
B2    C            FIRST     IFEQ *OFF
      C                      EXSR CLEAR
      C                      ADD  1          RRN
      C                      WRITESFLRCD                  WRITE BLANK LINE
E2    C                      ENDIF
      C                      MOVE RFILLB     SFLIB          FOR CLARITY
      C                      MOVELRFILLB     SFFILE
      C                      MOVELFNDFMT     SFFMT
      C                      EXSR GETTXT
B2    C                      DO   NUMKEY                  NUMBER OF KEY FIELDS
      C                      MOVEAAR,S       KEYDTA
      C                      TESTB'0'        ASEDES       79 ASCENDING/DESCENDING
B3    C                      SELEC
      C            *IN79     WHEQ *OFF
      C                      MOVE 'A'        SFASND
      C            *IN79     WHEQ *ON
      C                      MOVE 'D'        SFASND
E3    C                      ENDSL
      C                      MOVE DEPKEY     SFKEY
      C                      DO   B          C       40
B3    C            ARYF,C    IFEQ DEPKEY
      C                      MOVELARYT,C     SFTEXT    P
      C                      LEAVE
      C                      ENDIF
```

```
E3  C                    ENDDO
    C                    ADD  1         RRN     40
    C                    WRITESFLRCD
    C                    MOVE *BLANKS   SFLIB
    C                    MOVE *BLANKS   SFFILE
    C                    MOVE *BLANKS   SFFMT
    C                    MOVE *BLANKS   SFVALU
    C                    ADD  32        S
E2  C                    ENDDO
B2  C        SOON        IFNE *ZEROS                     SELECT/OMIT EXISTS
    C                    EXSR SELOMT
E2  C                    ENDIF
    C                    MOVE *BLANKS   SFCOMP
    C                    MOVE *BLANKS   SFRULE
    C                    ADD  160       I
E1  C                    ENDDO
    C        ENDGET      TAG
    C                    ENDSR
    *
    C        SELOMT      BEGSR
    C        SOOF        ADD  1         I1      40    OFFSET TO SEL/OMIT
    C                    MOVE *BLANKS   SFTEXT
B1  C                    DO   SOON
    C                    MOVEAAR,I1     KEYSEL
B2  C        COMP        IFEQ 'AL'
    C                    ITER
E2  C                    ENDIF
    C                    MOVE COMP      SFCOMP        KEY FIELD
    C                    MOVE RULE      SFRULE
    C        SOSO        ADD  1         I2      40
B2  C                    DO   NUMSO
    C                    MOVEAAR,I2     KEYSOS        OFFSET TO VARIABLE
    C                    MOVEASELVAR    A2
    C                    SUB  19        NL
B3  C        NL          IFGT *ZEROS
    C                    MOVEA*BLANKS   A2,NL
E3  C                    ENDIF
    C                    MOVEAA2,1      SFVALU        PART OF SEL/OMIT
    C                    MOVE CMPNAM    SFKEY
    C                    ADD  1         RRN     40
    C                    MOVE *BLANKS   SFASND
    C                    SETON                        59
    C                    WRITESFLRCD
    C                    SETOF                        59
    C        POFSET      ADD  1         I2
E2  C                    ENDDO
    C                    ADD  32        I1
E1  C                    ENDDO
    C                    ENDSR
    *
    C        CLEAR       BEGSR
    C                    MOVE *BLANKS   SFLIB
    C                    MOVE *BLANKS   SFFILE
    C                    MOVE *BLANKS   SFCOMP
    C                    MOVE *BLANKS   SFFMT
    C                    MOVE *BLANKS   SFRULE
    C                    MOVE *BLANKS   SFVALU
    C                    MOVE *BLANKS   SFKEY
    C                    MOVE *BLANKS   SFASND
    C                    MOVE *BLANKS   SFTEXT
    C                    ENDSR
    ** GET TEXT FOR EACH FIELD
    C        GETTXT      BEGSR
    C                    MOVE SFFILE    FFILNM
```

```
        C                      MOVE SFLIB       FFILLB
        C                      MOVEL'FLDSPC'    FSPNAM    P
        C                      MOVEL'QTEMP'     FSPLIB    P
        C                      CALL 'QUSLFLD'                    LIST FIELDS TO
        C                      PARM             FLDSPC            USER SPACE
        C                      PARM 'FLDL0100'LSTFMT   8
        C                      PARM             FFILLI
        C                      PARM SFFMT       RCDFMI
        C                      PARM '1'         OVRRID 1
        C                      Z-ADD1           FSTRPS
        C                      Z-ADD140         FSTRLN
        C                      MOVEL'FLDSPC'    FSPNAM    P
        C                      MOVEL'QTEMP'     FSPLIB    P
        C                      CALL 'QUSRTVUS'                   RETRIEVE USER SPACE
        C                      PARM             FLDSPC           GENERAL INFORMATION
        C                      PARM             FSTRPS
        C                      PARM             FSTRLN
        C                      PARM             FGENDS
        C           FOFFHD     ADD  1           FSTRPS
        C                      Z-ADDFSIZHD      FSTRLN
        C                      MOVEL'FLDSPC'    FSPNAM    P
        C                      MOVEL'QTEMP'     FSPLIB    P
        C           FOFFLS     ADD  1           FSTRPS
        C                      Z-ADDFSIZEN      FSTRLN
B1      C                      DO   FNUMLS                       DO FOR NUMBER OF
        C                      MOVEL'FLDSPC'    FSPNAM    P
        C                      MOVEL'QTEMP'     FSPLIB    P
        C                      CALL 'QUSRTVUS'                   RETRIEVE THE LIST
        C                      PARM             FLDSPC           BY WALKING THROUGH
        C                      PARM             FSTRPS           THE USER SPACE.
        C                      PARM             FSTRLN
        C                      PARM             FLIST
        C                      ADD  1           B       40
        C                      MOVELFFLDNM      ARYF,B
        C                      MOVELFFLDTX      ARYT,B
        C                      ADD  FSIZEN      FSTRPS
E1      C                      ENDDO
        C                      ENDSR
      ** CREATE USER SPACE FOR LISTING FIELDS
        C           SPACE1     BEGSR
        C                      MOVEL'FLDSPC'    FSPNAM    P
        C                      MOVEL'QTEMP'     FSPLIB    P
        C                      CALL 'QUSCRTUS'                   CREATE USER SPACE
        C                      PARM             FLDSPC
        C                      PARM *BLANKS     ATRSPC 10
        C                      PARM 1024        LENSPC
        C                      PARM *BLANKS     VALSPC  1
        C                      PARM '*CHANGE'   AUTSPC 10
        C                      PARM *BLANKS     TXTSPC 50
        C                      PARM '*YES'      RPLSPC 10
        C                      PARM             ERROR
        C                      ENDSR
```

THE DISPLAY FIELD COMMAND

If you ever have to use the Display File Field Description (DSPFFD) command when you are programming, you will want to take a look at this utility. The Display Field

(DSPFLD) command provides an easy-to-read display that shows all of the fields in a file. The buffer positions, key field identification, field description, record format length, and record format name are all condensed onto a single screen. The file field information can also be printed simply by pressing a function key. In Figure 11.5, we see an example of the DSPFLD command when it is run over our customer file.

Figure 11.5: Output from the Display Field (DSPFLD) Command

```
                           Display File Fields

Physical File  . . . . .: CUSTOMER      File Type . . . . . . .:      PF
Library  . . . . . . . .: TESTLIB       Record Length . . . . .:     132
Record Format. . . . . .: CUSREC        Number of fields. . . .:       8

Key   Field   Length Dec Type From   To Text
K1    CUST#      10       A      1    10 CUSTOMER#
      NAME       40       A     11    50 NAME
      ADDRES     30       A     51    80 ADDRESS
      CITY       30       A     81   110 CITY
      STATE       2       A    111   112 STATE
      ZIP         9       A    113   121 ZIP CODE
      SLSMAN      5       A    122   126 SALESMAN
      PHONE      10    0  P    127   132 PHONE NUMBER




                                                              Bottom


   F3=Exit        F12=Previous      F8=Print
```

The DSPFLD utility consists of three source members: the DSPFLD command in Figure 11.6, the DSPFLDDS display file in Figure 11.7, and the DSPFLDRG RPG program in Figure 11.8.

Figure 11.6: The Display Field (DSPFLD) Command Source

```
/*================================================================*/
/* To compile:                                                    */
/*                                                                */
/*          CRTCMD     CMD(XXX/DSPFLD) PGM(XXX/DSPFLDRG)          */
/*                                                                */
/*================================================================*/
           CMD        PROMPT('List Fields')

           PARM       KWD(FILE) TYPE(QUAL) MIN(1) PROMPT('File')
           PARM       KWD(RCDFMT) TYPE(*NAME) DFT(*FIRST) +
                        SPCVAL((*FIRST)) PROMPT('Record format')

QUAL:      QUAL       TYPE(*NAME) LEN(10)
           QUAL       TYPE(*NAME) LEN(10) DFT(*LIBL) +
                        SPCVAL((*LIBL)) PROMPT('Library')
```

Figure 11.7: The DSPFLDDS Display File Source

```
     *****************************************************************
     *   TO COMPILE:
     *      CRTDSPF FILE(XXXLIB/DSPFLDDS)
     *****************************************************************
     A                                        CF12
     A                                        CF03
     A          R SFLRCD                       SFL
     A            SFFLD      8A  O  8  8
     A            SFLEN      5Y 0O  8 17EDTCDE(3)
     A            SFTYPE     1A  O  8 28
     A            SFFROM     5Y 0O  8 31EDTCDE(3)
     A            SFTO       5Y 0O  8 37EDTCDE(3)
     A            SFTEXT    38A  O  8 43
     A            SFDEC      1A  O  8 25
     A            SFKEY      3A  O  8  2DSPATR(HI)
     A          R SFLCTL                       SFLCTL(SFLRCD)
     A                                        CF08(08 'print')
     A                                        OVERLAY
     A  21                                     SFLDSP
     A                                        SFLDSPCTL
     A  53                                     SFLEND(*MORE)
     A                                        SFLSIZ(0024)
     A                                        SFLPAG(0012)
     A                                     1 28'Display File Fields'
     A                                        DSPATR(HI)
     A                                     3  2'Physical File . . . . .:'
     A            OUTFIL    10A  O  3 28DSPATR(HI)
     A                                     4  2'Library  . . . . . . .:'
     A            OUTLIB    10A  O  4 28DSPATR(HI)
     A                                     7  8'Field'
     A                                        DSPATR(HI)
     A                                     7 16'Length'
     A                                        DSPATR(HI)
     A                                     7 32'From'
     A                                        DSPATR(HI)
     A                                     7 43'Text'
     A                                        DSPATR(HI)
     A                                     7 40'To'
     A                                        DSPATR(HI)
     A                                     5  2'Record Format. . . . . .:'
     A            OUTFMT    10A  O  5 28DSPATR(HI)
     A                                     3 43'File Type . . . . . . .:'
     A            OUTTYP     5A  O  3 70DSPATR(HI)
     A                                     7 23'Dec'
     A                                        DSPATR(HI)
     A                                     4 43'Record Length . . . . .:'
     A            OUTRLN     6Y 0O  4 69DSPATR(HI)
     A                                        EDTCDE(3)
     A                                     5 43'Number of fields. . . .:'
     A            RRN        4Y 0O  5 71DSPATR(HI)
     A                                        EDTCDE(3)
     A                                     7  2'Key'
     A                                        DSPATR(HI)
     A                                     7 27'Type'
     A                                        DSPATR(HI)
     A          R FORMAT1
     A                                    23  4'F3=Exit'
     A                                        COLOR(BLU)
     A                                    23 18'F12=Previous'
     A                                        COLOR(BLU)
     A                                    23 35'F8=Print'
     A                                        COLOR(BLU)
```

Figure 11.8: The DSPFLDRG RPG Program Source

```
     ******************************************************************
     *   TO COMPILE:
     *      CRTRPGPGM PGM(XXXLIB/DSPFLDRG)
     ******************************************************************
     FDSPFLDDSCF E                   WORKSTN
     F                                      RRN    KSFILE SFLRCD
     FQSYSPRT O    F     132     OF     PRINTER
     E                   AR        4096  1
     E                   AKEY       20 10
     E                   AK#        20  2 0
     IGENDS       DS
     I                                  B 113 1160SIZINP
     I                                  B 117 1200OFFHDR
     I                                  B 121 1240SIZHDR
     I                                  B 125 1280OFFLST
     I                                  B 133 1360NUMLST
     I                                  B 137 1400SIZENT
     IHEADER      DS
     I                                     1  10 OUTFIL
     I                                    11  20 OUTLIB
     I                                    21  30 FLDTYP
     I                                    21  25 OUTTYP
     I                                    31  40 OUTFMT
     I                                  B 41  440RCDLEN
     IINPUT       DS
     I                                     1  20 USRSPC
     I                                     1  10 SPCNAM
     I                                    11  20 SPCLIB
     I                                    29  48 FILLII
     I                                    29  38 FILNAI
     I                                    39  48 FILLBI
     I                                    49  58 RCDFMI
     ILIST        DS
     I                                     1  10 FLDNAM
     I                                     1   8 SFFLD
     I                                    11  11 SFTYPE
     I                                  B 13  160BUFERO
     I                                  B 17  200BUFERI
     I                                  B 21  240FLDLEN
     I                                  B 25  280DIGITS
     I                                  B 29  320DECMLS
     I                                    33  82 FLDDSC
     IERROR       IDS
     I                                  B  1   40BYTPRV
     I                                  B  5   80BYTAVA
     I                                     9  15 MSGID
     I                                    16  16 ERR###
     I                                    17 116 MSGDTA
     IRCVVR2      DS                      100
     IRCVVAR      DS                      4096
     I                                  B 62  630FMTNUM
     I                                  B 317 3200QDBFOS
     I                                   337 338 ACCTYP
     IFNDSEL      DS                      150
     I                                  B 117 1180NUMKEY
     I                                  B 136 1390OFFSET
     IKEYDTA      DS
     I                                     1  10 DEPKEY
     I            DS
     I                                  B  1   40STRPOS
     I                                  B  5   80STRLEN
     I                                  B  9  120LENSPC
```

320

```
        I                                 B  13  160RCVLEN
        I                                 B  17  200MSGKEY
        I                                 B  21  240MSGDLN
        I                                 B  25  280MSGQNB
        C           *ENTRY    PLIST
        C                     PARM              FILLIB 20
        C                     PARM              ENTFMT 10
        C                     MOVELFILLIB       SFILLB
        C                     MOVEL'FFDSPC'     SPCNAM      P
        C                     MOVEL'QTEMP'      SPCLIB      P
        C                     MOVELFILLIB       FILNAI
        C                     MOVE FILLIB       FILLBI
        C                     Z-ADD116          BYTPRV
        C           'QCPFMSG' CAT  'QSYS':3     MSGF
        C                     SETON                     53    MORE/BOTTOM
        C                     CALL 'QUSCRTUS'                 CREATE USER SPACE
        C                     PARM              USRSPC
        C                     PARM *BLANKS      ATRSPC 10
        C                     PARM 1024         LENSPC
        C                     PARM *BLANKS      VALSPC  1
        C                     PARM '*CHANGE'    AUTSPC 10
        C                     PARM *BLANKS      TXTSPC 50
        C                     PARM '*YES'       RPLSPC 10
        C                     PARM              ERROR
        *
        C                     CALL 'QUSROBJD'                 ATTEMPT TO RETRIEVE
        C                     PARM              RCVVR2         OBJECT DESC
        C                     PARM 100          RCVLEN
        C                     PARM 'OBJD0100'   FILFMT  8
        C                     PARM              FILLIB
        C                     PARM '*FILE'      OBJTYP  8
        C                     PARM              ERROR
        C           MSGID     IFNE *BLANKS                    FILE DOESN'T EXIST
        C                     EXSR SNDMSG                      SEND MESSAGE AND
        C                     GOTO END                         GET OUT
        C                     ENDIF
        *
        C                     EXSR GETKEY
        *
        C                     CALL 'QUSLFLD'                  LIST FIELDS TO
        C                     PARM              USRSPC         USER SPACE
        C                     PARM 'FLDL0100'   LSTFMT  8
        C                     PARM              FILLII
        C                     PARM ENTFMT       RCDFMI
        C                     PARM '1'          OVRRID  1
        C                     Z-ADD1            STRPOS
        C                     Z-ADD140          STRLEN
        C                     CALL 'QUSRTVUS'                 RETRIEVE USER SPACE
        C                     PARM              USRSPC         GENERAL INFORMATION
        C                     PARM              STRPOS
        C                     PARM              STRLEN
        C                     PARM              GENDS
        C           OFFHDR    ADD  1            STRPOS
        C                     Z-ADDSIZHDR       STRLEN
        C                     CALL 'QUSRTVUS'                 RETRIEVE HEADER INFO
        C                     PARM              USRSPC
        C                     PARM              STRPOS
        C                     PARM              STRLEN
        C                     PARM              HEADER
        C                     MOVEL'FFDSPC'     SPCNAM      P
        C                     MOVEL'QTEMP'      SPCLIB      P
        C           OFFLST    ADD  1            STRPOS
        C                     Z-ADDSIZENT       STRLEN
   B1   C                     DO   NUMLST                     DO FOR NUMBER OF
```

```
        C                       CALL 'QUSRTVUS'            RETRIEVE THE LIST
        C                       PARM           USRSPC      BY WALKING THROUGH
        C                       PARM           STRPOS      THE USER SPACE.
        C                       PARM           STRLEN
        C                       PARM           LIST
        C                       EXSR WRITER                WRITE RECORD
        C                       ADD  SIZENT    STRPOS
   E1   C                       ENDDO
   B1   C            RRN        IFGT 0
        C                       SETON                  21
   E1   C                       ENDIF
        C                       Z-ADDRCDLEN    OUTRLN
        C            ' '        CHEKROUTTYP    Z     10
        C**          Z          SUBSTOUTTYP:1  F5     5 P
        C                       MOVELOUTTYP    F5     5 P
        C            5          SUB  Z         Z
        C                       MOVE *BLANKS   OUTTYP
        C                       CAT  F5:Z      OUTTYP
        C                       WRITEFORMAT1
        C                       EXFMTSFLCTL
   B1   C            *IN08      IFEQ *ON                   PRINT LOOP
        C                       EXCPTHEDING
   B2   C            1          DO   9999      X     40
        C            X          CHAINSFLRCD          68
   B3   C            *IN68      IFEQ *OFF
        C                       EXCPTDETAIL
   E3   C                       ENDIF
   E2   C    N68                ENDDO
   E1   C                       ENDIF
        C            END        TAG
        C                       SETON                  LR
        *
        C            WRITER     BEGSR
        C                       Z-ADDDIGITS    SFLEN
        C                       MOVE DECMLS    SFDEC
   B1   C            SFLEN      IFEQ *ZEROS
        C                       Z-ADDFLDLEN    SFLEN
        C                       MOVE *BLANKS   SFDEC
   E1   C                       ENDIF
        C                       Z-ADDBUFERO    SFFROM
        C            SFFROM     ADD  FLDLEN    WORKF 60
        C            WORKF      SUB  1         SFTO
        C                       MOVELFLDDSC    SFTEXT
        C                       MOVE *BLANKS   SFKEY
   B1   C                       DO   20        I
   B2   C            AKEY,I     IFEQ SFFLD
   B3   C            AK#,I      IFLT 10
        C                       MOVE AK#,I     I1     1
        C            'K'        CAT  I1:0      SFKEY   P
   X3   C                       ELSE
        C                       MOVE AK#,I     I2     2
        C            'K'        CAT  I2:0      SFKEY   P
   E3   C                       ENDIF
        C                       LEAVE
   E2   C                       ENDIF
   E1   C                       ENDDO
        C                       ADD  1         RRN   40
        C                       WRITESFLRCD                WRITE BLANK LINE
        C                       ENDSR
        *
        C            GETKEY     BEGSR
        C                       CALL 'QDBRTVFD'            GET KEY FIELD INFO
        C                       PARM           RCVVAR       INTO RCVVAR
        C                       PARM 4096      RCVLEN
```

```
C                   PARM            RFILLB 20
C                   PARM 'FILD0100' FILFMT  8
C                   PARM            SFILLB 20
C                   PARM ENTFMT     RCDFMT 10
C                   PARM '0'        OVRRID  1        NO OVERRIDES
C                   PARM '*LCL'     SYSTEM 10        WHAT SYSTEM FILE ON
C                   PARM '*EXT'     FMTTYP 10        INTERNAL/EXTERNAL
C                   PARM            ERROR            ERROR CODE
C        MSGID      CABEQ'CPF5715'  ENDGET
C                   MOVEARCVVAR     AR,1
C                   Z-ADDQDBFOS     I      40        FILE HEADER OFFSET
B1 C                DO   FMTNUM
C                   MOVEAAR,I       FNDSEL
C        OFFSET     ADD  1          S      40
B2 C     NUMKEY     IFGT 20                          DON'T EXCEED ARRAY
C                   Z-ADD20         NUMKEY           ELEMENTS
E2 C                ENDIF
C                   Z-ADD0          JJ
B2 C                DO   NUMKEY                       NUMBER OF KEY FIELDS
C                   MOVEAAR,S       KEYDTA
C                   ADD  1          J      20
C                   ADD  1          JJ     20
C                   MOVEADEPKEY     AKEY,J
C                   MOVEAJJ         AK#,JJ
C                   ADD  32         S
E2 C                ENDDO
C                   ADD  160        I
E1 C                ENDDO
C        ENDGET     TAG
C                   ENDSR
   *
C        SNDMSG     BEGSR
C                   CALL 'QMHSNDPM'                  SEND ERROR MESSAGE
C                   PARM            MSGID
C                   PARM            MSGF   20
C                   PARM            FILLIB
C                   PARM 20         MSGDLN
C                   PARM '*DIAG'    MSGTYP 10
C                   PARM '*'        MSGQ   10
C                   PARM 1          MSGQNB
C                   PARM            MSGKEY
C                   PARM            ERROR            ERROR CODE
C                   ENDSR
   **
OQSYSPRT E  302           HEDING
O       OR        OF
O                               5 'DATE:'
O                   UDATE Y      14
O                               75 'PAGE:'
O                   PAGE  Z      80
O                               48 'DISPLAY FIELD FOR FILE'
O                   OUTFIL       59
   *
O        E  1           HEDING
O       OR        OF
O                               24 'PHYSICAL FILE...........'
O                   OUTFIL       35
O                               64 'FILE TYPE..............'
O                   OUTTYP       75
   *
O        E  1           HEDING
O       OR        OF
O                               24 'LIBRARY................'
O                   OUTLIB       35
```

```
O                                    64 'RECORD LENGTH..........'
O                         OUTRLNZ     75
   *
O         E  3           HEDING
O         OR       OF
O                                    24 'RECORD FORMAT..........'
O                         OUTFMT      35
O                                    64 'NUMBER OF FIELDS........'
O                         RRN    Z    75
   *
O         E  1           HEDING
O         OR       OF
O                                    22 'KEY     FIELD    LENGTH'
O                                    45 'DEC  TYPE  FROM    TO'
O                                    75 'TEXT...................'
   *
O         EF 1           DETAIL
O                         SFKEY        4
O                         SFFLD       16
O                         SFLEN Z     20
O                         SFDEC       27
O                         SFTYPE      32
O                         SFFROMZ     39
O                         SFTO  Z     45
O                         SFTEXT      88
```

THE REORGANIZE PHYSICAL FILE FILTER COMMAND

Those of us whose career paths closely paralleled the development of the family of IBM Midrange Systems initially found the AS/400 to be a bit of an enigma. All of the rules with which we were familiar regarding the placement of data had changed. Our trusty CATALOG was replaced with a variety of tools that we could use to determine how much disk was used and where the files were stored, but the days of using a single command to determine what had gobbled up all of your DASD were long gone.

In Search of Missing DASD...

Many improvements made to the AS/400 operating system make the task of tracking down the missing DASD easier. Print Disk Information (PRTDSKINF) can be used to help reveal some of the disk utilization. But the very nature of the AS/400 operating system can make tracking down the overall disk usage a difficult thing to expose.

One area where lost DASD can reside is in deleted records. When you delete a record on the AS/400, the record is simply blanked out, or more specifically, changed to *null* characters when the delete operation occurs. The deleted record is then ignored on subsequent I/O operations for that file. The significance of this point is that the "deleted" record still takes up the same amount of space on disk. This may not matter very much if the file was built to reuse deleted records (reusing deleted records is one of the options in the Create Physical File (CRTPF) and Change Physical File (CHGPF) commands), but most files are not configured this way because it can impact performance negatively.

Deleted records continue to take up space on the DASD until the file is reorganized. This occurs when, and if, Reorganize Physical File Member (RGZPFM) is run. Depending upon your AS/400 software, you may have hidden DASD that could be recovered on your system. Many AS/400 software packages do not reorganize physical files on a regular basis. Some do not perform this file maintenance at all.

If you are curious as to whether or not files on your system contain deleted records, you can use the Display File Description (DSPFD) over a few of the files to find out. You may be in for a little surprise.

The RGZPFFLTR command identifies those files on your system that contain deleted records and automatically reorganizes them for you. It also prints a status report informing you of how much DASD was regained by using the utility. You can also specify the percentage of deleted records that must exist in each file before the file reorganization occurs.

The Long and the Short of It

We employed this utility to greatly reduce the length of time that our monthend process took to complete. Our monthend used to reorganize all of the major files in the system whether they needed it or not. This was primarily because there was no easy way to tell which files had deleted records in them.

Because this utility selectively reorganizes the files based upon the percentage of deleted records, our monthend process now only reorganizes the files that need it. The amount of time our monthend process takes is reduced by more than 50 percent.

What's Under the Hood?

The command in Figure 11.9 accepts three parameters. The first, library name, also accepts the value *ALL, which causes the program to look at all files in the system. The second parameter is the percentage of deleted records that must exist in the file before the reorganization is performed. If a Y (for yes) is entered as the last parameter, the files that meet the established criteria are listed, but the reorganization is not performed.

Figure 11.9: The RGZPFFLTR Command Source

```
/*===============================================================*/
/* To compile:                                                   */
/*                                                               */
/*          CRTCMD      CMD(XXX/RGZPFFLTR) PGM(XXX/RGZPFRG)       */
/*                                                               */
/*===============================================================*/
          CMD           PROMPT('Reorganize Files Filter)')
          PARM          KWD(LIBRARY) TYPE(*CHAR) LEN(10) MIN(1) +
                        CHOICE('Name, *ALL') PROMPT('Library  . . +
                        . . . . . . . . .')
          PARM          KWD(PERCENT) TYPE(*DEC) LEN(2) DFT(10) +
                        MIN(0) PROMPT('Percent . . . . . . . . . +
                        . .')
          PARM          KWD(PRONLY) TYPE(*CHAR) LEN(1) RSTD(*YES) +
                        DFT(N) VALUES(Y N) MIN(0) +
                        PROMPT('Print only ? . . . . . . . . .') +
                        CHOICE('Y, N')
```

The RPG program for this utility is shown in Figure 11.10. The CL program is represented by Figure 11.11.

Figure 11.10: The RGZPFFRG RPG Program Source

```
*****************************************************************
     *   YOU MUST BE SIGNED ON AS QSECOFR TO COMPILE:
     *
     *      PRIOR TO V3R1 OF OS/400, KEY:
     *
     *         CRTRPGPGM PGM(XXXLIB/RGZPFFRG) USRPRF(*OWNER)
     *
     *      AFTER V2R3 OF OS/400, KEY:
     *
     *         CRTRPGPGM PGM(XXXLIB/RGZPFFRG) USRPRF(*OWNER) ALWNULL(*YES)
     *
     *      REMEMBER, YOU MUST COMPILE AS QSECOFR  AND *OWNER
     *
     *****************************************************************
FQADBXREFIF E           K         DISK
FQSYSPRT O   F     132       OF   PRINTER
IERROR       IDS
I                                 B   1   40BYTPRV
I                                 B   5   80BYTAVA
I                                     9  15 MSGID
I                                    16  16 ERR###
I                                    17 116 MSGDTA
I            DS
I                                 B   1   40RCVLEN
I                                 B   5   80MSGKEY
I                                 B   9  120MSGDLN
I                                 B  13  160MSGQNB
IVAR         DS                       500
I                                 B   1   40BYTTOT
I                                 B   5   80BYTAVL
I                                 B 141 1440NUMREC
I                                 B 145 1480NUMDEL
I                                 B 149 1520DSSIZ
```

```
I                               B 153 1560ACPSIZ
C           *ENTRY    PLIST
C                     PARM          LIB  10        LIBRARY
C                     PARM          PERC 20        PERCENTAGE DELETED
C                     PARM          PRONLY 1       PRINT ONLY ?
C                     Z-ADD116      BYTPRV
C                     SELEC
C           LIB       WHEQ '*ALL'                  ALL LIBRARIES
C           *LOVAL    SETLLQADBXREF
C                     OTHER                        ONLY ONE LIBRARY
C                     EXSR EXIST
C           LIB       SETLLQADBXREF
C                     ENDSL
C           ERR       IFNE *ON
C                     EXCPTHEADNG
C           *IN41     DOUEQ*ON
C           LIB       IFEQ '*ALL'
C                     READ QADBXREF           41
C                     ELSE
C           LIB       READEQADBXREF           41
C                     ENDIF
C           *IN41     IFEQ *OFF
C           DBXATR    IFEQ 'PF'                     ONLY LOOK AT
C           DBXTYP    ANDEQ'D'                      PHYSICAL FILES WITH
C                     MOVE *OFF     REORG  1
C                     ADD  1        TOTFIL 70
C                     EXSR RGZCHK
C           REORG     IFEQ *ON
C                     Z-ADDDSSIZ    B4SIZE 100
C                     Z-ADDACPSIZ   B4ACPS 100
C           PRONLY    IFNE 'Y'
C                     EXSR RGZFIL
C                     ENDIF
C                     EXSR PRINT
C                     ADD  1        TOTREO 70
C                     ENDIF
C                     ENDIF
C                     ENDIF
C                     ENDDO
C           ALLTOT    IFGT 1000000                 COMPRESS MEGABYTES
C           ALLTOT    DIV  1000000  TOTOUT 51H     SAVED
C                     MOVE 'MB'     TOTTYP 2
C                     ELSE
C           ALLTOT    IFGT 1024                     COMPRESS KILOBTYES
C           ALLTOT    DIV  1024     TOTOUT  H      SAVED
C                     MOVE 'KB'     TOTTYP
C                     ENDIF
C                     ENDIF
C                     EXCPTTOTAL
C                     ENDIF
C                     SETON                    LR
 * ENSURE THAT REQUESTED LIBRARY EXISTS
C           EXIST     BEGSR
C                     MOVE LIB      FILLIB 20
C                     MOVEL'QSYS'   FILLIB
C                     CALL 'QUSROBJD'               ATTEMPT TO RETRIEVE
C                     PARM          VAR            OBJECT DESC
C                     PARM 500      RCVLEN
C                     PARM 'OBJD0100'FILFMT  8
C                     PARM          FILLIB
C                     PARM '*LIB'   OBJTYP 8
C                     PARM          ERROR
C           MSGID     IFNE *BLANKS                  LIBRARY DOESN'T EXIST
C           'QCPFMSG' CAT  'QSYS':3 MSGF
```

```
C                        CALL 'QMHSNDPM'              SEND ERROR MESSAGE
C                        PARM          MSGID
C                        PARM          MSGF    20
C                        PARM          LIB
C                        PARM 10       MSGDLN
C                        PARM '*DIAG'  MSGTYP  10
C                        PARM '*'      MSGQ    10
C                        PARM 1        MSGQNB
C                        PARM          MSGKEY
C                        PARM          ERROR        ERROR CODE
C                        MOVE *ON      ERR     1
C                        ENDIF
C                        ENDSR
 * CALL CL PROGRAM TO PERFORM REORG OF FILE
C           RGZFIL      BEGSR
C                        CALL 'RGZPFFCL'
C                        PARM          DBXLIB
C                        PARM          DBXFIL
C                        EXSR RTVMBR                GET NEW SIZES
C                        ENDSR
 * SEE IF REORG NEEDS TO BE DONE
C           RGZCHK      BEGSR
C                        MOVE *OFF     REORG
C                        MOVELDBXFIL   FILLIB 20
C                        MOVE DBXLIB   FILLIB
C                        Z-ADD500      RCVLEN
C                        EXSR RTVMBR
C           NUMREC      IFEQ 0                     NO RECORDS IN FILE
C           NUMDEL      ANDNE0                     DELETED RECORDS DO
C                        MOVE *ON      REORG         EXIST, REORG IT
C                        ENDIF
C           NUMREC      IFNE 0                     RECORDS EXIST AND
C           NUMDEL      ANDNE0                     DELETED RECS ALSO
C           NUMDEL      ADD  NUMREC   TOTREC  90
C           TOTREC      IFNE 0
C           NUMDEL      DIV  TOTREC   RESLT   72  IF PERCENTAGE OF
C           RESLT       MULT 100      TSTPRC  20   DELETED RECORDS
C           TSTPRC      IFGE PERC                  EXCEEDS SPECIFIED,
C                        MOVE *ON      REORG        REORG
C                        ENDIF
C                        ENDIF
C                        ENDIF
C                        ENDSR
 * ACCUMULATE TOTALS AND PRINT DETAIL
C           PRINT       BEGSR
C           B4SIZE      ADD  B4ACPS   B4TOT  100
C           DSSIZ       ADD  ACPSIZ   AFTOT  100
C           B4TOT       SUB  AFTOT    DIFTOT 100
C                        ADD  DIFTOT   ALLTOT 100
C                        EXCPTDETAIL
C                        ENDSR
 * RETREIVE MEMBER DESCRIPTION
C           RTVMBR      BEGSR
C                        CALL 'QUSRMBRD'
C                        PARM          VAR
C                        PARM          RCVLEN
C                        PARM 'MBRD0200'FMTNAM  8
C                        PARM          FILLIB
C                        PARM '*FIRST' MEMBR  10
C                        PARM '0'      OVRPRC  1
C                        PARM          ERROR
C                        ENDSR
OQSYSPRT E  101           HEADNG
O     OR        OF
```

```
       O                                 9  'LIBRARY'
       O                                18  'FILE'
       O                                39  'BEFORE SIZE'
       O                                54  'AFTER SIZE'
       O                                69  'FILE SAVED'
       O                                84  'TOTAL SAVED'
OQSYSPRT EF  1              DETAIL
       O                   DBXLIB    12
       O                   DBXFIL    24
       O                   B4TOT  1  39
       O                   AFTOT  1  54
       O                   DIFTOT1   69
       O                   ALLTOT1   84
OQSYSPRT EF22              TOTAL
       O                                24  'TOTAL BYTES SAVED.......'
       O                   TOTOUT1   39
       O                   TOTTYP    42
OQSYSPRT EF  1             TOTAL
       O                                24  'PHYSICAL FILES PROCESSED'
       O                   TOTFILZ   39
OQSYSPRT EF  1             TOTAL
       O                                24  'FILES REORGANIZED.......'
       O                   TOTREOZ   39
```

Figure 11.11: The RGZPFFCL CL Program Source

```
/*********************************************************************/
/*    TO CREATE:                        .                          */
/*        CRTCLPGM PGM(XXXLIB/RGZPFFCL)                            */
/*********************************************************************/
PGM (&LIB &FILE)
DCL &LIB   *CHAR 10
DCL &FILE *CHAR 10
MONMSG CPF0000
            RGZPFM       FILE(&LIB/&FILE) KEYFILE(*FILE)
ENDPGM
```

THE FIND DISPLACED LOGICAL FILE COMMAND

If a logical file resides in a different library than the physical file(s) it is over, you can end up with some rather unintentional and undesirable results. This tool helps you to identify the *outlaw logical* file and do what it takes to bring it to justice.

We all have done it at one time or another. Our object library option in PDM is not what we thought it was or our library list is messed up when we went to compile that new logical file. In many cases, we end up with a job that does not complete normally and we go on to correct the situation.

But what if the conditions are such that the job did complete normally? The end result is that we create an outlaw logical file that resides in a different library than the physical file it is over.

This condition is potentially dangerous for a number of reasons. Among them are nasty little error messages that come up when a program is called that is looking for a logical file that is nowhere to be found in the library list. Another reason could be revealed during the Save/Restore process. If the physical file does not already reside on disk when the system attempts to restore the outlaw logical file, the system gives you an error message and the logical file is not restored.

What makes this situation alarming is that you may have an outlaw on your system and not even know it. He may be lurking around the next corner waiting to pounce upon some poor unsuspecting user at the worst possible time.

The good news is that you can do something about it. You can use this utility to sniff out those nasty varmints and put them back where they belong.

Finding the Bad Guys

The Find Displaced Logical File (FNDDSPLF) command may be run over a specific library, library list, or all libraries on your system. The program finds all outlaw logical files in the libraries specified and brings them up in a subfile display, as seen in Figure 11.12.

Figure 11.12: Output from the FNDDSPLF Command

```
                    Find Displaced Logical Files

      Physical     Library      Logical      Library     Created By   Created On
      CUST         TSTFILES     CUSTQPGMR    TESTLIB     QPGMR          8/14/95
      CUSTCRD      TSTFILES     CUSBYLIM     JOHNLIB     JOHN          11/23/94
      CUSTPLAN     TSTFILES     CUSPLAN1     JOHNLIB     JOHN          12/07/94
      TRANS        TSTFILES     TRNBYDAT     WILSONLIB   WILSON         8/04/95
      CUSXREF      TSTFILES     CUSBYZIP     WILSONLIB   WILSON         8/14/95
      TRANS        TSTFILES     TRNBYCOD     QPGMR       QPGMR          8/14/95




                                                                  Bottom

      F3=Exit
```

The program displays outlaw logical files even if the physical file they are over is not in the libraries specified. If the physical file and the logical file meet the designated search criteria, you see the record listed twice in the subfile. To give you an idea of how long this program takes to run, it ran in less than 1 minute on a fully loaded E20 with over 7,000 files filling 4.7 gigabytes of DASD.

How It is Done

The program is a simple subfile display program over the system file QADBLDNC. This file is the *Dependency logical multiple-format file* over the QADBFDEP file that can be found in library QSYS. The QADBLDNC file is used to define the relationship between all of the physical and logical files on your system.

The command (Figure 11.13), display file (Figure 11.14), and RPG program (Figure 11.15) that follow are all you need for this handy utility. Refer to the compile notes found in the source members for instructions.

Figure 11.13: The FNDDSPLF Command

```
/*==================================================================*/
/* To compile:                                                      */
/*                                                                  */
/*          CRTCMD     CMD(XXX/DSPFLD) PGM(XXX/FNDDSPRG)            */
/*                                                                  */
/*==================================================================*/
           CMD        PROMPT('Find Displaced Logical Files')
           PARM       KWD(LIBRARY) TYPE(*CHAR) LEN(10) DFT(*LIBL) +
                        SPCVAL((*ALL)) MIN(0) CHOICE('Name, +
                        *LIBL, *ALL') PROMPT(Library:)
```

Figure 11.14: The FNDDSPDS Display File Source

```
      **********************************************************************
      *   TO COMPILE:
      *      CRTDSPF FILE(XXXLIB/FNDDSPDS)
      **********************************************************************
     A                                        CA03(03 'End of Program')
     A                                        PRINT(*LIBL/QSYSPRT)
     A          R SFLRCD                       SFL
     A            DBFFIL    10A  O  4  5
     A            DBFLIB    10A  O  4 18
     A            DBFFDP    10A  O  4 31
     A            DBFLDP    10A  O  4 44
     A            CRE8BY    10   O  4 57
     A            WHEN      6Y  OO  4 70EDTCDE(Y)
     A          R SFLCTL                       SFLCTL(SFLRCD)
     A                                        SFLSIZ(0032)
     A                                        SFLPAG(0016)
     A                                        OVERLAY
```

```
A   21                                 SFLDSP
A                                      SFLDSPCTL
A   41                                 SFLEND(*MORE)
A                                   1 26'Find Displaced Logical Files'
A                                      DSPATR(HI)
A                                   3  5'Physical'
A                                      DSPATR(HI)
A                                   3 18'Library'
A                                      DSPATR(HI)
A                                   3 31'Logical'
A                                      DSPATR(HI)
A                                   3 44'Library'
A                                      DSPATR(HI)
A                                   3 57'Created By'
A                                      DSPATR(HI)
A                                   3 70'Created On'
A                                      DSPATR(HI)
A        R FMT1
A                                  22  6'F3=Exit'
A                                      COLOR(BLU)
```

Figure 11.15: The FNDDSPRG RPG Program

```
        ***********************************************************************
        *   TO COMPILE:
        *     CRTRPGPGM PGM(XXXLIB/FNDDSPRG)
        ***********************************************************************
FFNDDSPDSCF E              ·     WORKSTN
F                                       RRN   KSFILE SFLRCD
FQADBLDNCIF E          K         DISK
E                    AR     4096  1
E                    ALIB       50 10
IERROR      IDS
I                                   B   1    40BYTPRV
I                                   B   5    80BYTAVA
I                                       9   15 MSGID
I                                      16   16 ERR###
I                                      17  116 MSGDTA
I           DS
I                                   B   1    40RCVLEN
I                                   B   5    80MSGKEY
I                                   B   9   120MSGDLN
I                                   B  13   160MSGQNB
IRCVVAR     DS                        4096
I                                   B   1    40BYTTOT
I                                   B   5    80BYTAVL
I                                   B  65   680SYS#
I                                   B  69   720PRD#
I                                   B  73   760CUR#
I                                   B  77   800USR#
IRCVVR1     DS                         460
I                                      66   670WHENYR
I                                      68   710WHENMD
I                                     220  229 CRE8BY
IFILLIB     DS
I                                       1   10 FLIB
I                                      11   20 FSYS
I               'No outlaw logicals f-C        CONER1
I               'ound in'
I               'Now searching files -C        CONMS1
```

```
I                      'for outlaw logicals'
C              *ENTRY   PLIST
C                       PARM              INLIB   10
C              'QCPFMSG' CAT  'QSYS':3   MSGF
C                       Z-ADD116          BYTPRV
C                       MOVE *OFF         ERR
C                       MOVE INLIB        LIB     10
   *   Make sure library exists
C              LIB      IFNE '*ALL'
C              LIB      ANDNE'*LIBL'
C                       EXSR EXIST
C                       ENDIF
C              ERR      IFEQ *OFF
C                       Z-ADD40           MSGDLN
C                       MOVELCONMS1       MDATA      P
C                       MOVEL'CPF9898'    MSGID
C                       MOVEL'*STATUS'    MSGTYP
C                       MOVEL'*EXT'       MSGQ
C                       Z-ADD0            MSGQNB
C                       EXSR SNDERR
C                       SELEC
C              LIB      WHEQ '*ALL'
C              *LOVAL   SETLLQDBFDEP
C              LIB      WHEQ '*LIBL'
C                       EXSR LIBLST
C              LIB      SETLLQADBLDNC
C                       OTHER
C              LIB      SETLLQADBLDNC
C                       ENDSL
C              *IN41    DOUEQ*ON
C              LIB      IFEQ '*ALL'
C              LIB      OREQ '*LIBL'
C                       READ QDBFDEP                  41
C                       ELSE
C              LIB      READEQADBLDNC                 41
C                       ENDIF
C              *IN41    IFEQ *OFF
C              .DBFLIB  IFNE DBFLDP
C                       MOVE *BLANKS      MSGID
C                       EXSR GETCRT                       GET CREATED INFO
C              MSGID    IFEQ 'CPF9812'
C                       ITER
C                       ENDIF
C                       Z-ADD0            WHEN
C                       MOVELWHENMD       WHEN
C                       MOVE WHENYR       WHEN
C                       ADD  1            RRN     40
C                       WRITESFLRCD
C                       ENDIF
C                       ELSE
C              INLIB    IFEQ '*LIBL'
C                       ADD  1            I
C              ALIB,I   IFNE *BLANKS
C                       MOVEAALIB,I       LIB
C              LIB      SETLLQADBLDNC
C                       SETOF                            41
C                       ENDIF
C                       ENDIF
C                       ENDIF
C                       ENDDO
   *
C              RRN      IFNE *ZEROS
C                       SETON                            21
C                       WRITEFMT1
```

```
C                      EXFMTSFLCTL
C                      ELSE
 *   No libraries found with outlaw logicals
C                      Z-ADD38        MSGDLN
C                      MOVELCONER1    MDATA      P
C          MDATA       CAT  LIB:1     MDATA
C                      MOVEL'CPF9898' MSGID
C                      MOVEL'*DIAG '  MSGTYP
C                      MOVEL'*    '   MSGQ
C                      Z-ADD1         MSGQNB
C                      EXSR SNDERR
C                      ENDIF
C                      ENDIF
C                      SETON                      LR
 *   Get who created logical file and when
C          GETCRT      BEGSR
C                      MOVELDBFFDP    FILLIB 20
C                      MOVELDBFLDP    FSYS
C                      CALL 'QUSROBJD'
C                      PARM           RCVVR1
C                      PARM 460       RCVLEN
C                      PARM 'OBJD0300'FILFMT  8
C                      PARM           FILLIB
C                      PARM '*FILE'   OBJTYP 10
C                      PARM           ERROR
C                      ENDSR
 *   Make sure requested library exists
C          EXIST       BEGSR
C                      MOVELLIB       FILLIB 20
C                      MOVEL'QSYS'    FSYS
C                      CALL 'QUSROBJD'           ATTEMPT TO RETRIEVE
C                      PARM           RCVVAR       OBJECT DESC
C                      PARM 5000      RCVLEN
C                      PARM 'OBJD0100'FILFMT  8
C                      PARM           FILLIB
C                      PARM '*LIB'    OBJTYP
C                      PARM           ERROR
C          MSGID       IFNE *BLANKS              LIBRARY DOESN'T EXIST
C                      Z-ADD10        MSGDLN
C                      MOVELLIB       MDATA
C                      MOVEL'*DIAG '  MSGTYP
C                      MOVEL'*    '   MSGQ
C                      Z-ADD1         MSGQNB
C                      EXSR SNDERR
C                      ENDIF
C                      ENDSR
 *   Send error back to caller
C          SNDERR      BEGSR
C                      CALL 'QMHSNDPM'           SEND ERROR MESSAGE
C                      PARM           MSGID
C                      PARM           MSGF   20
C                      PARM           MDATA  50
C                      PARM           MSGDLN
C                      PARM           MSGTYP 10
C                      PARM           MSGQ   10
C                      PARM           MSGQNB
C                      PARM           MSGKEY
C                      PARM           ERROR       ERROR CODE
C                      MOVE *ON       ERR     1
C                      ENDSR
 *   Get library list
C          LIBLST      BEGSR
C                      CALL 'QUSRJOBI'           GET LIBRARY LIST
C                      PARM           RCVVAR
```

```
C                       PARM 5000      RCVLEN
C                       PARM 'JOBI0700'FILFMT  8
C                       PARM '*'       JOBNAM 26
C                       PARM           INTJOB 16
C                       MOVEARCVVAR    AR,1
C           SYS#        MULT 11        I       40        IGNORE SYSTEM LIBS
C                       ADD  81        I
C                       Z-ADD1         J       40
C                       DO   PRD#                        PRODUCT LIBRARIES
C                       MOVEAAR,I      ALIB,J
C                       ADD  1         J
C                       ADD  11        I
C                       ENDDO
C                       DO   CUR#                        CURRENT LIBRARIES
C                       MOVEAAR,I      ALIB,J
C                       ADD  1         J
C                       ADD  11        I
C                       ENDDO
C                       DO   USR#                        USER LIBRARIES
C                       MOVEAAR,I      ALIB,J
C                       ADD  1         J
C                       ADD  11        I
C                       ENDDO
C                       MOVEAALIB,1    LIB
C                       Z-ADD1         I
C                       ENDSR
```

THE WORK WITH OBJECT REFERENCE COMMAND

It is a basic law of programming: Program complexity grows until it exceeds the capability of the programmer to maintain it. Change management systems have been created (costing in the tens of thousands of dollars) to help alleviate this basic rule.

The Art of Change Management

One common problem with change management is trying to locate all the programs that reference a file, a data area, or even another program. Changing an object can be a scary thing if you do not know how many other objects in the system may be affected. Wouldn't it be nice to have a command that shows all objects that reference another?

In order to have such a command, you need to build a reference file. The Build Object Reference (BLDOBJREF) command submits a program to build an object reference file that shows all objects that reference another object. The program creates one record in the file for each reference. An inquiry program can be written to access the reference file and then you have a very useful change management tool. The Work with Object Reference (WRKOBJREF) command is designed to perform just such a function.

Before you take the time to implement this tool, be aware that the tool is not perfect. The reference file for this tool is created using the Display Program Reference (DSPPGMREF) command, which can not pick up programs called using the QCMDEXC API. If your programs use the QCMDEXC command extensively, this tool may not be as useful as you would like.

Running the Work with Object Reference (WRKOBJREF) Command

All you need to do to run the Work with Object Reference command is to key WRKOBJREF and press F4 (you must have built your object reference summary file prior to the execution of this command). You see a prompt screen similar to that in Figure 11.16.

Figure 11.16: Running the WRKOBJREF Command

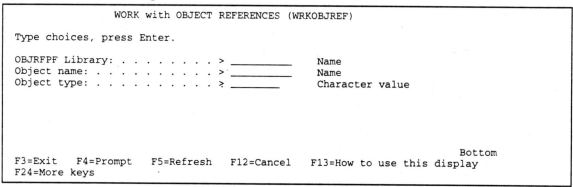

```
                    WORK with OBJECT REFERENCES  (WRKOBJREF)

 Type choices, press Enter.

 OBJRFPF Library: . . . . . . . . >  _____      Name
 Object name: . . . . . . . . . . >  _____      Name
 Object type: . . . . . . . . . . >  _____        Character value




                                                                     Bottom
 F3=Exit    F4=Prompt    F5=Refresh    F12=Cancel    F13=How to use this display
 F24=More keys
```

Fill in the prompt with the library name, object name, and object type (e.g., *FILE, *PGM, *DTAARA) and press Enter. If the type you specify happens to be a file, you are prompted for an extra set of parameters, shown in Figure 11.17. These parameters are necessary to determine whether or not the object you specify happens to be a physical file. If so, you may specify that the search of reference occurrences include any logical files that may be related to the physical file.

Figure 11.17: Running the WRKOBJREF Command on Physical Files

```
                  WORK with OBJECT REFERENCES (WRKOBJREF)

 Type choices, press Enter.

 OBJRFPF Library: . . . . . . . . > TESTLIB       Name
 Object name: . . . . . . . . . . > CUSTOMER      Name
 Object type: . . . . . . . . . > *FILE           Character value
 Is Object a Physical File?:  . .   Y             Y, N
 Include logicals over file?: . .   Y             N, Y
 Physical file library: . . . . .   *LIBL         Character value




                                                            Bottom
 F3=Exit    F4=Prompt    F5=Refresh    F12=Cancel    F13=How to use this display
 F24=More keys
```

Once you establish your search criteria and press Enter, you see an Object Reference
display similar to Figure 11.18.

Figure 11.18: Sample Output from the WRKOBJREF Command

```
                      Work with Object References

  Object name. . . . . CUSTOMER

   Type Options, press Enter.
    1=Source

   Name      Library    Text                              Useage   Logical
   CUSSUM    TESTLIB    Customer Summary Report           INPUT    CSBYNUM
   FONLST    TESTLIB    Customer Phone Book               INPUT    PHYSICAL
   LSTCUS    TESTLIB    Customer List Program             INPUT    CUSBYNAM
   QRYCUS    TESTLIB    Customer Query Program            INPUT    PHYSICAL
   RCDLCK    TESTLIB    Record lock error program         UPDATE   PHYSICAL


                                                            Bottom
    F3=Exit      F12=Previous
```

GETTING STARTED WITH *WRKOBJREF*

Because of the number of source members required to make the BLDOBJREF and
WRKOBJREF commands work, we put together a CL program that builds all of the
required objects for you. The first thing you need to do is get all of the source members
into your desired library. Put them in a physical source file named SOURCE (you can use

the CRTSRCPF command to create the file, if needed). Then compile the OBJMAKECL program, and call it. The OBJMAKECL program builds everything you need to run the WRKOBJREF and BLDOBJREF commands.

Compile the OBJMAKECL program as follows:

```
CRTCLPGM PGM(XXXLIB/OBJMAKECL)
```

To run the OBJMAKECL program, simply key:

```
CALL OBJMAKECL PARM('XXXLIB')
```

> **Note**: XXXLIB is the library where you have put the OBJREF source members.

Once the OBJMAKECL program has been run, you are ready to build your Object Reference pointer file. To do so, simply press BLDOBJREF and press F4. You are prompted for the libraries you want to include in your Object Reference pointer file and the date and time at which you want the command to execute.

How often you need to run the BLDOBJREF command depends upon how much your programs change. If you are in a development environment like ours, you may want to incorporate this command into your daily startup programs, as we have. The data in your Object Reference pointer files can obviously only be current to the last time you ran the BLDOBJREF command.

THE VALUE OF WRKOBJREF

We find this tool to be tremendously valuable when we have to change existing objects in our system. The command provides a quick way to determine what is involved, as well as a list of the source members that need to be changed.

There are two commands in this utility: BLDOBJREF and WRKOBJREF. BLDOBJREF (Figure 11.19) is used to build the work files. Figures 11.20 through 11.30 make up the display files, RPG programs, and CL programs used to build or work with the files created by the BLDOBJREF command. WRKOBJREF (Figure 11.31) is used to display the object reference instances. Even though compile notes have been added in the remarks sections of these source members, the OBJMAKECL command described previously should take care of all of this for you.

Figure 11.19: The BLDOBJREF Command

```
            CMD           PROMPT('BUILD OBJECT REFERENCE')
            PARM          KWD(LIB) TYPE(*NAME) PROMPT('LIBRARY FOR FILE:') MIN(1)
            PARM          KWD(LIST) TYPE(LIST1) MIN(1) MAX(100) +
                            PROMPT('LIST OF LIBRARIES:')
            PARM          KWD(JOBQ) TYPE(*CHAR) LEN(10) DFT(QBATCH) +
                            PMTCTL(*PMTRQS) PROMPT('JOB QUEUE:')
            PARM          KWD(SCDATE) TYPE(*CHAR) LEN(6) DFT(*CURRENT) +
                            SPCVAL((*CURRENT 000000)) PMTCTL(*PMTRQS) +
                            PROMPT('SCHEDULE DATE:')
            PARM          KWD(SCTIME) TYPE(*CHAR) LEN(4) DFT(*CURRENT) +
                            SPCVAL((*CURRENT 0000)) PMTCTL(*PMTRQS) +
                            PROMPT('SCHEDULE TIME (MILITARY):')
            PARM          KWD(JOBN) TYPE(*CHAR) LEN(10) DFT(BUILDREF) +
                            PMTCTL(*PMTRQS) PROMPT('JOB NAME:')
LIST1:      ELEM          TYPE(*NAME) LEN(10) MIN(1) EXPR(*YES) +
                            PROMPT('LIBRARY NAME')
```

Figure 11.20: The OBJCRLGL CL Program

```
/****************************************************************************/
/*   TO CREATE:                                                             */
/*        CRTCLPGM PGM(XXXLIB/OBJCRLGL)                                      */
/****************************************************************************/
PGM (&FILE &LIB)

DCL VAR(&FILE) TYPE(*CHAR) LEN(10)
DCL VAR(&LIB) TYPE(*CHAR) LEN(10)

MONMSG CPF0000

            IF            COND(&LIB *EQ '          ') THEN(DO)
            CHGVAR        VAR(&LIB) VALUE('*LIBL')
            ENDDO

            CLRPFM        FILE(QTEMP/OBJRFLOG)

            DSPDBR        FILE(&LIB/&FILE) OUTPUT(*OUTFILE) +
                            OUTFILE(QTEMP/OBJRFLOG)

ENDPGM
```

Figure 11.21: The OBJDETTY CL Program

```
/*******************************************************************************/
/*    TO CREATE:                                                              */
/*        CRTCLPGM PGM(XXXLIB/OBJDETTY)                                       */
/*******************************************************************************/
PGM ((&OBJNAM) (&OBJLIB) (&FILATR))

DCL &FILATR *CHAR 3
DCL &OBJNAM *CHAR 10
DCL &OBJLIB *CHAR 10

MONMSG (CPF0000)

IF COND(&OBJLIB *EQ '          ') THEN(DO)
CHGVAR VAR(&OBJLIB) VALUE('*LIBL')
ENDDO

            RTVMBRD    FILE(&OBJLIB/&OBJNAM) FILEATR(&FILATR)

ENDPGM
```

Figure 11.22: The OBJDSP CL Program

```
/*******************************************************************************/
/*    TO CREATE:                                                              */
/*        CRTCLPGM PGM(XXXLIB/OBJDSP)                                         */
/*******************************************************************************/
PGM (&OBJ &LIB)

DCL VAR(&OBJ) TYPE(*CHAR) LEN(10)
DCL VAR(&LIB) TYPE(*CHAR) LEN(10)

MONMSG CPF0000

            IF         COND(&LIB *EQ '          ') THEN(DO)
            CHGVAR     VAR(&LIB) VALUE('*LIBL')
            ENDDO

            DSPOBJD    OBJ(&LIB/&OBJ) OBJTYPE(*ALL) +
                         OUTPUT(*OUTFILE) OUTFILE(QTEMP/OBJDSPPF)

            OVRDBF     FILE(OBJDSPPF) TOFILE(QTEMP/OBJDSPPF)

            CALL       QGPL/OBJDSP1 PARM(&OBJ &LIB)
ENDPGM
```

Figure 11.23: The OBJHS RPG Program

```
          *******************************************************************
          *   TO COMPILE:
          *      CRTRPGPGM PGM(XXXLIB/OBJHS)
          *******************************************************************
          *
          *    PROGRAM NAME - OBJHS
          *    FUNCTION      - TAKE FILE FROM DSPPGMREF AND WRITE PERTINENT
          *                    INFO TO FILE.
          *
          FPGMREFO IF  E                     DISK
          FOBJRFPF O   E                     DISK
          *
          C           1          SETLLPGMREFO
          *
B1        C           *IN50      DOUEQ*ON
          C                      READ PGMREFO                    50
          *
B2        C           *IN50      IFEQ *ON
          C                      LEAVE
E2        C                      ENDIF
          *
          C                      MOVELWHLIB      OBJLIB
          C                      MOVELWHPNAM     OBJNAM
          C                      MOVELWHTEXT     OBJTXT
          C                      MOVELWHFNAM     OBRNAM
          C                      MOVELWHLNAM     OBRLIB
          C                      MOVELWHFUSG     OBRUSE
          C                      MOVELWHOTYP     OBRTYP
          C                      WRITEOBJREC
E1        C                      ENDDO
          *
          C                      SETON                     LR
```

Figure 11.24: The OBJHSTCL CL Program

```
/**************************************************************************/
/*    TO CREATE:                                                         */
/*        CRTCLPGM PGM(XXXLIB/OBJHSTCL)                                   */
/**************************************************************************/
PGM   (&LIBRARY &REPADD &REFLIB)

DCL &LIBRARY *CHAR 10
DCL &REPADD *CHAR 1
DCL &REFLIB  *CHAR 10

          DSPPGMREF   PGM(&LIBRARY/*ALL) OUTPUT(*OUTFILE) +
                        OUTFILE(QTEMP/PGMREFO) OUTMBR(*FIRST)

          OVRDBF      FILE(OBJRFPF) TOFILE(&REFLIB/OBJRFPF)
          OVRDBF      FILE(PGMREFO) TOFILE(QTEMP/PGMREFO)

IF COND(&REPADD *EQ 'R') THEN(DO)
CLRPFM &REFLIB/OBJRFPF
ENDDO

CALL OBJHS

          DLTOVR PGMREFO
          DLTOVR OBJRFPF

ENDPGM
```

Figure 11.25: The OBJMAKECL CL Program

```
/**************************************************************************/
/*    TO CREATE:                                                         */
/*        CRTCLPGM PGM(XXXLIB/OBJMAKECL)                                  */
/**************************************************************************/
PGM (&LIB)

DCL &LIB *CHAR 10
DCL &MSGDTA *CHAR 50
DCL &NOADD *CHAR 1

          ADDLIBLE    &LIB
          MONMSG      MSGID(CPF2103) EXEC(DO)
          CHGVAR      &NOADD '1'
          ENDDO

          CHGVAR      VAR(&MSGDTA) VALUE('Creating OBJRFPF file')
          SNDPGMMSG   MSGID(CPF9898) MSGF(QSYS/QCPFMSG) +
                        MSGDTA(&MSGDTA) TOPGMQ(*EXT) MSGTYPE(*STATUS)
          CRTPF       FILE(&LIB/OBJRFPF) SRCFILE(&LIB/SOURCE)

          CHGVAR      VAR(&MSGDTA) VALUE('Creating PGMREFO file')
          SNDPGMMSG   MSGID(CPF9898) MSGF(QSYS/QCPFMSG) +
                        MSGDTA(&MSGDTA) TOPGMQ(*EXT) MSGTYPE(*STATUS)
          DSPPGMREF   PGM(&LIB/*ALL) OUTPUT(*OUTFILE) +
                        OUTFILE(QTEMP/PGMREFO) OUTMBR(*FIRST)

          CHGVAR      VAR(&MSGDTA) VALUE('Creating OBJRFLOG file')
          SNDPGMMSG   MSGID(CPF9898) MSGF(QSYS/QCPFMSG) +
```

```
                    MSGDTA(&MSGDTA) TOPGMQ(*EXT) MSGTYPE(*STATUS)
    DSPDBR          FILE(&LIB/OBJRFPF) OUTPUT(*OUTFILE) +
                    OUTFILE(QTEMP/OBJRFLOG)

    CHGVAR          VAR(&MSGDTA) VALUE('Creating OBJRFDSP display file')
    SNDPGMMSG       MSGID(CPF9898) MSGF(QSYS/QCPFMSG) +
                    MSGDTA(&MSGDTA) TOPGMQ(*EXT) MSGTYPE(*STATUS)
    CRTDSPF         FILE(&LIB/OBJRFDSP) SRCFILE(&LIB/SOURCE)

    CHGVAR          VAR(&MSGDTA) VALUE('Creating OBJRF RPG program     ')
    SNDPGMMSG       MSGID(CPF9898) MSGF(QSYS/QCPFMSG) +
                    MSGDTA(&MSGDTA) TOPGMQ(*EXT) MSGTYPE(*STATUS)
    CRTRPGPGM       PGM(&LIB/OBJRF) SRCFILE(&LIB/SOURCE)

    CHGVAR          VAR(&MSGDTA) VALUE('Creating OBJHS RPG program     ')
    SNDPGMMSG       MSGID(CPF9898) MSGF(QSYS/QCPFMSG) +
                    MSGDTA(&MSGDTA) TOPGMQ(*EXT) MSGTYPE(*STATUS)
    CRTRPGPGM       PGM(&LIB/OBJHS) SRCFILE(&LIB/SOURCE)

    CHGVAR          VAR(&MSGDTA) VALUE('Creating OBJCRLGL CLP program ')
    SNDPGMMSG       MSGID(CPF9898) MSGF(QSYS/QCPFMSG) +
                    MSGDTA(&MSGDTA) TOPGMQ(*EXT) MSGTYPE(*STATUS)
    CRTCLPGM        PGM(&LIB/OBJCRLGL) SRCFILE(&LIB/SOURCE)

    CHGVAR          VAR(&MSGDTA) VALUE('Creating OBJDETTY CLP program ')
    SNDPGMMSG       MSGID(CPF9898) MSGF(QSYS/QCPFMSG) +
                    MSGDTA(&MSGDTA) TOPGMQ(*EXT) MSGTYPE(*STATUS)
    CRTCLPGM        PGM(&LIB/OBJDETTY) SRCFILE(&LIB/SOURCE)

    CHGVAR          VAR(&MSGDTA) VALUE('Creating OBJDSP CLP program    ')
    SNDPGMMSG       MSGID(CPF9898) MSGF(QSYS/QCPFMSG) +
                    MSGDTA(&MSGDTA) TOPGMQ(*EXT) MSGTYPE(*STATUS)
    CRTCLPGM        PGM(&LIB/OBJDSP)  SRCFILE(&LIB/SOURCE)

    CHGVAR          VAR(&MSGDTA) VALUE('Creating OBJHSTCL CLP program ')
    SNDPGMMSG       MSGID(CPF9898) MSGF(QSYS/QCPFMSG) +
                    MSGDTA(&MSGDTA) TOPGMQ(*EXT) MSGTYPE(*STATUS)
    CRTCLPGM        PGM(&LIB/OBJHSTCL) SRCFILE(&LIB/SOURCE)

    CHGVAR          VAR(&MSGDTA) VALUE('Creating OBJREFBLDS CLP program ')
    SNDPGMMSG       MSGID(CPF9898) MSGF(QSYS/QCPFMSG) +
                    MSGDTA(&MSGDTA) TOPGMQ(*EXT) MSGTYPE(*STATUS)
    CRTCLPGM        PGM(&LIB/OBJREFBLDS) SRCFILE(&LIB/SOURCE)

    CHGVAR          VAR(&MSGDTA) VALUE('Creating OBJREFBSBM CLP program ')
    SNDPGMMSG       MSGID(CPF9898) MSGF(QSYS/QCPFMSG) +
                    MSGDTA(&MSGDTA) TOPGMQ(*EXT) MSGTYPE(*STATUS)
    CRTCLPGM        PGM(&LIB/OBJREFBSBM) SRCFILE(&LIB/SOURCE)

    CHGVAR          VAR(&MSGDTA) VALUE('Creating WRKOBJREF command      ')
    SNDPGMMSG       MSGID(CPF9898) MSGF(QSYS/QCPFMSG) +
                    MSGDTA(&MSGDTA) TOPGMQ(*EXT) MSGTYPE(*STATUS)
    CRTCMD          CMD(&LIB/WRKOBJREF) PGM(&LIB/OBJRF) +
                    SRCFILE(&LIB/SOURCE)

    CHGVAR          VAR(&MSGDTA) VALUE('Creating BLDOBJREF command      ')
    SNDPGMMSG       MSGID(CPF9898) MSGF(QSYS/QCPFMSG) +
```

```
                    MSGDTA(&MSGDTA) TOPGMQ(*EXT) MSGTYPE(*STATUS)
        CRTCMD      CMD(&LIB/BLDOBJREF) PGM(&LIB/OBJREFBSBM) +
                    SRCFILE(&LIB/SOURCE)

        IF          COND(&NOADD *NE '1') THEN(DO)
        RMVLIBLE    &LIB
        ENDDO

ENDPGM
```

Figure 11.26: The OBJREFBLDS CL Program

```
/****************************************************************************/
/*    TO CREATE:                                                            */
/*        CRTCLPGM PGM(XXXLIB/OBJREFBLDS)                                    */
/****************************************************************************/
PGM (&LIB &LIST)

            DCL         VAR(&LIB) TYPE(*CHAR) LEN(10)
            DCL         VAR(&BLDLIB) TYPE(*CHAR) LEN(10)
            DCL         VAR(&REPADD) TYPE(*CHAR) LEN(1) VALUE('R')
            DCL         VAR(&LIST) TYPE(*CHAR) LEN(1902)
            DCL         VAR(&X) TYPE(*DEC) LEN(3 0) /* Count of nbr */
            DCL         VAR(&Y) TYPE(*DEC) LEN(5 0) VALUE(1) /* +
                          Displacement */
            DCL         VAR(&Z) TYPE(*DEC) LEN(5 0) /* Pos of values */
            DCL         VAR(&WORK) TYPE(*CHAR) LEN(2)
            DCL         VAR(&LSTCNT) TYPE(*DEC) LEN(5 0)
            DCL         VAR(&DISPCNT) TYPE(*DEC) LEN(5 0)

/*    GLOBAL MONITOR MESSAGE    */
            MONMSG      MSGID(CPF0000)

/*    IF REFERENCE FILE DOESN'T EXIST, CREATE IT FROM BASE COPY IN QGPL    */
            CHKOBJ      OBJ(&LIB/OBJRFPF) OBJTYPE(*FILE)
            MONMSG      MSGID(CPF9801) EXEC(DO)
            CRTDUPOBJ   OBJ(OBJRFPF) FROMLIB(QGPL) OBJTYPE(*FILE) +
                          TOLIB(&LIB)
            ENDDO

            OVRDBF      FILE(OBJRFPF) TOFILE(&LIB/OBJRFPF)
            CLRPFM      FILE(&LIB/OBJRFPF)

            CHGVAR      VAR(&WORK) VALUE(%SST(&LIST 1 2)) /* Nbr of +
                          lists */
            CHGVAR      VAR(&LSTCNT) VALUE(%BIN(&WORK 1 2))
/*    BEGIN LOOP FOR EACH LIST                                      */
 LOOP:
            CHGVAR      VAR(&X) VALUE(&X + 1) /* Next list */
            CHGVAR      VAR(&Y) VALUE(&Y + 2) /* Next displacement */

/*    EXTRACT DISPLACEMENT VALUE    */
            CHGVAR      VAR(&WORK) VALUE(%SST(&LIST &Y 2))
            CHGVAR      VAR(&DISPCNT) VALUE(%BIN(&WORK 1 2))

            CHGVAR      VAR(&Z) VALUE(&DISPCNT + 3) /* Bgn pos +
                          within list */

/*    GET LIBRARY NAME                  */
```

```
                CHGVAR      VAR(&BLDLIB) VALUE(%SST(&LIST &Z 10))

/*  DISPLAY PROGRAM REFERENCES TO WORK FILE IN QTEMP  */
                DSPPGMREF   PGM(&BLDLIB/*ALL) OUTPUT(*OUTFILE) +
                              OUTFILE(QTEMP/PGMREFO) OUTMBR(*FIRST *ADD)

                IF          (&X *LT &LSTCNT) GOTO LOOP /* Loop back */

/*  CALL PROGRAM TO WRITE RECORDS TO REFERENCE FILE    */
                OVRDBF      FILE(OBJRFPF) TOFILE(&LIB/OBJRFPF)
                OVRDBF      FILE(PGMREFO) TOFILE(QTEMP/PGMREFO)
                CALL        PGM(OBJHS)
                DLTOVR PGMREFO
                DLTOVR OBJRFPF

ENDPGM
```

Figure 11.27: The OBJREFBSBM CL Program

```
/*******************************************************************/
/*    TO CREATE:                                                   */
/*         CRTCLPGM PGM(XXXLIB/OBJREFBSBM)                         */
/*******************************************************************/
PGM (&LIB &LIST &JOBQ &SCCDATE &SCCTIME &JOBN)

                DCL         VAR(&LIST) TYPE(*CHAR) LEN(1902)
                DCL         VAR(&LIB) TYPE(*CHAR) LEN(10)
                DCL         VAR(&JOBQ) TYPE(*CHAR) LEN(10)
                DCL         VAR(&JOBN) TYPE(*CHAR) LEN(10)
                DCL         VAR(&SCCDATE) TYPE(*CHAR) LEN(6)
                DCL         VAR(&SCCTIME) TYPE(*CHAR) LEN(4)
                DCL         VAR(&SCCDATE8) TYPE(*CHAR) LEN(8) +
                              VALUE(*CURRENT)
                DCL         VAR(&SCCTIME8) TYPE(*CHAR) LEN(8) +
                              VALUE(*CURRENT)

/*    GLOBAL MONITOR MESSAGE     */
                MONMSG      MSGID(CPF0000)

/*    IF SUBMITTING ON DATE OTHER THAN CURRENT THEN USE THAT DATE    */
                IF          COND(&SCCDATE *NE '000000') THEN(DO)
                CHGVAR      VAR(&SCCDATE8) VALUE(&SCCDATE)
                ENDDO

/*    IF SUBMITTING ON TIME OTHER THAN CURRENT THEN USE THAT TIME    */
                IF          COND(&SCCTIME *NE '0000') THEN(DO)
                CHGVAR      VAR(&SCCTIME8) VALUE(&SCCTIME)
                ENDDO

/*    SUBMIT THE JOB TO CREATE THE FILE                     */
                SBMJOB      CMD(CALL PGM(OBJREFBLDS) PARM(&LIB &LIST)) +
                              JOB(&JOBN) JOBQ(&JOBQ) SCDDATE(&SCCDATE8) +
                              SCDTIME(&SCCTIME8)

/*    SEND JOB SUBMITTED MESSAGE BACK TO USER               */
                SNDPGMMSG   MSGID(CPF9898) MSGF(QCPFMSG) MSGDTA('JOB' +
                              *BCAT &JOBN *TCAT ' has been submitted +
                              to batch.') MSGTYPE(*DIAG)

ENDPGM
```

Figure 11.28: The OBJRF RPG Program

```
      ********************************************************************
      *   TO COMPILE:
      *      CRTRPGPGM PGM(XXXLIB/OBJRF)
      ********************************************************************
      FOBJRFDSPCF  E                    WORKSTN
      F                                           RRN    KSFILE SFLRCD
      F                                                  KINFDS INFO
      FOBJRFPF IF  E          K         DISK                                UC
      FOBJRFLOGIF  E                    DISK                                UC
      IINFO        DS
      I                                           197 206 WSID
      I                                           370 371 CHAR
      I                                         B 370 3710BIN
      I                                         B 378 3790FSTL
      IERROR       IDS
      I                                         B   1   40BYTPRV
      I                                         B   5   80BYTAVA
      I                                             9  15 MSGID
      I                                            16  16 ERR###
      I                                            17 116 MSGDTA
      I            DS
      I                                         B   1   40MSGDLN
      I                                         B   5   80MSGQNB
      I                                         B   9  120MSGKY
      I            SDS
      I                                           254 263 USER
      I                               *PARMS      PARMS
      I                    'OVRDBF FILE(OBJRFPF)-C        REST'
      I                    ' TOFILE('
      I                    '/OBJRFPF)'              C        FILENM
      I                    'NO REFERENCES EXIST -C        NOREF
      I                    'FOR THIS OBJECT  - P-
      I                    'RESS ENTER'
      C            *ENTRY    PLIST
      C                      PARM           PASLIB 10        LIBRARY NAME
      C                      PARM           PASOBJ 10        OBJECT NAME
      C                      PARM           PASTYP  8        OBJECT TYPE
      C                      PARM           PHYFIL  1        PHYSICAL FILE?
      C                      PARM           LOGYN   1        LOGICAL TOO?
      C                      PARM           LOGLIB 10        LOGICAL LIBRARY
      C                      MOVEL'*'       PGMQ   10
      C                      MOVELREST      CMD       P      OVERRIDE TO
      C                      CAT  PASLIB:0  CMD              CORRECT OBJRFPF
      C                      CAT  FILENM:0  CMD              FILE/LIBRARY
      C                      Z-ADD50        LEN
      C                      CALL 'QCMDEXC'
      C                      PARM           CMD    50
      C                      PARM           LEN   155
      C                      OPEN OBJRFPF                 99
      C                      MOVE PASOBJ    SCNNAM 10
      B1  C        PASTYP    IFEQ '*FILE'                    OBJECTS A FILE
      C            LOGYN     ANDEQ'Y'                        LOGICALS TO BE USED
      C            PHYFIL    ANDEQ'Y'                        PHYSICAL FILES ONLY
      C                      CALL 'OBJCRLGL'                 CREATE FILE OF NAMES
      C                      PARM           SCNNAM           OF LOGICALS
      C                      PARM           LOGLIB
      C                      OPEN OBJRFLOG                99
      B2  C        *IN99     IFEQ *OFF
      C                      SETON                        82
      E2  C                  ENDIF
      E1  C                  ENDIF
```

```
        C         SCNNAM      SETLLOBJRFPF
        C                     EXSR LODSFL                          LOAD SUBFILE
        C                     SETOF                       21
B1      C         RRN         IFNE *ZEROS
        C                     SETON                       21       DISPLAY SFLRCD
        C                     Z-ADD1      DSPRRN
X1      C                     ELSE
        C                     EXSR ERRSR
        C                     WRITEMSGCTL
        C                     SETON                       03
E1      C                     ENDIF
B1      C         *IN03       DOUEQ*ON
        C         FOUND       ORNE 'Y'
B2      C         *IN03       IFEQ *OFF
        C                     WRITEFORMAT1
E2      C                     ENDIF
        C                     EXFMTSFLCTL
        C                     MOVE *BLANKS    FOUND   1
B2      C         *IN03       IFEQ *OFF                   NOT END OF JOB
        C         *IN21       ANDEQ*ON
        C                     Z-ADDFSTL   DSPRRN  40      SAVE CURRENT PAGE
        C                     EXSR OPTION                 LOOK FOR SELECTIONS
E2      C                     ENDIF
E1      C                     ENDDO
        C                     SETON                       LR
        CSR       OPTION      BEGSR                       LOOK FOR OPTION RQSTS
B1      C         *IN55       DOUEQ*ON
        C                     READCSFLRCD                 55
B2      C         *IN55       IFEQ *OFF
B3      C         SEL         IFNE *BLANKS
        C                     MOVE 'Y'        FOUND
        C                     CALL 'OBJDSP'               SEU SOURCE
        C                     PARM            DOBJNM
        C                     PARM            DOBJLB
        C                     MOVE *BLANKS    SEL
        C                     UPDATSFLRCD
E3      C                     ENDIF
E2      C                     ENDIF
E1      C                     ENDDO
        CSR                   ENDSR
        CSR       LODSFL      BEGSR                       LOAD SUBFILE
B1      C         MORELG      DOUEQ*BLANKS                UNTIL NO MORE LOGICAL
        C                     MOVE *BLANKS    MORELG  1   S ARE FOUND
B2      C         *IN51       DOUEQ*ON
        C         SCNNAM      READEOBJRFPF                51
B3      C         *IN51       IFEQ *ON
        C                     LEAVE
E3      C                     ENDIF
        *
        * IF OBJECT REFERENCED MORE THAN ONCE IN SAME PROGRAM, ONLY WANT IT
        *   SHOWN IN THE THE SUBFILE ONCE
        *
        C                     MOVELOBJLIB     F20     20
        C                     MOVE OBJNAM     F20
B3      C         F20         IFEQ DUPES
        C                     ITER
E3      C                     ENDIF
        C                     MOVE F20        DUPES   20
        *
        C                     MOVE OBJNAM     DOBJNM
        C                     MOVE OBJLIB     DOBJLB
        C                     MOVELOBJTXT     DOBJTX
        C                     MOVE *BLANKS    DUSEDS
B3      C         OBRTYP      IFEQ '*FILE'                TRANSLATE FILE USEAGE
```

```
       C                            MOVEL'UNKNOWN' DUSEDS    P        TYPE CODE TO ENGLISH
B4     C                            SELEC
       C                   OBRUSE   WHEQ '01'
       C                            MOVEL'INPUT'   DUSEDS    P
       C                   OBRUSE   WHEQ '02'
       C                            MOVEL'OUTPUT'  DUSEDS    P
       C                   OBRUSE   WHEQ '03'
       C                            MOVEL'WRKSTN'  DUSEDS    P
       C                   OBRUSE   WHEQ '04'
       C                            MOVEL'UPDATE'  DUSEDS    P
       C                   OBRUSE   WHEQ '06'
       C                            MOVEL'UPD/ADD' DUSEDS    P
       C                   OBRUSE   WHEQ '09'
       C                   OBRUSE   OREQ '11'
       C                            MOVEL'DEL/CRT' DUSEDS    P
E4     C                            ENDSL
E3     C                            ENDIF
B3     C          DLOGNM            IFEQ *BLANKS
B3     C          *IN82             ANDEQ*ON
       C                            MOVEL'PHYSICAL'DLOGNM
E3     C                            ENDIF
       C                            ADD  1         RRN       40
       C                            WRITESFLRCD
E2     C                            ENDDO
B2     C          *IN82             IFEQ *ON                          IF LOGICALS ARE TO BE
       C                            READ OBJRFLOG                  52 INCLUDED IN SEARCH,
B3     C          *IN52             IFEQ *OFF                         PUT NEXT LGL NAME
       C                            MOVELWHREFI    SCNNAM    P        LOOP TO TOP
       C                            MOVELWHREFI    DLOGNM    P
       C                            MOVE 'X'       MORELG
       C          SCNNAM            SETLLOBJRPF
E3     C                            ENDIF
E2     C                            ENDIF
E1     C                            ENDDO
       C                            ENDSR
       C          ERRSR             BEGSR
       C                            Z-ADD116       BYTPRV
       C          'QCPFMSG'  CAT    'QSYS':3 MSGF
       C                            MOVE 'CPF9898' MSGID
       C                            MOVELNOREF     MSGDTA    P
       C                            Z-ADD60        MSGDLN
       C                            Z-ADD0         MSGQNB
       C                            CALL 'QMHSNDPM'                   SEND ERROR MESSAGE
       C                            PARM           MSGID
       C                            PARM           MSGF      20
       C                            PARM           MSGDTA
       C                            PARM           MSGDLN
       C                            PARM '*DIAG'   MSGTYP 10
       C                            PARM '*'       MSGQ   10
       C                            PARM           MSGQNB
       C                            PARM           MSGKY
       C                            PARM           ERROR             ERROR CODE
       C                            ENDSR
```

Figure 11.29: The OBJRFDSP Display File

```
A*******************************************************************
A*   TO COMPILE:
A*     CRTDSPF FILE(XXXLIB/OBJRFDSP)
A*******************************************************************
A                                          DSPSIZ(24 80 *DS3)
A                                          PRINT
A                                          CA03(03)
A                                          CA12(03)
A            R SFLRCD                      SFL
A   40                                     SFLNXTCHG
A              DOBJNM     10A  O  9  4
A              DOBJLB     10A  O  9 15
A              DOBJTX     38A  O  9 26
A              DUSEDS      7A  O  9 65
A              DLOGNM      8A  O  9 73
A              SEL         1A  B  9  2DSPATR(HI)
A            R SFLCTL                      SFLCTL(SFLRCD)
A                                          CHGINPDFT
A                                          SFLSIZ(0024)
A                                          SFLPAG(0012)
A                                          OVERLAY
A   21                                     SFLDSP
A                                          SFLDSPCTL
A   51                                     SFLEND(*MORE)
A              DSPRRN      4S 0H           SFLRCDNBR
A                                      1 26'Work with Object References'
A                                          DSPATR(HI)
A                                          DSPATR(UL)
A                                      3  3'Object name. . . .'
A N21                                      DSPATR(ND)
A              SCNNAM     10A  O  3 22
A N21                                      DSPATR(ND)
A   21N82                               8  2' Name       Library    Text    -
A                                                                    Useage-
A                                          '
A                                          DSPATR(HI)
A   21 82                               8  2' Name       Library    Text    -
A                                                                    Useage-
A                                          . Logical'
A                                          DSPATR(HI)
A   21                                  5  4'Type Options, press Enter.'
A                                          COLOR(BLU)
A   21                                  6  5'1=Source'
A                                          COLOR(BLU)
A            R FORMAT1
A                                          TEXT('Command keys')
A                                     23  4'F3=Exit'
A                                          COLOR(BLU)
A                                     23 17'F12=Previous'
A                                          COLOR(BLU)
A            R MSGSFL                       SFL
A                                          SFLMSGRCD(24)
A              MSGKEY                       SFLMSGKEY
A              PGMQ                         SFLPGMQ
A            R MSGCTL                       SFLCTL(MSGSFL)
A                                          OVERLAY
A                                          ALARM
A                                          SFLSIZ(3) SFLPAG(1)
A                                          SFLDSP SFLINZ
A   90                                     SFLEND
A              PGMQ                         SFLPGMQ
```

Figure 11.30: The OBJRFPF Physical File

```
      R OBJREC
        OBJNAM       10           COLHDG('OBJECT NAME')
        OBJLIB       10           COLHDG('OBJECT LIBRARY')
        OBJTXT       40           COLHDG('OBJECT TEXT')
        OBRNAM       10           COLHDG('REFERENCED OBJECT')
        OBRLIB       10           COLHDG('REFERENCED LIBRARY')
        OBRTYP       10           COLHDG('REFERENCED TYPE')
        OBRUSE        2           COLHDG('FILE USEAGE')
      K OBRNAM
      K OBRLIB
      K OBJNAM
      K OBJLIB
```

Figure 11.31: The WRKOBJREF Command

```
        CMD        PROMPT('WORK with OBJECT REFERENCES')
        PARM       KWD(LIB) TYPE(*NAME) PROMPT('OBJRFPF Library:') +
                     MIN(1)
        PARM       KWD(NAME) TYPE(*NAME) PROMPT('Object name:') +
                     MIN(1)
        PARM       KWD(TYPE) TYPE(*CHAR) LEN(8) PROMPT('Object type:') +
                     MIN(1)
        PARM       KWD(PHYFIL) TYPE(*CHAR) LEN(1) RSTD(*YES) +
                     VALUES(Y N) DFT(Y) PMTCTL(TYPE) PROMPT('Is +
                     Object a Physical File?:')
        PARM       KWD(LOGYN) TYPE(*CHAR) LEN(1) RSTD(*YES) +
                     DFT(Y) VALUES(N Y) PMTCTL(ATTR) +
                     PROMPT('Include logicals over file?:')
        PARM       KWD(LOGLIB) TYPE(*CHAR) LEN(10) DFT(*LIBL) +
                     PMTCTL(ATTR) PROMPT('Physical file library:')
TYPE:   PMTCTL     CTL(TYPE) COND((*EQ *FILE))
ATTR:   PMTCTL     CTL(PHYFIL) COND((*EQ Y))
```

FINAL WORDS ABOUT TOOLS IN THE TOOLBOX

We have not observed any programmers whom we feel had too many tools in their toolbox. It is our position that you simply can not have too many weapons in your arsenal.

If a tool can improve your productivity enough that the amount of time saved by the tool surpasses the amount of time spent developing it, the development time was time well spent. If a tool eliminates or helps to reduce certain errors from getting into production, implementation of the tool should be considered seriously.

Appendix A

Companion Diskette Contents

The companion diskette that accompanies this book contains source code for many of the figures. Table A.1 represents a cross reference for the figures and files on the diskette.

Table A.1: Diskette Cross-reference Information

Figure	File Name	Description
2.8	CUSSFLDS	DDS for Customer Subfile
2.9	CUSSFL	RPG Program for Customer Subfile
2.10	SLIDEDSP	DDS for State Lookup Window Subfile
2.11	SLIDE	RPG for State Lookup Window Subfile Program

Figure	File Name	Description
2.15	PRINTER	DDS for Physical File PRINTER
2.16	PRINTERS	DDS for Logical File PRINTERS
2.17	LOOKUPDS	DDS for Display File LOOKUPDS
2.18	LOOKUP	RPG Specifications for Program LOOKUP
3.3	BAREXDSP	Sample DDS for Menu Bar in Figures 3.1 and 3.2
3.4	BAREX	The BAREX RPG Program to Present a Menu Bar
3.6	REQUEST	DDS for File Request
3.7	REQ001RG	REQ001RG RPG Attention Window Program
3.8	REQ001DS	DDS for the REQ001DS System Request Window
4.11	RCDLCKDS	DDS for Sample Record Lock Program
4.12	RCDLCK	Sample RPG Program for Record Locks
6.2	QRYCUS	Using QCMDEXC to Run OPNQRYF from within an RPG Program
6.3	LSTCUS	Using QCMDEXC to Override Printer Attributes
6.4	LCUSTDSP	Customer List Prompt Screen Display File
6.6	LCUST	Using QCMDEXC to Submit Jobs from within an RPG program
6.7	EXIST2	RPG API Program to Validate Printer Existence
7.3	CUSSUM	Using Sort Array (SORTA) to Resequence Array Elements
7.4	FONLST	Multicolumn Customer Phone List Using Arrays to

Figure	File Name	Description
		Format Output
9.2	GETDAT	Sample of the Retrieve Object Description API
9.3	EXIST	Sample RPG Program to Validate Object Existence
9.4	MSGEX	Sample RPG Program Using the Send Program Message (QMHSNDPM) API
9.5	MSGEXDSP	DDS for the MSGEX RPG Program Using the QMHSNDPM Send Program Message API
9.10	DSPDBA	DSPDBA RPG Program
9.11	DSPDBADS	DSPDBADS Display File
9.12	DSPPATH	DSPPATH Command
9.13	SIZDOC	Retrieve and Add Size of Documents in a Folder
9.14	MOVSPL	Move Spool File Entries
11.3	DSPPTHDS	Source for the DSPPTHDS Display File
11.4	DSPPTHRG	Source for the DSPPTHRG RPG Program
11.6	DSPFLD	The Display Field (DSPFLD) Command Source
11.7	DSPFLDDS	The DSPFLDDS Display File Source
11.8	DSPFLDRG	The DSPFLDRG RPG Program Source
11.9	RGZPFFLT	The RGZPFFLTR Command Source
11.10	RGZPFFRG	The RGZPFFRG RPG Program Source
11.11	RGZPFFCL	The RGZPFFCL CL Program Source

Figure	File Name	Description
11.13	FNDDSPLF	The FNDDSPLF Command
11.14	FNDDSPDS	The FNDDSPDS Display File Source
11.15	FNDDSPRG	The FNDDSPRG RPG Program
11.19	BLDOBJRF	The BLDOBJREF Command
11.20	OBJCRLGL	The OBJCRLGL CL Program
11.21	OBJDETTY	The OBJDETTY CL Program
11.22	OBJDSP	The OBJDSP CL Program
11.23	OBJHS	The OBJHS RPG Program
11.24	OBJHSTCL	The OBJHSTCL CL Program
11.25	OBJMAKE	The OBJMAKECL CL Program
11.26	OBJREFBD	The OBJREFBLDS CL Program
11.27	OBJREFBSB	The OBJREFBSBM CL Program
11.28	OBJRF	The OBJRF RPG Program
11.29	OBJRFDSP	The OBJRFDSP Display File
11.30	OBJRFPF	The OBJRFPF Physical File
11.31	WRKOBJRF	The WRKOBJREF Command

Source for files used in the examples:

FILE: CUSTOMER   Customer File

FILE: PRINTER   Printer Description File

FILE: PRINTERS   Printer File by Description

FILE: REQUEST   Request File

FILE: STATES   States Description File

Source for the File Information Data Structure in Appendix B:

FILE: FILINFDS   RPG Input Specifications for the
                        File Information Data Structure

TRANSFERRING THE SOURCE

The companion diskette includes source code for program samples and utilities listed in this appendix. Because the diskette is a PC diskette, you need a PC and PC Support (or another file-transfer utility) to transfer the source to the AS/400. In addition, your system needs the RPG compiler.

To transfer the source, follow these steps:

1. Sign on to the AS/400 with a user profile that has *PGMR user class.

2. If you want, create a library to contain all the software you're about to install. For example, you could call it POWERRPG for ease of identification:

```
CRTLIB LIB(POWERRPG)
```

3. Create a source physical file called SOURCE in the library of your choice. You MUST name this file SOURCE:

```
CRTSRCPF FILE(POWERRPG/SOURCE) RCDLEN(92) TEXT('Power RPG/III source')
```

where POWERRPG is the name of the library selected.

4. Transfer all source code to the source file just created. The preceding cross-reference table is provided to allow you to match the figures in the book to the file names found on the diskette.

5. Due to PC file naming conventions, all file names had to be limited to eight characters. Some of the file names had to be changed to transfer them to the PC diskette. For that reason, you need to rename the following source members once they have been transferred to the AS/400:

PC File Name	AS/400 Source Member Name
BLDOBJRF	BLDOBJREF
OBJMAKE	OBJMAKECL
OBJREFBD	OBJREFBLDS
OBJREFSB	OBJREFSBM
RGZPFFLT	RGZPFFLTR
WRKOBJRF	WRKOBJREF

COMPILING THE SOURCE

You will find instructions on how to compile each source member in the first few lines of each source member itself. For the most part, the compiles are very straightforward.

In the example below, POWERRPG represents the name of the library where the source members reside and XXX is the name of the source member to compile.

For CL programs:

```
CRTCLPGM PGM(POWERRPG/XXX) SRCFILE(POWERRPG/SOURCE)
```

For Display Files:

```
CRTDSPF FILE(POWERRPG/XXX) SRCFILE(POWERRPG/SOURCE)
```

For RPG programs:

```
CRTRPGPGM PGM(POWERRPG/XXX) SRCFILE(POWERRPG/SOURCE)
```

All of the objects for the Work with Object Reference (WRKOBJREF) utility found in Chapter 11 (Figures 11.20 through 11.31) can be created automatically by running the OBJMAKECL program.

Compile the OBJMAKECL program as follows:

```
CRTCLPGM PGM(POWERRPG/OBJMAKECL)
```

To run the OBJMAKECL program, key the following:

```
CALL OBJMAKECL PARM('POWERRPG')
```

Appendix B

File Information Data Structure

The File Information Data Structure is described in its entirety in Chapter 4. We have included a complete listing of the RPG Input Specifications for the data structure for you here (and on the companion diskette) so you may include it in your programs if you desire to do so.

The RPG specifications are followed by a short description of each field. This is intended for those occasions where you are looking for a particular piece of information and don't know where it is. You need to refer to Chapter 4 for a more complete description of the fields.

Figure B.1: Source Code for the File Information Data Structure

```
     **
     **
FDISPLAY CF   E                    WORKSTN
F                                           KINFDS INFO
IINFO         DS
     ***
     ***   COMMON FIELDS
     ***
I                                      1    8 F1NAME
I                                      9    9 F1OPEN
I                                     10   10 F1EOF
I                                     11  150F1STAT
I                                     16   21 F1OPCO
I                                     22   29 F1ROUT
I                                     30   37 F1STMT
I                                     38  420F1RESN
I                                     38   45 F1RECD
I                                     46   52 F1MSGI
I                                     53   66 F1UNUS
I                                     67  700F1SIZE
I                                     71  720F1INP
I                                     73  740F1OUT
I                                     75  760F1MODE
     ***
     ***   OPEN FEEDBACK INFORMATION
     ***
I                                     81   82 F1ODPT
I                                     83   92 F1FNAM
I                                     93  102 F1FLIB
I                                    103  112 F1SNAM
I                                    113  122 F1SLIB
I                                  B 123 1240F1SNBR
I                                  B 125 1260F1RCDL
I                                  B 127 1280F1MAXK
I                                    129  138 F1FMBR
I                                  B 147 1480F1FTYP
I                                  B 152 1530F1LINE
I                                  B 154 1550F1COLS
I                                  B 156 1590F1RCNT
I                                    160  161 F1ACCT
I                                    162  162 F1DUPK
I                                    163  163 F1SRC
I                                    164  173 F1UFCP
I                                    174  183 F1UFCO
I                                  B 184 1850F1VOLI
I                                  B 186 1870F1BLKL
I                                  B 188 1890F1OVRF
I                                  B 190 1910F1BLKI
I                                    197  206 F1REQR
I                                  B 207 2080F1OPNC
I                                  B 211 2120F1BASD
I                                    214  215 F1OPNI
I                                  B 216 2170F1FMTL
I                                  B 218 2190F1CCSI
I                                  B 227 2290F1NUMD
     ***
     ***   I/O FEEDBACK INFORMATION
     ***
I                                  B 243 2460F1WRTC
I                                  B 247 2500F1REDC
I                                  B 251 2540F1WRTR
```

```
  I                                    B 255 2580F1OTHC
  I                                      260 260 F1OPER
  I                                      261 270 F1IFMT
  I                                      271 272 F1CLAS
  I                                      273 282 F1DEVN
  I                                    B 283 2860F1IRLN
   ***
   ***    DEVICE SPECIFIC FEEDBACK, PRINTERS
   ***
  I                                    B 367 3680F1CURL
  I                                    B 369 3720F1CURP
  I                                      401 402 F1PMAJ
  I                                      403 4040F1PMIN
   ***
   ***    DEVICE SPECIFIC FEEDBACK, DATABASE FILES
   ***
  I                                    B 367 3700F1SIZB
  I                                      371 374 F1JFIL
  I                                    B 377 3780F1LOK#
  I                                    B 379 3800F1MAXF
  I                                    B 381 3840F1OERR
  I                                      385 385 F1POSB
  I                                      386 386 F1DELB
  I                                    B 387 3880F1KEY#
  I                                    B 393 3940F1KEYL
  I                                    B 395 3960F1MBR#
  I                                    B 397 4000F1RRN
  I                                      4012400 F1KEYV
   ***
   ***    DEVICE SPECIFIC FEEDBACK, WORKSTATION FILE
   ***
  I                                      367 368 F1FLAG
  I                                      369 369 F1AID
  I                                      370 371 F1CSRL
  I                                    B 372 3750F1DATL
  I                                    B 376 3770F1SRRN
  I                                    B 378 3790F1SFLM
  I                                    B 380 3810F1SFL#
  I                                      382 383 F1WCSR
  I                                      401 402 F1MAJR
  I                                      403 404 F1MINR
   ***
   ***********************************************************************
   ***
   ***    FIELD DESCRIPTIONS
   ***
   ***********************************************************************
   ***
   ***    COMMON FIELDS
   ***
   *   F1NAME - FILE NAME AS USED BY THR RPG PROGRAM
   *   F1OPEN - FILE OPEN INDICATOR (1 = OPEN)
   *   F1EOF  - AT END OF FILE? (1 = END OF FILE)
   *   F1STAT - STATUS CODE
   *   F1OPCO - LAST USED RPG OP CODE ON FILE
   *   F1ROUT - RPG ROUTINE THAT WAS PROCESSING THE FILE
   *   F1STMT - RPG SOURCE STATMENT NUMBER
   *   F1RESN - USER SPECIFIED RETURN CODE FOR SPECIAL FILES
   *   F1RECD - RECODR FORMAT NAME (OR REC INDICATOR IF INTERNALLY DESC)
   *   F1MSGI - SYSTEM ERROR MESSAGE ID
   *   F1UNUS - UNUSED
   *   F1SIZE - TOTAL CHARACTERS THAT FIT ON WORKSTATION DISPLAY
   *   F1INP  - NATIONAL LANGUAGE INPUT CAPABILITY
   *   F1OUT  - NATIONAL LANGUAGE OUTPUT CAPABILITY
```

```
    *   F1MODE - NATIONAL LANGUAGE PERFERRED MODE
    ***
    ***   OPEN FEEDBACK INFORMATION
    ***
    *   F1ODPT - OPEN DATA PATH TYPE
    *   F1FNAM - FILE NAME AS KNOWN BY THE SYSTEM
    *   F1FLIB - LIBRARY NAME WHERE FILE RESIDES
    *   F1SNAM - SPOOLED FILE NAME
    *   F1SLIB - SPOOLED FILE LIBRARY NAME
    *   F1SNBR - SPOOLED FILE NUMBER
    *   F1RCDL - FILE RECORD LENGTH
    *   F1MAXK - MAXIMUM KEY LENGTH
    *   F1FMBR - MEMBER NAME
    *   F1FTYP - TYPE OF FILE SUBTYPE CODE
    *   F1LINE - NUMBER OF LINES ON THE WORKSTATION
    *   F1COLS - NUMBER OF COLUMNS ON THE WORKSTATION
    *   F1RCNT - NUMBER OF RECORDS IN FILE WHEN OPENED
    *   F1ACCT - TYPE OF DATA FILE ACCESS
    *   F1DUPK - DUPLICATE KEY ALLOWED INDICATOR (D=DUPLICATES U=UNIQUE)
    *   F1SRC  - SOURCE FILE INDICATOR (Y=YES, IT'S A SOURCE FILE)
    *   F1UFCP - USER FILE CONTROL BLOCK PARAMETERS
    *.  F1UFCO - USER FILE CONTROL BLOCK PARAMETER OVERIDES
    *   F1VOLI - OFFSET TO LOCATION OF VOLUMNE ID ON TAPE
    *   F1BLKL - BLOCKED INPUT/OUTPUT LIMIT
    *   F1OVRF - OVERFLOW LINE NUMBER
    *   F1BLKI - BLOCKED INPUT/OUTPUT OFFSET
    *   F1REQR - REQUESTER NAME
    *   F1OPNC - OPEN COUNT
    *   F1BASD - NUMBER OF MEMBERS BASED ON FILE
    *   F1OPNI - OPEN IDENTIFIER
    *   F1FMTL - MAXIMUM FORMAT RECORD LENGTH
    *   F1CCSI - DATABASE CCSID
    *   F1NUMD - NUMBER OF DEVICES DEFINED
    ***
    ***   I/O FEEDBACK INFORMATION
    ***
    *   F1WRTC - NUMBER OF WRITES PERFORMED
    *   F1REDC - NUMBER OF READS PERFORMED
    *   F1WRTR - NUMBER OF WRITES AND READS PERFORMED
    *   F1OTHC - NUMBER OF OTHER I/O'S PERFORMED
    *   F1OPER - CURRENT OPERATION
    *   F1IFMT - RECORD FORMAT NAME
    *   F1CLAS - DEVICE CLASS
    *   F1DEVN - DEVICE NAME
    *   F1IRLN - RECORD LENGTH
    ***
    ***   DEVICE SPECIFIC FEEDBACK, PRINTERS
    ***
    *   F1CURL - CURRENT LINE NUMBER
    *   F1CURP - CURRENT PAGE NUMBER
    *   F1PMAJ - MAJOR RETURN CODE
    *   F1PMIN - MINOR RETURN CODE
    ***
    ***   DEVICE SPECIFIC FEEDBACK, DATABASE FILES
    ***
    *   F1SIZB - SIZE OF DATABASE FEEDBACK AREA
    *   F1JFIL - JOINED FILE INDICATORS
    *   F1LOK# - NUMBER OF LOCKED RECORDS
    *   F1MAXF - MAXIMUM NUMBER OF FIELDS
    *   F1OERR - OFFSET TO FIELD MAPPING ERROR BIT MAP
    *   F1POSB - CURRENT FILE POSITION
    *   F1DELB - CURRRENT RECORD DELETED INDICATION
    *   F1KEY# - NUMBER OF KEY FIELDS
    *   F1KEYL - KEY LENGTH
```

```
     *   F1MBR# - DATA MEMBER NUMBER
     *   F1RRN  - RELATIVE RECORD NUMBER IN MEMBER
     *   F1KEYV - KEY VALUES
     ***
     ***   DEVICE SPECIFIC FEEDBACK, WORKSTATION FILE
     ***
     *   F1FLAG - DISPLAY FLAGS
     *   F1AID  - AID BYTE
     *   F1CSRL - CURSOR LOCATION
     *   F1DATL - ACTUAL DATA LENGTH
     *   F1SRRN - SUBFILE RELATIVE RECORD NUMBER
     *   F1SFLM - SUBFILE MINIMUM RELATIVE RECORD NUMBER
     *   F1SFL# - NUMBER OF RECORDS IN SUBFILE
     *   F1WCSR - ACTIVE WINDOW CURSOR LOCATION
     *   F1MAJR - MAJOR RETURN CODE
     *   F1MINR - MINOR RETURN CODE
```

Index

—W—

windows, 83
   DDS window, 26
   DDS window program sample, 91
   removing windows, 89
   subfiles within DDS windows, 45
   window subfile example, 48
Work with Object Reference command, 308, 335
WRKACTJOB (Work with Active Jobs), 291
WRKOBJREF (Work with Object Reference), 335
WRKOBJREF command, 308

WRKSBMJOB (Work with Submitted Jobs), 291, 300

—X—

XFOOT (Cross Foot) op code, 165
XLATE
   using to translate brackets to parentheses, 180
   using to translate lowercase-character strings to
      uppercase, 179
XLATE (Translate) op code, 127, 169
XLATE (Translate) performs single-character
   substitution within character strings, 179